Instant Pot Cookbook

500 Healthy, Easy and Quick-to-Make Recipes for the Instant Pot Pressure Cooker

Jessica Williams

Table of Contents

Chapter 7 Vegetable Recipes 127

Introduction

Eating healthy gets much easier with this delicious collection of Instant Pot recipes. This Instant Pot cookbook makes it easier and tastier for beginner Instant Pot users who love to eat a real homemade meal daily. This cooking appliance cuts down cooking time without sacrificing the delicious taste of the foods. Cooking has become easier after the invention of this great cooking device – the Instant Pot. Whether you are a skilled cook or a novice, the Instant Pot opens up a world of possibilities when cooking.

This Instant Pot cookbook was developed by a seasoned cook for maximum health and flavor. In this cookbook, you will find flavorful, nutritious, simple yet mouthwatering Instant Pot recipes. Every single recipe comes with detailed directions and a complete ingredients list that will leave you with no excuses not to cook a perfect meal and to look forward to enjoying its delicious taste. Meticulously planned, rich, and delicious recipes in this book ensure that there are no leftovers, no waste, and no guesswork, which is important for a beginner like you.

Next time you cook for your family members, partner, friends, or whomever, they will absolutely love these meals. This guide is your ultimate guide to Instant Pot cooking. This cookbook will not only let you know all the important facts about cooking but also will show you 500 easy Instant Pot recipes. Recipes include breakfasts, snacks, appetizers, pasta, side dishes, rice, grains, beans, soups, stews, vegetables, poultry, pork, beef, lamb, fish, seafood and desserts. If you do not own an Instant Pot now, then the recipes in this cookbook will definitely convince you to get one. Click "Buy Now" to purchase this book and start your new life!

Chapter 1 Instant Pot

Ten pro tips for the Instant Pot:

1. Read the user manual before using the Instant Pot. This is a must.
2. If you haven't used an Instant Pot before, then do not worry. The Instant Pot has a few safety features, so you are safe. The device includes a safety lid lock, an anti-block shield, a steam release valve, and overheat protection. New versions have the unique ability to automatically seal the steam release.
3. Stick to the rule: Add one cup of liquid to the inner pot of your Instant Pot. Remember, your instant pot cannot make steam without liquid.
4. Your Instant Pot can cook without monitoring and stirring. However, do not leave it unattended when pressure cooking your meal just to be safe.
5. Never fill your Instant Pot more than 2/3 of the way, including liquids. When cooking foods that expand, such as grains and beans, your instant pot shouldn't be more than 1/3 full.
6. Just as with regular cooking, pressure cooking in phases is the best option for many recipes. Cut larger pieces of food into uniform sizes to ensure even cooking. If you tend to pressure cook meat and vegetables at the same time, sauté your vegetables first, set them aside, then pressure cook the meat. Also, you can brown the meat and cook it quickly using the "Manual" setting.
7. Read and know the entire recipe before beginning to cook in the Instant Pot. Reading instructions from a professional is always handy since you cannot add ingredients and check your meal later. Some important things to know include cook time, the number of servings, food sense, necessary items, and so forth. In this way, you will know when to add your ingredients, which pressure level to use, as well as the pressure release method.
8. Undercook rather than overcook. If you are not sure how long to cook something, remember, less is more. You can always cook your food a few minutes longer, but you cannot fix an overcooked meal.
9. Pay attention to the cooking temperature; otherwise, your food will dry out or burn. This is a common mistake with the Instant Pot. Use the "Manual" mode to choose the exact temperature.
10. Make sure you buy the right sized Instant Pot, according to the number of people you usually cook for.

Using the Instant Pot buttons:

1. Manual: This feature allows you to adjust cook time and pressure. This makes it the most utilized function since you can select parameters according to your recipe.
2. Soup/Broth: This is an ideal program for hearty soups, broth, and sauces. This feature allows your soup to simmer gently without boiling too heavily.
3. Meat/Stew: This program cooks tender, juicy, and flavorful meat to perfection. This feature makes your Instant Pot a real game-changer.
4. Bean/Chili: Ideally, you should pre-soak beans for a creamier texture.

5. Slow Cook: You can use this button for slow cooking and gentle simmering.
6. Sauté: You can sauté or brown items before pressure cooking, or you can finish them (thicken the liquid or brown the meat) just as you would in a skillet or a pot. The Sauté function allows you to sear, sauté, brown, and simmer.
7. Rice: with this setting, you will need to adjust the cooking time for white rice: 4 to 8 minutes, jasmine rice: 4 to 5 minutes, brown rice, 22 to 28 minutes, wild rice: 25 to 30 minutes.
8. Multigrain: Use this program to cook grains. First, measure out dry ingredients, measure out the exact amount of water, rinse your grains, cover, and press button.
9. Porridge: This program is best for congee, porridge, and oatmeal.
10. Steam: Use this program to cook delicate items such as fruits, vegetables, fish, and seafood. You can use your instant pot as a traditional steamer.
11. Yogurt: This is a fully automated program for making yogurt at home.
12. Keep Warm/Cancel: Once you have done cooking, use this function to keep your food hot or to stop the pressure-cooking mode.

10 safety features of the Instant Pot

1. Safety lid lock: Automatic lid lock during high inside pressure.
2. Steam release: Automatic release of extra pressure.
3. Anti-block shield: Prevents tiny food particles going into the steam release valve and pipe
4. Automatic pressure control: Monitors inside pressure and prevents it from going higher than a specified safety level.
5. Automatic temperature control: Monitors inside temperature and prevents it from going higher than the specified safety level.
6. Safe lid position: Automatic stoppage of the cooking process, if the lid is not in its locked position.
7. Overheat prevention: Detects uneven heat distribution and prevents food burning or sticking at the bottom.
8. Electric fuse: Detects unexpected electric/current supply and shuts down the cooking process.

Chapter 2 Breakfast Recipes

Breakfast Muffins

Cook time: 14 minutes |Serves: 8| Per serving: Calories 282; Carbs 1g; Fat 12g; Protein 24g

Ingredients:

- Shredded Pepper Jack Cheese – ¼ cup
- Bacon slices – 4
- Eggs - 4
- Green onion – 1, chopped
- Pinch of garlic powder
- Pinch of pepper
- Salt – ¼ tsp.
- Water – 1 ½ cups

Directions:

Set your Instant Pot or IP to Sauté. Cook the bacon until crispy, about a few minutes. Wipe off the bacon grease, pour the water inside and lower the rack. In a bowl, beat the eggs along with salt, pepper, and garlic powder. Crumble the bacon and add to this mixture. Stir in the cheese and onion. Pour the mixture into 4 silicone muffin cups. Arrange them on the rack and close the lid. Cook on High for 8 minutes. Serve.

Shakshuka

Cook time: 15 minutes |Serves: 6 | Per serving: Calories 504; Carbs 7g; Fat 39g; Protein 29g

Ingredients:

- Ground chorizo – 1 pound
- Eggs – 6
- Cumin – ½ tbsp.
- Diced onion – ½ cup
- Red bell pepper – 1, diced
- Canned diced tomatoes – 28 ounces
- Minced garlic – 1 tsp.
- Coconut oil – 1 tsp.
- Pepper – ¼ tsp.
- Salt – ½ tsp.
- Water – 1 ½ cup

Directions:

Press Sauté and melt the coconut oil in it. Add the onions and peppers and sauté for 3 minutes. Add garlic and cook for 30 seconds more. Add chorizo and cook until browned. Stir in the tomatoes. Transfer the mixture to a baking dish. Clean and pour the water into the instant pot and lower the rack. Crack the eggs into the baking dish and place it on the rack. Close the lid and cook on High for 10 minutes. Serve.

Bacon and Sausage Omelet
Cook time: 25 minutes |Serves: 6| Per serving: Calories 222; Carbs 3.5g; Fat 15.5g; Protein 16.8g

Ingredients:

- Eggs – 6
- Bacon slices – 6, cooked and crumbled
- Sausage links – 6, sliced
- Onions – 1, diced
- Milk – ½ cup
- Garlic powder – ¼ tsp.
- Salt – ¼ tsp.
- Pepper – ¼ tsp.
- Water – 1 ½ cups

Directions:

Pour the water into the instant pot and lower the rack. Beat the eggs along with the milk and seasonings. Add the remaining ingredients. Grease a baking dish with cooking spray. Pour the egg mixture into it. Place the dish on the rack and close the lid. Cook on Manual for 25 minutes. Serve.

Eggs and Avocado Stir-Fry
Cook time: 10 minutes |Serves: 2| Per serving: Calories 350; Carbs 2.6g; Fat 32.7g; Protein 8.4g

Ingredients:

- Medium avocado – 1, pitted and cubed
- Eggs – 2 large, beaten
- Green onions – 2 tbsps. finely chopped
- Olive oil – 1 tsp.
- Butter – 1 tbsp.
- Sea salt – ½ tsp.
- Black pepper – ¼ tsp. ground
- Red chili flakes – ¼ tsp.

Directions:

Melt the butter in the instant pot. Press the Sauté button and add avocado cubes. Season with salt and pepper and cook for 3 to 4 minutes. Stirring occasionally. Now, add the green onions, eggs, and olive oil to taste. Add 2 tbsps. of milk for a creamier texture. Cook until the eggs are set, about 3 minutes. Transfer the dish to the serving plate. Top with heavy cream and serve.

Egg Spinach Cups
Cook time: 8 minutes| Serves: 4 | Per serving: Calories 114; Carbs 2g; Fat 7g; Protein 11g

Ingredients:

- Eggs – 6
- Shredded mozzarella cheese – ½ cup
- Chopped baby spinach – 1 cup
- Crumbled feta cheese – ¼ cup
- Tomato – 1, chopped
- Salt – ½ tsp.
- Pepper – 1 tsp.
- Garlic powder – ¼ tsp.
- Water – 1 ½ cups

Directions:

Add water in the instant pot and lower the trivet. Beat the eggs along with the spices. Stir in the cheeses and tomato. Grease 4 ramekins and divide the spinach between them. Pour the egg mixture over. Arrange the ramekins inside the instant pot and close the lid. Cook on High for 8 minutes. Serve.

Breakfast Casserole
Cook time: 15 minutes |Serves: 6| Per serving: Calories 484; Carbs 4.2g; Fat 38.9g; Protein 26.1g

Ingredients:

- Olive oil – 1 tbsp.
- Broccoli – 1 medium, chopped
- Pork sausages – 12 oz. cooked and cut into inch slices
- Cheddar cheese – 1 cup, grated
- Eggs – 10
- Salt – ½ tsp.
- Whipping cream – ¾ cup
- Garlic – 2 cloves, minced
- Ground black pepper – ¼ tsp.

Directions:

Grease the inside the instant pot with olive oil. Layer half of the broccoli, then half of the sausages and half of the cheese. Repeat with the rest of the ingredients. In a bowl, whisk the eggs and salt. Add the cream, garlic, and pepper. Whisk well. Pour the mixture over the ingredients in the instant pot. Cover and cook 15 minutes on High. Serve.

Instant Pot Pancakes
Cook time: 10 minutes |Serves: 1| Per serving: Calories 334; Carbs 3g; Fat 29g; Protein 17g

Ingredients:

- Eggs – 2
- Cream cheese – 2 ounces
- Cinnamon – ½ tsp.
- Swerve – 1 tsp.
- Butter – 2 tsps.

Directions:

In a blender, place the cream cheese, eggs, swerve, and cinnamon. Blend until smooth. Melt half of the butter in the instant pot on Sauté. Add half of the butter and cook for 3 minutes. Flip and cook the other side for 1 to 2 minutes. Repeat with the other half of the batter. Serve.

Breakfast Quiche
Cook time: 20 minutes |Serves: 6| Per serving: Calories 178; Carbs 3.8g; Fat 11.2g; Protein 15.3g

Ingredients:

- Diced tomatoes – 1 cup
- Chopped spinach – 3 cups
- Grated Parmesan cheese – ¼ cup
- Milk – ½ cup
- Green onions – 3, chopped
- Eggs – 12
- Tomato – ½, sliced
- Garlic salt – ½ tsp.
- Pepper – ¼ tsp.
- Water – 1 ½ cups

Directions:

Pour the water into the instant pot. Grease the baking dish with cooking spray. Combine the spinach, green onions, and diced tomatoes in it. Beat the eggs along with milk, salt, and pepper. Pour the mixture over the tomatoes and spinach. Sprinkle with parmesan cheese and top with tomato slices. Place the baking dish on the rack and close the lid. Cook on High for 20 minutes. Serve.

Coconut Pancakes
Cook time: 5 minutes| Serves: 3| Per serving: Calories 350; Carbs 4.2g; Fat 31.3g; Protein 12.1g

Ingredients:

- Almond flour – 1 cup
- Baking powder – 1 tsp.
- Cream cheese – ½ cup, softened
- Large eggs – 3, beaten
- Coconut milk – 2 tbsps.
- Coconut butter – 1 tbsp. melted
- Powdered stevia – 1 tsp.
- Cherry extract – 1 tsp.
- Nutmeg – ¼ tsp. ground

Directions:

In a bowl, combine the coconut flour, stevia, nutmeg, and baking powder. Mix well. Now, add cream cheese, eggs, coconut milk, cherry extract, and nutmeg. Beat until smooth and creamy.

Grease the stainless-steel insert with coconut butter. Pour 1/3 of the mixture and cover. Cook 5 minutes on High and open. Remove the pancake and repeat with the remaining batter. Top with some plain yogurt and sprinkle with some shredded coconut. Serve.

Pumpkin Bread

Cook time: 25 minutes| Serves: 4| Per serving: Calories 275; Carbs 5.8g; Fat 21.8g; Protein 10.7g

Ingredients:

- Pumpkin puree – ½ cup
- Large eggs – 2, beaten
- Almond flour – 1 cup
- Almond milk – ¼ cup
- Almond butter – 1 tbsp. melted
- Salt – ½ tsp.
- Nutmeg – ¼ tsp. ground
- Pumpkin pie spice – ½ tsp.
- Turmeric powder – ¼ tsp.

Directions:

In a bowl, combine the flour, pumpkin pie spice, turmeric, nutmeg, salt, and baking powder. Stir until combined and add eggs, milk, and pumpkin puree. Mix well and set aside. Grease a springform pan with melted butter. Add the dough and cover with aluminum foil. Pour 1 cup of water and place a trivet on the bottom and place the pan on top. Cover the pot and cook 25 minutes on Low. Cool completely. Slice and serve.

Eggs in Avocado Boats

Cook time: 20 minutes |Serves: 2| Per serving: Calories 421; Carbs 2.3g; Fat 41.3g; Protein 7.6g

Ingredients:

- Avocado – 1, sliced in half
- Whole eggs – 2
- Butter – 3 tbsps.
- Dried oregano – 1 tsp.
- Pink Himalayan salt – ½ tsp.

Directions:

Slice the avocado in half and generously brush with butter. Set aside. Place the steamer insert in the Instant Pot. Add avocados and gently crack eggs in each avocado and sprinkle with salt and oregano. Pour in one cup of water in the inner pot and cover. Cook 20 minutes on Low. Serve.

Cheesy Breakfast Bagels

Cook time: 15 minutes |Serves: 3| Per serving: Calories 367; Carbs 3.5g; Fat 29g; Protein 20g

Ingredients:

- Almond flour – ¾ cup

- Mozzarella cheese – 1 ½ cups, grated and melted
- Egg – 1
- Cream cheese – 2 tbsps.
- Xanthan gum – 1 tsp.
- Pinch of sea salt
- Water – 1 ½ cups
- Butter – 1 tbsp. melted

Directions:

Pour the water into the Instant Pot and place in a trivet. Beat the egg along with xanthan gum and salt. Whisk in the cheeses. Stir in the flour. Form a log out of the dough and divide it into three equal pieces. Make three bagel shape rings and flatten them. Brush with the butter. Arrange on a greased baking tray and place on the trivet. Cover and cook on Manual for 15 minutes. Serve.

Oatmeal with Blueberries
Cook time: 4 minutes |Serves: 3| Per serving: Calories 405; Carbs 78.2g; Fat 5.5g; Protein 13.4g

Ingredients:

- Water – 3 cups
- Cinnamon – 1 stick
- Vanilla bean – 1
- Old-fashioned oats – 1 ½ cups
- Sea salt – 1 pinch
- Grated nutmeg – 1 pinch
- Fresh blueberries – ½ cup
- Honey – 3 tbsps.

Directions:

Place the water, cinnamon, vanilla, oat, salt, and nutmeg in the Instant Pot. Mix. Cover and cook 4 minutes on High. Do a natural release and open. Top with blueberries and honey. Serve.

Quinoa and Bulgur Porridge
Cook time: 6 minutes |Serves: 5| Per serving: Calories 349; Carbs 46.2g; Fat 11.9g; Protein 14.5g

Ingredients:

- Coconut milk – 3 cups, unsweetened
- Water – 1 cup
- Chia seeds – 3 tbsps.
- Quinoa – 1 cup, rinsed and drained
- Bulgur – ½ cup
- Grated nutmeg – 1 pinch
- Sea salt – 1 pinch
- Ground cardamom – ½ tsp.
- Ground anise – ½ tsp.
- Ground cloves – ¼ tsp.

- Black currants – ½ cup
- Honey for serving

Directions:

Add everything in the Instant Pot, except for the honey. Cover and cook on High for 6 minutes. Do a natural release and open. Serve with honey.

Pumpkin Pie Oatmeal
Cook time: 8 minutes |Serves: 4| Per serving: Calories 360; Carbs 66.5g; Fat 5.9g; Protein 10.9g

Ingredients:

- Rolled old fashioned oats – 2 cups
- Maple syrup – ½ cup
- Vanilla essence – ½ tsp.
- Pumpkin pie spice – 1 tsp.
- Pumpkin puree – ½ cup
- Milk – 1 ¾ cup
- Water - 2 cups

Directions:

Add 1-cup of water to the Instant Pot. Set pot on Sauté to boil the water. Meanwhile, in a bowl, mix the maple syrup, oats, vanilla, milk, pumpkin pie spice, pumpkin puree, and 1 cup water. Cover the bowl with aluminum foil. Press Cancel and add trivet into the Pot. Position the dish on top of the trivet. Cover and cook on High for 8 minutes. Do a natural release and open. Cool and serve.

Savory Breakfast Grits
Cook time: 15 minutes |Serves: 6| Per serving: Calories 184; Carbs 6.2g ; Fat 15g ; Protein 6.5g

Ingredients:

- Milk – 1 cup
- Water – 2 ½ cups
- Cheddar cheese – 1 cup, shredded
- Olive oil – 2 Tbsps.
- Grits – 1 cup

Directions:

Pour two cups of water into the Instant Pot and place in a trivet. In a bowl, mix 2 tbsps. Of olive oil, the rest of the water, and grits. Cover the bowl with aluminum foil. Place the bowl on top of the trivet. Close the lid. Cook on High for 15 minutes. Then do a quick release. Remove the bowl from the Instant Pot and transfer the grit mixture to a large bowl. Add cheese and milk to the grit mixture and stir until the cheese has melted. Serve.

Spinach Bacon Frittata
Cook time: 15 minutes |Serves: 4| Per serving: Calories 120; Carbs 1.9g ; Fat 8.5g ; Protein 9.2g

Ingredients:

- Eggs – 6
- Bacon – ¼ cup, cooked and chopped
- Tomato – ½ cup, chopped
- Fresh spinach – 1 cup
- Italian seasoning – ½ tsp.
- Heavy cream – 2 ½ tsps.
- Pepper – ¼ tsp.
- Salt – ¼ tsp.
- Water - 1 ½ cups for the pot

Directions:

Whisk eggs with spices and heavy cream in a bowl. Spray a baking pan with cooking spray. Add bacon, tomato, and spinach to the pan. Pour egg mixture over the bacon mixture. Cover the pan with aluminum foil. Pour 1 ½ cups water into the Instant Pot and place in the trivet. Place the baking pan on top of the trivet and cover the Instant Pot. Cook on High for 15 minutes. Do a quick release and open. Serve.

Fluffy Pancake
Cook time:17 minutes |Serves: 2| Per serving: Calories 480; Carbs 74.1 g ; Fat 14.7g ; Protein 14.3g

Ingredients:

- Egg – 1
- Olive oil – 1 ½ tbsps.
- Buttermilk – 1 ¼ cups
- Baking soda – ¾ tsp.
- Baking powder – ¾ tsp.
- Brown sugar – 3 tbsps.
- All-purpose flour – 1 cup

Directions:

Mix the flour, baking soda, baking powder, and sugar in a bowl. Add oil, buttermilk, and eggs and whisk until mixed. Spray a springform pan with cooking spray. Pour batter into the prepared pan. Pour 1 cup of water into the Instant Pot and place in a trivet. Place the pan on top of the trivet. Cover and cook on Low for 17 minutes. Do a natural release and open the lid. Slice and serve.

Cheese Mushroom Frittata
Cook time: 15 minutes| Serves: 2| Per serving: Calories 262; Carbs 18.5 g ; Fat 18.5g ; Protein 20g

Ingredients:

- Eggs – 4
- Swiss cheese slices – 2, cut each slice into 4 pieces

- Mushrooms – 4 oz. sliced
- White pepper – 1/8 tsp.
- Onion powder – 1/8 tsp.
- Heavy cream – 2 tsps.
- Salt – ¼ tsp.
- Water – 1 ½ cups for the pot

Directions:

In a bowl, whisk eggs with spices, salt, and heavy cream. Spray a baking pan with cooking spray. Add sliced mushrooms to the pan then pour egg mixture over the mushrooms. Arrange cheese slices on top of the mushroom and egg mixture. Cover the pan with aluminum foil. Pour 1 ½ cups water to the Instant Pot and place in a trivet. Place the pan on top of the trivet and close the pot. Cook on High for 15 minutes. Do a quick release, open, and serve.

Banana Nut Oatmeal
Cook time: 3 minutes |Serves: 2| Per serving: Calories 218; Carbs 28.8g ; Fat 8g ; Protein 8.9g

Ingredients:

- Banana – 1, chopped
- Walnuts – ¼ cup, chopped
- Honey – 1 tsp.
- Milk – 2 cups
- Water – 2 cups
- Steel-cut oats – 1 cup

Directions:

Add water, milk, and oats to the Instant Pot and mix well. Cover and then cook on High for three minutes. Do a natural release and open the lid. Add walnuts, banana, and honey to the oats and stir well. Serve.

Apple Dates Oatmeal
Cook time: 4 minutes |Serves: 2| Per serving: Calories 122; Carbs 28.9 g ; Fat 1g ; Protein 1.9g

Ingredients:

- Vanilla – ¼ tsp.
- Cinnamon – ¼ tsp.
- Dates – 2, chopped
- Apple – 1, chopped
- Water – ½ cup
- Instant Oatmeal – ¼ cup

Directions:

Add everything in the Instant Pot and mix. Cover the pot and cook on High for 4 minutes. Do a natural release and open. Stir well and serve.

Blueberry French Toast Casserole

Cook time: 25 minutes |Serves: 4| Per serving: Calories 212; Carbs 35.7g ; Fat 4.2g ; Protein 8.8g

Ingredients:

- French bread slices – 4, cut into pieces
- Blueberries – 1 cup
- Cinnamon – ½ tsp.
- Vanilla – ½ tsp.
- Brown sugar – ¼ cup
- Eggs – 2
- Milk – 1 cup

Directions:

In a bowl, whisk eggs with vanilla, cinnamon, sugar, and milk. Add bread pieces and blueberries and mix to coat well. Spray baking dish with cooking spray. Pour mixture into the baking dish. Pour ¾ cup of water into the Instant Pot and place a trivet in the pot. Place baking dish on top of the trivet and close the lid. Cook on High for 25 minutes. Do a natural release. Open and serve.

Apple Oatmeal

Cook time: 20 minutes |Serves: 2 | Per serving: Calories 236; Carbs 42.9g ; Fat 6.2g ; Protein 6g

Ingredients:

- Steal-cut oats – 1 cup
- Coconut oil – 2 tsps.
- Apple – 1 cup, chopped
- Water – 2 ½ cups
- Brown sugar – 3 tbsps.
- Vanilla extract – 1 tsp.
- Ground cinnamon – ½ tsp.

Directions:

Press Sauté on your Instant Pot. Place the coconut oil, sugar, apple, vanilla extract, and ground cinnamon in the Instant Pot. Add oats and stir. Press Sauté and stir the mixture for 5 minutes. Then add mixture and mix. Close the lid and cook the oatmeal for 13 minutes on High. Then do a quick release. Mix up the meal and serve.

French Toast Pudding

Cook time: 16 minutes |Serves: 5 |Per serving: Calories 387; Carbs 59.6 g ; Fat 14.5g ; Protein 8.9g

Ingredients:

- Bananas – 4, chopped
- Almond milk – 1 cup
- Vegan French bread – 4 slices
- Maple syrup – 2 tbsps.
- Vanilla extract – 1 tsp
- Vegan butter – 1 tbsp.
- Ground cinnamon – 1 tsp.
- Ground cloves – ¼ tsp.
- Water – 1 cup, for cooking

Directions:

Pour water into the Instant Pot. Chop the bread and place it in a round pan. Blend together the maple syrup, chopped bananas, vanilla extract, ground cinnamon, and ground cloves until smooth. Pour the mixture over the bread. Cover the pan with the foil and secure the edges well. Place the pan in the IP. Close the lid and cook on High for 16 minutes. Do a quick release. Open the lid and remove the foil. Add the butter and stir gently. Serve.

Morning Muffins
Cook time: 10 minutes |Serves: 5| Per serving: Calories 152; Carbs 13.1 ; Fat 10.8g ; Protein 4.5g

Ingredients:

- Banana – 1, chopped
- Vanilla extract – 1 tsp.
- Cocoa powder - 1 tbsp.
- Flax meal – 4 tbsps.
- Vegan butter – 4 tsps.
- Brown sugar – 3 tsps.
- Almond milk – 2 tbsps.
- Baking powder – ½ tsp.
- Water – 1 cup, for cooking
- Oil to grease the muffin molds

Directions:

Blend chopped banana until smooth and transfer it in the mixing bowl. Add cocoa powder, vanilla extract, flax meal, butter, Brown sugar, almond milk, and baking powder. Mix up the mixture and place it in the greased muffin molds. Fill ½ part of every muffin mold. Pour water in the Instant Pot and place in a rack. Place the muffin tray on the rack and close the lid. Cook the muffins for 10 minutes on High. Cool and serve.

Miso Oat Porridge
Cook time: 4 minutes |Serves: 4| Per serving: Calories 394 ; Carbs 16.9 g ; Fat 36g ; Protein 5.7g

Ingredients:

- Steel-cut oats – 1 cup
- Miso paste – 1 tsp.
- Tahini - 1 tbsp.
- Avocado – ½, peeled
- Nutritional yeast – ½ tsp.
- Almond milk – 2 cups
- Chives – ½ tsp. chopped

Directions:

Mix together the almond milk, nutritional yeast, and tahini. Then pour the mixture into the Instant Pot. Add the oats and stir gently. Close the lid. Cook the oats on High for 4 minutes. Do natural pressure. Meanwhile, mash the avocado well. Add miso paste and chives. Stir until smooth. Transfer the cooked oats in a bowl and add avocado mash. Stir and serve.

Buckwheat with Pecans
Cook time: 5 minutes |Serves: 6| Per serving: Calories 468; Carbs 56.2 g ; Fat 26g ; Protein 10.1g

Ingredients:

- Buckwheat – 2 cups
- Pecans – ¼ cup, chopped
- Raisins – 1 tbsp. chopped
- Vanilla extract - 1 tsp.
- Maple syrup – 4 tbsps.
- Water – 2 cups
- Coconut milk – 2 cups

Directions:

Place buckwheat in the Instant Pot. Add water, vanilla extract, and coconut milk. Close the lid and cook the buckwheat on High for 5 minutes. Do a natural release. Open and add raisins, maple syrup, chopped pecans in the buckwheat and stir well. Serve.

Rice Pudding
Cook time: 8 minutes |Serves:4 | Per serving: Calories 376; Carbs 81.1g ; Fat 2g ; Protein 5.5g

Ingredients:

- Rice - 1 ½ cups
- Rice milk – 3 cups
- All-purpose flour – 1 tbsp.
- Brown sugar – 2 tbsps.
- Turmeric – ¼ tsp.
- Vanilla extract – 1 tsp.

Directions:

In a bowl, combine ½-cup rice milk and flour. Add sugar, turmeric, and vanilla extract. Then pour it in the Instant Pot bowl. Add rice, and remaining milk. Stir to mix. Close and cook on High for 8 minutes. Do a natural release. Open the lid and stir. Serve.

Chia Pudding
Cook time: 5 minutes |Serves: 2| Per serving: Calories 475; Carbs 49.8g ; Fat 41.1g ; Protein 10g

Ingredients:

- Chia seeds – ½ cup
- Brown sugar - 1 tbsp.
- Maple syrup – 1 tbsp.
- Almond milk – 1 cup
- Vanilla extract – ½ tsp.
- Banana – 1, sliced

Directions:

Pour almond milk in the Instant Pot. Add maple syrup, vanilla extract, and sugar. Stir. Close lid, then cook on High for 5 minutes. Do a quick release. Cool the mixture and add sliced banana and chia seeds. Mix up gently. Serve.

Zucchini Frittata
Cook time:12 minutes |Serves: 5| Per serving: Calories 83; Carbs 7.3g ; Fat 4.9g ; Protein 4.1g

Ingredients:

- Firm tofu – 6 oz.
- Zucchini – 1
- Red onion – 1, diced
- Almond milk – ¼ cup
- Salt – 1 tsp.
- Ground black pepper – 1 tsp.
- Wheat flour – 2 tbsps.
- Olive oil – ½ tsp.

Directions:

Grate zucchini and scrambled tofu. Mix up together zucchini, tofu, onion, and almond milk. Add salt, ground black pepper, and wheat flour. Mix well. Brush the Instant Pot bowl with olive oil. Transfer the zucchini mixture into it. Flatten with a spatula. Close and cook 12 minutes on High pressure. Do a natural release. Open and serve.

Tapioca Porridge
Cook time: 17 minutes| Serves: 4| Per serving: Calories 366; Carbs 29.5g ; Fat 28.6g ; Protein 2.8g

Ingredients:

- Tapioca pearls - ½ cup
- Tapioca flour – 1 tbsp.
- Almond milk – 2 cups
- Maple syrup – 1 tbsp.

Directions:

In the Instant Pot, mix together tapioca pearls, tapioca flour, and almond milk. Close and cook on High for 17 minutes. Then do a natural release. Open the lid and add syrup. Mix and serve.

Quinoa Breakfast Bowl

Cook time: 14minutes |Serves: 3| Per serving: Calories 459; Carbs 30.8g ; Fat 35.4g ; Protein 8.8g

Ingredients:

- Quinoa – ½ cup, soaked
- Almond milk – 1 ½ cups
- Coconut shredded – 1 tbsp.
- Maple syrup – 2 tsps.
- Vanilla extract – 1 tsp.
- Ground cinnamon – ½ tsp.
- Hemp seeds – 1 tbsp.

Directions:

Place quinoa and almond milk in the Instant Pot bowl. Add vanilla extract and stir gently. Close the lid and press Rice. Cook quinoa for 14 minutes on Low. Then transfer cooked quinoa in a bowl and add maple syrup, coconut shred, and ground cinnamon. Add hemp seeds and mix the mixture well. Serve.

Breakfast Hash

Cook time: 25 minutes |Serves: 5| Per serving: Calories 126 ; Carbs 25.8g ; Fat 1g ; Protein 6g

Ingredients:

- Mushroom – 1 cup, chopped
- Zucchini – 1, chopped
- Red potatoes – 2, chopped
- Red sweet pepper – 1, chopped
- Vegetable broth – 1/3 cup
- Salt – 1 tsp.
- Fresh dill – 1 tbsp. chopped
- Ground black pepper – ½ tsp.
- Pinto beans – 1/3 cup, canned
- Fresh parsley – 1 tbsp. chopped

- Olive oil - 1 tbsp.

Directions:

Press Sauté and pour olive oil. Add zucchini and potatoes. Sprinkle the vegetables with salt, and ground black pepper. Sauté the vegetables for 5 minutes. Then add the mushrooms, and sweet pepper. Add dill and parsley. Then add pinto beans and vegetable broth. Mix up the hash and close. Cook for 20 minutes on Sauté mode. Serve.

Potato Pancakes

Cook time: 15 minutes |Serves: 4| Per serving: Calories 159; Carbs 29g; Fat 3.7g ; Protein 3.2g

Ingredients:

- Potatoes – 3, peeled
- Wheat flour – 2 tbsps.
- Cornstarch – 1 tsp.
- Salt – 1 tsp.
- Ground black pepper – ½ tsp.
- Chives – 1 tbsp.
- Fresh dill – 1 tsp. chopped
- Olive oil – 1 tbsp.

Directions:

Grate potatoes and mix them up with wheat flour, cornstarch, salt, black pepper, chives, and fresh dill. Separate the mixture into 4 parts. Preheat the Instant Pot and add olive oil. Place the first part of the potato mixture in the Instant pot and then flatten it to make the shape of a pancake. Cook on Sauté for 4 minutes on each side. Repeat and serve.

Cinnamon Apple Porridge

Cook time: 7 minutes |Serves: 4| Per serving: Calories 232; Carbs 45g ; Fat 4g ; Protein 7g

Ingredients:

- Quinoa – 1 cup, rinsed
- Water – 1 ½ cups
- Maple syrup – 2 tbsps.
- Ground cinnamon – 2 tbsps.
- Vanilla extract – ½ tsp.
- Salt – ¼ tsp.
- Apple – 1, chopped
- Nondairy milk – 1 cup

Directions:

In the Instant Pot, stir together the apple, salt, vanilla, cinnamon, maple syrup, water, and quinoa. Cover and cook on High for 7 minutes. Stir in the milk and serve.

Oats with Milk and Blueberry
Cook time: 10 minutes |Serves: 4| Per serving: Calories 328; Carbs 47g ; Fat 13g ; Protein 10g

Ingredients:

- Steel-cut oats – 2 cups
- Water – 4 ½ cups
- Non-dairy milk – 1 cup
- Agave or maple syrup – 2 tbsps.
- Salt – ¼ tsp.
- Chia seeds – ¼ to ½ cup
- Chopped walnuts – 1 cup
- Fresh blueberries – 1 cup

Directions:

In the Instant Pot, stir together the water and oats. Cover and cook on High for 10 minutes. Open and add the milk. Stir in agave and salt. Top with blueberries, walnuts, and chia seeds and serve.

Kale and Sweet Potato Mini Quiche
Cook time:17 minutes |Serves: 7 | Per serving: Calories 150; Carbs 16g ; Fat 5g ; Protein 14g

Ingredients:

- Firm tofu – 1 (14-ounce package) lightly pressed
- Non-dairy milk – ¼ cup
- Nutritional yeast – ¼ cup
- Cornstarch – 1 tbsp.
- Sea salt – ½ tsp. plus more for seasoning
- Garlic powder – ½ tsp.
- Onion powder – ½ tsp.
- Ground turmeric – ½ tsp.
- Shredded sweet potato – ½ cup
- Kale leaves – 1 handful, chopped
- Water – 1 cup, plus 1 tbsp.
- Freshly ground black pepper

Directions:

In a food processor, combine turmeric, onion powder, garlic powder, salt, cornstarch, yeast, milk, and tofu. Blend until smooth. Press Sauté on the Instant Pot. Add 1 tbsp. water, kale, and sweet potato. Sauté for 1 to 2 minutes. Stir the veggies into the tofu mixture and spoon the mixture into a prepared mold. Cover the mold tightly with aluminum foil. Place on the trivet. Add the remaining

1 cup of water to the Instant Pot and place the trivet with the mold in the Instant Pot. Cover and cook on High for 15 minutes. Serve.

Buckwheat Porridge

Cook time: 3 minutes |Serves: 2| Per serving: Calories 438; Carbs 51g ; Fat 28g ; Protein 6.2g

Ingredients:

- Raw buckwheat – 1 cup
- Coconut milk – 3 cups, divided
- Banana – 1
- Dried cranberries – ¼ cup
- Splash of vanilla
- Dash of cinnamon

Directions:

Add everything in the Instant Pot and cover. Cook on High for 3 minutes. Open and add another splash of milk. Stir to thicken. Serve.

Mexican Breakfast Casserole

Cook time: 5 minutes |Serves: 4 | Per serving: Calories 422; Carbs 60g ; Fat 3g ; Protein 11g

Ingredients:

- Cooked brown rice – 2 cups
- Pinto beans – 1 large can
- Diced green tomatoes with chili pepper – 1 can
- Cilantro – 1 tsp.
- Tomato paste – 1 small can
- Lime zest
- Water – 1 ½ cup

Directions:

Except for the lime zest, combine and mix everything in the Instant Pot. Cover and cook for 5 minutes on High. Do a natural release and serve with lime zest.

Creamy Wheat Cereal

Cook time: 2 minutes |Serves: 2| Per serving: Calories 538; Carbs 58g; Fat32g ; Protein 12g

Ingredients:

- Ground wheat berries – 2 cups
- Agave nectar – 1 tbsp.
- Coconut milk – 2 cups
- Splash of vanilla
- Cocoa powder – 1 tbsp.

Directions:

In the Instant Pot, add everything and mix. Cover and cook on High for 2 minutes. Do a natural release. Serve.

Hash Browns
Cook time:10 minutes |Serves: 4| Per serving: Calories 211; Carbs 23g ; Fat 12g ; Protein 1g

Ingredients:

- Hash browns – 1 (1-pound) package
- Green onions – 1 small bunch
- Parsley – 1 tsp.
- Coconut oil – 1 tbsp.
- Salt and pepper to taste

Directions:

In the Instant Pot, add all the ingredients. Cover and cook on High for 10 minutes. Do a natural release and open. Serve.

Breakfast Shake
Cook time: 5 minutes| Serves: 3| Per serving: Calories 333; Carbs 8g; Fat 26g ; Protein 18g

Ingredients:

- Butter – 2 tbsps. softened
- Full-fat coconut milk – ½ cup
- Liquid stevia – 10 drops
- Pecans – 1 tbsp. chopped
- Cashews – 1 tbsp. chopped
- Macadamia nuts – 1 tbsp. chopped
- Cinnamon – ½ tsp. ground
- Turmeric – ½ tsp. ground
- Heavy whipping cream – ¼ cup
- Mixed dark berries – ¼ cup
- Whey protein powder – 2 scoops
- Ice cubes to serve
- Water – 1 ½ cups

Directions:

Pour 1 ½ cups of water into a blender. Press sauté on the Instant Pot and melt the butter. Pour in the coconut milk. Then add the berries, whipping cream, turmeric, cinnamon, macadamia nuts, cashews, pecans, and stevia. Stir continuously. Press Cancel when mixed well. Pour the mixture into the blender. Add the protein powder and blend well. Serve with ice.

Fat Burning Shake

Cook time: 5 minutes |Serves:3 | Per serving: Calories 434; Carbs 5.4 g ; Fat 45.1g ; Protein 10.8g

Ingredients:

- Butter – 2 tbsps. softened
- Full-fat coconut milk – ¾ cup
- Liquid stevia – 10 drops
- Unflavored MCT oil – 3 tbsps.
- Pecans – 2 tbsps. chopped
- Walnuts – 2 tbsps. chopped
- Sugar-free chocolate chips – 2 tbsps.
- Coconut oil – 1 tbsp.
- Vanilla extract – ½ tsp.
- Turmeric – ½ tsp. ground
- Mint – ½ tsp. chopped
- Whey protein powder – 2 scoops
- Ice cubes
- Water – 1 ¼ cups

Directions:

Pour water into the blender. Press sauté and melt the butter in the Instant Pot. Pour in the coconut milk. Then add the turmeric, vanilla, coconut oil, chocolate chips, walnuts, pecans, mint, MCT oil, and stevia. Stir continuously. Press Cancel when mixed. Pour into the blender and add the protein powder. Blend until mixed. Serve with ice.

Bacon and Egg Bake

Cook time: 19 minutes |Serves: 3| Per serving: Calories 302; Carbs 4.5g ; Fat 23.9g ; Protein 17.6g

Ingredients:

- Eggs – 5
- Bacon – 3 slices, cooked and finely chopped
- Avocado oil – 2 tbsps.
- Kale – ½ cup, chopped
- Broccoli – ½ cup, chopped
- Heavy whipping cream – ½ cup
- Cayenne pepper – ½ tsp. ground
- Basil – ½ tsp. dried
- Kosher salt and pepper to taste
- Water – 1 cup

Directions:

Add 1-cup of water into the Instant Pot and place in the trivet. In a bowl, combine basil, salt, black pepper, cayenne pepper, whipping cream, broccoli, kale, oil, bacon, and eggs. Mix well. Place in a dish and cover with foil. Place on top of the trivet. Close and cook 19 minutes on High. Do a natural release and open. Serve.

Bacon and Sausage Omelet
Cook time:25 minutes |Serves: 6| Per serving: Calories 222; Carbs 3.5g ; Fat 15g ; Protein 16g

Ingredients:

- Eggs – 6
- Bacon slices – 6, cooked and crumbled
- Sausage links – 6, sliced
- Onions – 1, diced
- Almond milk – ½ cup
- Garlic powder – ¼ tsp.
- Salt – ¼ tsp.
- Pepper – ¼ tsp.
- Water – 1 ½ cups

Directions:

Pour the water into the Instant Pot and lower the rack. Beat the eggs along with the milk and seasonings. Add the remaining ingredients. Grease a baking dish with cooking spray. Pour the egg mixture into it. Place the dish on the rack and cover. Cook on Manual for 25 minutes. Serve.

Chapter 3 Snacks and Appetizers

Garlic Brussels Sprouts
Cook time:6 minutes |Serves: 4| Per serving: Calories 128; Carbs 6g ; Fat 8g ; Protein 4g

Ingredients:

- Minced garlic – 2 tsps.
- Brussels sprouts – 1 pound, trimmed, and halved
- Water – ½ cup
- Coconut oil – 2 tbsps.
- Chopped yellow onion – ½ cup
- Salt and black pepper to taste

Directions:

Press Sauté and add oil to the Instant Pot. Then add garlic and onions. Stir-fry for 2 minutes. Add the rest of the ingredients and mix. Cover and cook 2 minutes on High. Do a quick release and open the lid. Drain excess liquid and serve on a plate.

Ginger Eggplants
Cook time: 8 minutes |Serves: 4| Per serving: Calories 346; Carbs 6g ; Fat 28g ; Protein 4g

Ingredients:

- Garlic – 4 cloves, minced
- Chopped onion – 1
- Coconut oil – 4 tbsps.
- Eggplants – 2, sliced into 3-inch in length
- Ginger – 1 tsp. minced
- Coconut aminos – ¼ cup
- Lemon juice – 1 tsp.
- Water – ¼ cup

Directions:

Press Sauté and add oil to the Instant Pot. Add the eggplant and stir-fry for 2 minutes. Add in the onions and garlic and stir-fry until fragrant. Add the lemon juice, coconut aminos, and ginger. Mix and add some water if needed. Close and cook 6 minutes on High. Serve.

Lemon Radish
Cook time: 7 minutes| Serves: 4| Per serving: Calories 76; Carbs 4g ; Fat 5g; Protein 6g

Ingredients:

- Radishes – 2 cups, peeled and cut into rounds

- Chicken stock – ½ cup
- Melted ghee – 2 tbsps.
- Grated lemon zest – 1 tbsp.
- Salt and black pepper to taste
- Chopped chives – 1 tbsp.

Directions:

Add the radishes, with salt, pepper, stock, and lemon zest. Stir to mix well. Close and cook 8 minutes on High. Open the lid and add ghee and chives. Serve.

Ginger Broccoli
Cook time: 10 minutes |Serves: 5| Per serving: Calories 188; Carbs 9g ; Fat 13g ; Protein 6g

Ingredients:

- Ginger – 2 tbsps. sliced
- Broccoli – 2 heads, cut into florets
- Olive oil – 3 tbsps.
- Garlic – 3 cloves, minced
- Sesame oil – 3 tbsps.
- Coconut aminos – 2 tbsps.

Directions:

Press Sauté and add oil to the Instant Pot. Add the garlic, and ginger and cook until translucent and softened. Add the other ingredients and mix well. Cover and cook 6 minutes on High. Open and serve.

Boiled Peanuts
Cook time: 30 minutes |Serves: 8| Per serving: Calories 168; Carbs 11.1g ; Fat 10.6g ; Protein 7.5g

Ingredients:

- Green peanuts in shells – 2 cups
- Water – 2 cups
- Salt – 2 tsps.
- Cayenne pepper – 1 tsp.
- Taco seasoning – 1 tsp.

Directions:

Place green peanuts, water, salt, cayenne pepper, and taco seasoning in the Instant Pot. Close and cook on High for 30 minutes. Open and drain water and transfer peanuts into the serving bowl. Serve.

Candied Pecans
Cook time: 20 minutes |Serves: 30| Per serving: Calories 28; Carbs 0.8g ; Fat 2.7g ; Protein 0.3g

Ingredients:

- Butter – 1 tsp.
- Raw pecans – 4 cups
- Erythritol – ¼ cup
- Ground cinnamon – 1 tsp.
- Ground nutmeg – ½ tsp.
- Ground ginger – 1/8 tsp.
- Cayenne pepper – 1/8 tsp.
- Pinch of sea salt
- Water – ½ cup

Directions:

Add the butter in the instant pot and press Sauté. Then, except for water, add all the ingredients and cook and stir for 5 minutes. Then cover and cook on High for 10 minutes. Meanwhile, preheat the oven to 350F. When finished cooking, transfer the pecans onto a baking sheet. Bake for 5 minutes. Remove from the oven, cool and serve.

Deviled Eggs
Cook time: 6 minutes |Serves: 4| Per serving: Calories 132; Carbs 1g ; Fat 11g ; Protein 6g

Ingredients:

- Eggs – 4
- Mayonnaise – 2 tbsps.
- Olive oil – 1 tbsp.
- Dijon mustard – 1 tsp.
- Apple cider vinegar – ½ tsp.
- Sriracha – ¼ tsp.
- Paprika to taste
- Water – 1 cup for the pot

Directions:

Arrange a steamer basket in the bottom of the instant pot and add 1 cup water. Place eggs into the steamer basket. Cook on High for 6 minutes. Open and peel the eggs and cut in half lengthwise. Remove the yolks and transfer into a bowl. Mash the egg yolks with a fork. Except for paprika, add remaining ingredients and mix well. Fill the egg whites with this mixture. Sprinkle with paprika and serve.

Avocado Deviled Eggs
Cook time: 6 minutes| Serves: 6| Per serving: Calories 213; Carbs 1g ; Fat 18g ; Protein 7g

Ingredients:

- Eggs – 6
- Avocados – 2, sliced
- Chopped fresh cilantro – 1 tbsp.

- Serrano chile – 1, minced
- Fresh lime juice – 1 tbsp.
- Sour cream – 1 tbsp.
- Salt to taste
- Minced chives – 1 tbsp.
- Water – 1 cup for the pot

Directions:

Steam the eggs in the Instant Pot for 6 minutes on High. Then peel the eggs and cut in half lengthwise. Remove the yolks from egg halves and place them in a bowl. In a bowl, mash the avocado with a fork. Except for chives, add 2 egg yolks and remaining ingredients. Mix well. Fill the egg whites with this mixture. Sprinkle with chives and serve.

Chive Salmon Bites
Cook time: 10 minutes |Serves: 4| Per serving: Calories 180; Carbs 7g ; Fat 3g ; Protein 9g

Ingredients:

- Lemon juice – 1 tbsp.
- Oil – 1 tbsp.
- Salmon fillets – 1 pound, skinless, boneless, and cubed
- Garlic – 2 cloves, minced
- Chives – 1 tbsp. chopped
- Lime zest – 1 tbsp. grated
- Water – 1 cup

Directions:

In a bowl, mix the salmon cubes with the rest of the ingredients except the chives and water and mix. Add the water and the steamer basket in the pot. Add the salmon on top of the steamer basket and cover. Cook on High for 10 minutes. Open and serve sprinkled with chives.

Sweet Brussels
Cook time:4 minutes |Serves: 2| Per serving: Calories 68; Carbs 6g ; Fat 4g ; Protein 2.5g

Ingredients:

- Brussels sprouts – ½ pound, trimmed
- Butter – 1 tbsp.
- Maple syrup – 1 ½ tsps.
- Pinch of salt
- Orange zest – 1 tsp.
- Pinch of pepper
- Orange juice – 3 tbsps.

Directions:

Add the ingredients in the instant pot and mix. Close and cook for 4 minutes on High. Serve.

Bacon Cheese Muffins

Cook time: 8 minutes |Serves: 3| Per serving: Calories 170; Carbs 1g ; Fat 13g ; Protein 12g

Ingredients:

- Cheddar cheese – 4 tbsps. shredded
- Lemon pepper seasoning – ¼ tsp.
- Precooked bacon – 4 slices, crumbled
- Green onion – 1, diced
- Eggs – 4
- Water – 1 ½ cups for the pot

Directions:

Arrange the steamer basket inside the pot and add 1 ½ cups of water. Whisk the eggs in a bowl. Add the lemon pepper and beat again. Divide the bacon, green onion, and cheese into 4 muffin cups. Top with the egg mixture and stir to mix. Arrange the cups on the steamer basket. Cover and cook on High for 8 minutes. Serve.

Prosciutto Wrapped Asparagus

Cook time: 3 minutes |Serves: 2| Per serving: Calories 124; Carbs 5.5g ; Fat 4g ; Protein 17g

Ingredients:

- Asparagus spears – ½ pound
- Sliced prosciutto – 5 ounces
- Water – 2 cups for the pot

Directions:

Wrap the prosciutto slices around asparagus spears. Arrange a steamer basket in the bottom of the instant pot and add 2 cups of water. Arrange the asparagus over the trivet. Cook 3 minutes on High and serve.

Tofu Wraps

Cook time: 5 minutes| Serves: 6| Per serving: Calories 41; Carbs 2g ; Fat 2g ; Protein 3.6g

Ingredients:

- Lettuce leaves – 6
- Chili pepper – 1 tsp.
- Soy sauce – 1 tbsp.
- Brown sugar – 1 tsp.
- Water – 3 tbsps.
- Salt – ½ tsp.
- Firm tofu – 8 oz. chopped
- Mustard – 1 tsp.
- Olive oil – 1 tsp.
- Fresh parsley – 1 oz. chopped

Directions:

Make the tofu sauce: whisk together chili pepper, soy sauce, sugar, water, salt, mustard, and olive oil. Then combine together tofu and sauce. Let it marinate for 10 minutes. Press Sauté on the Instant Pot. Place the tofu and all marinade inside. Sauté and stir for 5 minutes. Remove the mixture from the IP and chill it until it reaches room temperature. Fill the lettuce leaves with chopped parsley and tofu. Sprinkle tofu wraps with the remaining cooked marinade and serve.

Pumpkin Hummus
Cook time:25 minutes |Serves: 6| Per serving: Calories 212; Carbs 24g ; Fat 10g ; Protein 7.7g

Ingredients:

- Pumpkin puree – ½ cup
- Chickpea – 1 ½ cups, soaked
- Tahini – 2 tsps.
- Harissa – 1 tsp.
- Olive oil – 4 tbsps.
- Garlic – 1 clove, peeled
- Water – 5 cups

Directions:

Place chickpeas and water in the Instant Pot. Add the garlic clove and cover. Cook for 25 minutes on High. Open and drain the liquid. Transfer the cooked chickpeas and garlic clove in the food processor. Add tahini, pumpkin puree, harissa, and olive oil. Blend until smooth. Serve.

Spicy Edamame Snack
Cook time: 11 minutes |Serves: 6| Per serving: Calories 89; Carbs 7.5g ; Fat 4g ; Protein 5.6g

Ingredients:

- Edamame beans – 1 cup
- Minced garlic – 1 tsp.
- Butter - 1 tbsp.
- Cayenne pepper – ½ tsp.
- Sesame seeds – 1 tbsp.
- Soy sauce – ¼ cup
- Salt – ¼ tsp.
- Brown sugar – ½ tsp.
- Water – 1 cup, for cooking

Directions:

Pour water into the Instant Pot. Add edamame beans and salt. Close and cook on High for 6 minutes. Meanwhile, mix minced garlic, cayenne pepper, sesame seeds, sugar, and soy sauce. Transfer cooked edamame beans in the bowl. Clean the pot and add butter and melt it on Sauté.

Add soy sauce mixture and boil for 5 minutes. Chill the sauce. Pour the sauce over the edamame beans and mix. Serve.

Vegan Nuggets

Cook time: 6 minutes| Serves: 8| Per serving: Calories 200; Carbs 31g ; Fat 5.1g ; Protein 7.9g

Ingredients:

- Panko bread crumbs – ½ cup
- Turmeric – 1 tbsp.
- Rolled oats – 4 oz.
- Onion – 1, diced
- Olive oil – 1 tbsp.
- Ground black pepper – ½ tsp.
- Salt – 1 tsp.
- Coconut milk – 1 tbsp.
- Chickpeas – 1 cup, canned
- Tomato sauce – 1 tbsp.
- Water – ½ cup for cooking

Directions:

Preheat the Instant Pot on Sauté. Add olive oil and diced onion. Cook and stir for 4 to 5 minutes. Then transfer to a food processor. Add rolled oats, ground black pepper, salt, coconut milk, canned chickpeas, and tomato sauce. Blend the mixture until smooth. In another bowl, mix together turmeric, and panko breadcrumbs. Make medium size nuggets from the chickpea mixture. Then coat nuggets in the panko bread mixture. Pour water into the Instant Pot and insert rack. Place the pot on the rack and put nuggets inside. Close and cook on High for 3 minutes. Serve.

Spring Rolls

Cook time: 4 minutes| Serves: 3| Per serving: Calories 22; Carbs 4.5g ; Fat 0.2g ; Protein 2g

Ingredients:

- Red cabbage – ¼ cup, shredded
- Fresh parsley – 2 oz. chopped
- Mushrooms – 1 cup, chopped
- Carrot – 1 cut into wedges
- Soy sauce – 1 tbsp.
- Paprika – 1 tsp.
- Lemon juice – 1 tbsp.
- Lime zest – ¼ tsp.
- Chili flakes – ½ tsp.
- Spring roll wraps – 6
- Water – 1 cup, for cooking

Directions:

In a bowl, mix shredded red cabbage, fresh parsley, chopped mushrooms, carrot, soy sauce, paprika, lemon juice, lime zest, and chili flakes. Fill the spring roll wraps with the cabbage mixture. Wrap the spring roll wraps. Pour water in the Instant Pot and insert steamer rack inside. Place prepared spring rolls on the steamer rack. Close and cook on High for 4 minutes. Open and serve.

Lettuce Wraps
Cook time: 4 minutes |Serves: 4 | Per serving: Calories 209; Carbs 15.7g ; Fat 7.3g ; Protein 20.1g

Ingredients:

- Lettuce leaves – 4
- Parmesan – 3 oz. grated
- Cucumber – 1, chopped
- Chives – 1 tbsp. chopped
- Tempeh – 8 oz. chopped
- Italian seasoning - 1 tbsp.
- Tomato sauce – 3 tbsps.
- Tomato juice – ¼ cup
- Brown sugar – 1 tsp.
- Turnip – 1/3 cup, chopped

Directions:

In the Instant Pot, combine chopped tempeh, Italian seasoning, tomato sauce, tomato juice, sugar, and turnip. Mix and close the lid. Cook on High for 4 minutes and open. Mix up grated Parmesan, chopped cucumber, and chives. Place the mixture on the lettuce leaves. Chill the tempeh mixture and transfer it over the vegetables. Wrap the lettuce leaves and serve.

Garlic Toast
Cook time: 2 minutes |Serves: 2| Per serving: Calories 153; Carbs 17.7g ; Fat 8g ; Protein 3.1g

Ingredients:

- Bread slices – 4
- Minced garlic – 1 tbsp.
- Olive oil - 1 tbsp.

Directions:

Preheat the Instant Pot. Then add the olive oil. Add the bread slices and cook then on Sauté for 1 minute on each side. Remove the bread slices from the Instant Pot and rub with minced garlic from each side. Serve.

Crispy Chickpea
Cook time: 57 minutes |Serves: 4| Per serving: Calories 219; Carbs 31g ; Fat 6.5g ; Protein 9.6g

Ingredients:

- Chickpeas – 7 oz.
- Water – 4 cups
- Salt – 1 tsp.
- Taco seasoning – 1 tbsp.
- Olive oil - 1 tbsp.
- Ground black pepper – 1 tsp.

Directions:

Place chickpeas, salt, and water in the Instant Pot. Close and cook on High for 50 minutes. Open and drain water and dry the chickpeas on paper towels. Then add olive oil, taco seasoning, and ground black pepper. Mix well. Cook them in the Instant Pot on Sauté for 7 minutes. Chill the cooked chickpeas and serve.

Herbed Tomato

Cook time: 20 minutes |Serves: 4| Per serving: Calories 30; Carbs 6.4g ; Fat 0.4g ; Protein 1.5g

Ingredients:

- Tomatoes – 4
- Fresh cilantro – 1 oz. chopped
- Garlic – 3 cloves, peeled
- Ground black pepper - 1 tsp.
- Salt - ½ tsp.
- Oregano – 1 tsp.
- Apple cider vinegar - 1 tbsp.
- Water – 1/3 cup

Directions:

Cut tomatoes into the halves and place them in the Instant Pot. Add fresh cilantro, garlic, ground black pepper, salt, oregano, apple cider vinegar, and water. Close the lid and cook on Sauté for 20 minutes. Stir it from time to time. Cool and serve.

Lentil Crackers

Cook time: 8 minutes |Serves: 8| Per serving: Calories 135; Carbs 16.6g ; Fat 5g ; Protein 7.7g

Ingredients:

- Green lentils – 1 cup, cooked
- Flax meal – ½ cup
- Ground black pepper – 1 tsp.
- Salt – 1 tsp.
- Dried parsley - 1 tsp.
- Coconut oil – 4 tsps.
- A drizzle of oil for the Instant Pot

Directions:

In a food processor, blend lentils until smooth and transfer to a bowl. Add flax meal, ground black pepper, salt, dried parsley, and coconut oil. Mix it up and knead the dough. Roll the lentil dough with the rolling pin. Then make medium size crackers from the dough. Press Sauté on the Instant Pot. Add a drizzle of oil in the instant pot and cook the crackers 2 minutes on each side or until crunchy. Repeat to finish all the crackers. Serve.

BBQ Cauliflower Florets

Cook time:15 minutes| Serves:2 | Per serving: Calories 89; Carbs 15.8g ; Fat 2.9g ; Protein 1.3g

Ingredients:

- Cauliflower florets - 1 cup
- BBQ sauce – 4 tbsps.
- Turmeric – 1 tsp.
- Paprika – 1 tsp.
- Cayenne pepper – 1 tsp.
- Water – ¼ cup
- Olive oil - 1 tsp.

Directions:

Place cauliflower florets in a bowl. Add BBQ sauce, turmeric, paprika, cayenne pepper, water, and olive oil. Mix and set aside for 10 to 15 minutes to marinate. Then transfer it in the Instant Pot, add all the remaining BBQ sauce mixture. Sauté the cauliflower for 10 to 15 minutes or until cooked. Serve.

Buffalo Brussel Sprouts

Cook time: 10 minutes| Serves: 4| Per serving: Calories 29; Carbs 3.5g ; Fat 1.3g ; Protein 0.8g

Ingredients:

- Brussel sprouts - 1 cup
- Buffalo sauce – 5 tbsps.
- Olive oil – 1 tsp.
- Water – 1 cup, for cooking

Directions:

Pour water in the Instant Pot. Add Brussels sprouts and cook on High for 4 minutes. Do a quick release. Drain water and pour olive oil in the Instant Pot. Add buffalo sauce and mix well. Cook Brussels sprouts on Sauté for 5 minutes. Serve.

Green Croquettes

Cook time: 5 minutes| Serves: 4| Per serving: Calories 155; Carbs 20.6 g ; Fat 6.8g ; Protein 4.4g

Ingredients:

- Sweet potatoes – 2, peeled, boiled
- Fresh spinach – 1 cup
- Peanuts – 1 tbsp.
- Flax meal – 3 tbsps.
- Salt – 1 tsp.
- Ground black pepper – 1 tsp.
- Olive oil – 1 tbsp.
- Dried oregano – ½ tsp.
- Wheat flour – ¾ cup

Directions:

Mash the sweet potatoes and place them in a bowl. Add flax meal, salt, dried oregano, and ground black pepper. Then blend the spinach with peanuts until smooth. Add the green mixture in the sweet potato. Mix. Make medium size croquettes and coat them in the wheat flour. Preheat Instant Pot on Sauté mode well. Add olive oil. Roast croquettes for 1 minute on each side or until golden brown. Serve.

Polenta Fries
Cook time: 10minutes| Serves: 10| Per serving: Calories 244; Carbs 16.7g ; Fat 19.4g ; Protein3.2g

Ingredients:

- Polenta – 1 cup
- Milk – 3 cups
- Salt – 1 tsp.
- Ground black pepper – 1 tsp.
- Dried cilantro - 1 tsp.
- Ground cumin – ½ tsp.
- Butter - 1 tbsp.
- Olive oil - 1 tbsp.

Directions:

Place the polenta in the Instant Pot. Add milk and salt. Then add black pepper, dried cilantro, and ground cumin. Mix well. Close and cook for 6 minutes on High. Open and add the butter. Mix well. Transfer the polenta into a square pan and flatten well. Chill until solid. Then cut solid polenta into 10 sticks. Brush every stick with olive oil. Clean and preheat the Instant Pot on Sauté. Cook the polenta stick in the Instant Pot, for 1 minute on each side. Serve.

Spicy Cauliflower and Tomatoes
Cook time: 7 minutes |Serves: 4| Per serving: Calories 74; Carbs 3.3g ; Fat 1.7g ; Protein 4.5g

Ingredients:

- Chopped tomatoes – 2

- Chopped small onion – ½
- Green chile – 1
- Olive oil – 1 tsp.
- Ground cumin – 1 tsp.
- Ground turmeric – ½ tsp.
- Paprika – ½ tsp.
- Salt and black pepper to taste
- Cauliflower head – 1, cut into small florets
- Water – ½ cup
- Chopped fresh cilantro – 1 tbsp.

Directions:

Add onion, tomato, and green chile in a food processor and pulse until smooth. Add oil in the Instant Pot and press Sauté. Then add the pureed onion mixture and cook for 2 to 3 minutes. Add the spices and cook for 1 minute. Stir in cauliflower and water. Cover and cook on Low for 3 minutes. Serve.

Garlic Mashed Potatoes

Cook time: 12 minute |Serves: 6| Per serving: Calories 352; Carbs 43g ; Fat 16g ; Protein 9g

Ingredients:

- Chicken broth – 1 (32 oz) carton
- Little potatoes – 3 lbs.
- Salted butter – 1 stick
- Cream cheese – ½ block
- Milk – ½ cup
- Minced garlic – 3 tsps.
- Salt and pepper to taste
- Dried chives – 2 tbsps.

Directions:

Add the broth, and potatoes in the pot. Season and cover. Cook for 12 minutes on Steam. Then open and drain the broth. In a bowl place potato, and add garlic, milk, cream cheese and butter. Season and mash the potatoes with all the ingredients. Serve.

Deviled Egg Salad

Cook time: 12 minutes| Serves: 5| Per serving: Calories 313; Carbs 1.3g ; Fat 26g ; Protein 16g

Ingredients:

- Eggs – 10
- Raw bacon – 5 strips
- Mayonnaise – 2 tbsps.

- Dijon mustard – 1 tsp.
- Smoked paprika – ¼ tsp.
- Green onion – 1 stalk
- Salt and pepper to taste

Directions:

Grease a cake pan that fits inside the IP. Add the raw eggs in the cake pan. Pour 1 cup of water into the bottom of the IP. Then place the steam rack, and place the cake pan on top of it. Cook on High for 6 minutes. Remove the cake pan and flip the pan to remove the egg loaf from the pan. Chop up the loaf and place in a bowl. Clean the inner bowl and place it again into the IP. Add chopped bacon, press Sauté and cook until crispy. Add the bacon and the fat to the chopped eggs. Add smoked paprika, mustard, mayonnaise and season with salt and pepper. Mix, garnish with chopped green onion. Serve.

Braised Kale and Carrot Salad
Cook time: 8 minutes| Serves: 5| Per serving: Calories 41; Carbs 5g ; Fat 5g ; Protein 2g

Ingredients:

- Kale – 10 ounces, roughly chopped
- Ghee – 1 tbsp.
- Onion – 1, sliced
- Medium carrots – 3, chopped
- Garlic – 5 cloves, chopped
- Chicken broth – ½ cup
- Fresh ground pepper
- Vinegar as needed
- Red pepper flakes - ½ tsp.

Directions:

Press Sauté, add ghee and melt it. Add chopped carrots and onion and Sauté for a while. Pile the kale on top. Pour chicken broth and season with pepper. Close and cook on High for 8 minutes. Open, stir and add vinegar and sprinkle with pepper flakes. Serve.

Shrimp Salad
Cook time: 6 minutes |Serves: 4| Per serving: Calories 170; Carbs 7g ; Fat 9g ; Protein 6g

Ingredients:

- Shrimp – 1 pound, peeled and deveined
- Baby arugula – 2 cups
- Balsamic vinegar – 1 tbsp.
- Tomato paste – 2 tbsps.
- Spring onions – 2, chopped
- Oil – ½ tsp.

- Chili powder – ½ tsp.
- Oregano – ½ tsp. chopped
- Garlic – ½ tsp. minced

Directions:

Heat oil on Sauté. Add onions and cook for 2 minutes. Add the rest of the ingredients except the arugula and the vinegar. Cover and cook on High for 4 minutes. Open and transfer the shrimp mixture to a bowl. Add the arugula and vinegar. Mix and serve.

Parmesan Asparagus
Cook time: 8 minutes| Serves: 4| Per serving: Calories 114; Carbs 3g ; Fat 10g ; Protein 3g

Ingredients:

- Full-fat butter – 3 tbsps.
- Grated Parmesan cheese – 3 tbsps.
- Trimmed asparagus – 1 pound
- Garlic cloves – 3, minced

Directions:

Arrange the garlic and asparagus in a large piece of foil and top with butter. Fold the edges to make a pocket. Add 1-cup water in the pot and place a trivet. Arrange the pocket over the trivet. Close and press Steam. Cook 8 minutes on High. Open and top with cheese. Serve.

Cinnamon Carrots
Cook time: 4 minutes| Serves: 6 | Per serving: Calories 98; Carbs 3g ; Fat 8g ; Protein 4g

Ingredients:

- Erythritol – 2 tbsps. powdered
- Cinnamon – ½ tsp. ground
- Baby carrots – 2 pounds, trimmed
- Butter – 1/3 cup
- Salt to taste
- Water – ½ cup

Directions:

Add all the ingredients and mix well. Close and cook 4 minutes on High. Open and serve.

Perfect Chicken Wings
Cook time:15 minutes |Serves: 4| Per serving: Calories 330; Carbs 1g ; Fat 12g ; Protein 49g

Ingredients:

- Chicken wings – 1 ½ pounds
- Tomato paste – ¼ cup

- Liquid stevia – 2 to 3 drops
- Fresh lemon juice – 1 tbsp.
- Salt and freshly ground black pepper to taste
- Water – 1 cup for the pot

Directions:

Arrange a steamer trivet in the bottom of the Instant Pot and add 1-cup water. Place the pan on top of the trivet. Place the chicken wings on top of the trivet, standing vertically. Cover and cook on High for 10 minutes. Preheat the oven to the broiler. Meanwhile, in a bowl, add remaining ingredients and beat until mixed. Open the pot and transfer the chicken wings to a bowl of sauce. Coat the wings with sauce. Arrange the chicken wings onto a parchment paper-lined baking sheet and broil for 5 minutes. Serve hot with remaining sauce.

Muffins
Cook time: 8 minutes |Serves: 3| Per serving: Calories 170 ; Carbs 1g ; Fat 13g ; Protein 12g

Ingredients:

- Cheddar cheese – 4 tbsps. shredded
- Lemon pepper seasoning – ¼ tsp.
- Precooked bacon – 4 slices, crumbled
- Green onion – 1, diced
- Eggs – 4

Directions:

Arrange the steamer basket inside the pot and add 1 ½ cups of water. Whisk the eggs in a bowl. Add the lemon pepper and beat again. Divide the bacon, green onion, and cheese into 4 muffin cups. Top with the egg mixture and stir to mix. Arrange the cups on the steamer basket. Cover and cook for 8 minutes. Serve.

Pecans Snacks
Cook time: 20 minutes| Serves: 30| Per serving: Calories 28; Carbs 1g ; Fat 2.7g ; Protein 0.3g

Ingredients:

- Butter – 1 tsp.
- Raw pecans – 4 cups
- Erythritol – ¼ cup
- Ground cinnamon – 1 tsp.
- Ground nutmeg – ½ tsp.
- Ground ginger – 1/8 tsp.
- Cayenne pepper – 1/8 tsp.
- Pinch of sea salt
- Filtered water – ½ cup

Directions:

Add the butter in the instant pot and press Sauté. Then, except for water, add all the ingredients and cook and stir for 5 minutes. Cover and cook on High for 10 minutes. Meanwhile, preheat the oven to 350F. When done, remove the lid and transfer the pecans onto a baking sheet. Bake for 5 minutes. Remove from the oven, cool and serve.

Cauliflower Mac and Cheese
Cook time: 5 minutes| Serves: 4| Per serving: Calories 134; Carbs 3g; Fat 11g ; Protein 6g

Ingredients:

- Cauliflower rice – 2 cups
- Cream cheese – 2 tbsps.
- Half-and-half – ½ cup
- Grated sharp cheddar cheese – ½ cup
- Salt and ground black pepper to taste

Directions:

In a bowl, mix the cheddar cheese, cauliflower, half-and-half, cream cheese, salt, and pepper. Cover the bowl with aluminum foil. Pour 2 cups of water into the Instant Pot and place a trivet in the Pot. Place the bowl on the trivet. Cover and cook on High for 5 minutes. Open and remove the bowl. Remove the foil. Place the cooked cauliflower under the broiler and broil for 3 to 5 minutes or until cheese is brown and bubbling. Serve.

Meatballs
Cook time: 5 minutes |Serves: 8| Per serving: Calories 223; Carbs 1.42g ; Fat 9.9g ; Protein 22.4g

Ingredients:

- Ground beef – 1 ½ pounds
- Finely chopped bacon – ½ cup
- Almond flour – ½ cup
- Garlic powder – 1 tsp.
- Parsley flakes – ½ tsp.
- Ground black pepper and salt to taste
- Ketchup – 1 ½ cups
- Steak sauce – ½ cup
- Filtered water – 2 cups
- Shredded Parmesan cheese - ¼ cup

Directions:

Except for ketchup, steak sauce, water, and cheese, add all the ingredients in a bowl and mix well. Make equal sized meatballs from the mixture. In another bowl, add ketchup, steak sauce, and water and mix well. At the bottom of the IP, please meatballs and top with ketchup mixture. Cook on High for 5 minutes. Open and sprinkle with cheese. Serve.

Egg & Cheese Salad

Cook time: 5 minutes |Serves: 8| Per serving: Calories 113; Carbs 3.1g ; Fat 8.3g ; Protein 6.7g

Ingredients:

- Eggs – 8
- Grated hard cheese – 1 + ½ cups
- Garlic – 2 large cloves, grated
- Mayonnaise – 1/3 cup
- Yellow or Dijon mustard – 1 tsp.
- Pinch of salt
- Water – 1 cup for the pot

Directions:

Place a trivet on the bottom of the IP and add 1 cup of water. Place the eggs on top of the trivet. Cook for 5 minutes on High. Then open and remove the eggs and place them in cold water. To make the salad: peel and finely dice the eggs in a bowl. Reserve 1 egg yolk. Add the rest of the ingredients and mix well. Garnish with the egg yolk, fresh parsley, and black pepper. Serve.

Hot Pizza Dip

Cook time: 18 minutes |Serves: 10| Per serving: Calories 158; Carbs 6.9g; Fat 11.6g ; Protein 3.9g

Ingredients:

- Romano cheese – ½ cup, shredded
- Mozzarella cheese – ½ cup, shredded
- Green olives – ½ cup, pitted and sliced
- Oregano – ½ tsp.
- Garlic salt – ½ tsp.
- Cream cheese – 10 ounces
- Tomato sauce - 1 cup
- Basil – ½ tsp.
- Water – 1 ½ cups for the pot.

Directions:

Add water and a trivet in the Instant Pot. Grease a souffle dish with cooking spray. Place the cream cheese at the bottom of the dish. Add the tomato sauce and mozzarella cheese. Scatter sliced olives. Add oregano, basil, and garlic salt. Top with Romano cheese Place the dish on the trivet. Cover and cook for 18 minutes on High. Serve.

Fingerling Potatoes with Herbs

Cook time: 19 minutes| Serves: 6| Per serving: Calories 391; Carbs 19.9g; Fat 35g; Protein 2.4g

Ingredients:

- Fingerling potatoes – 1 ½ pounds
- Thyme – 2 sprigs
- Rosemary – 2 sprigs

- Shallot powder – ½ tsp.
- Porcini powder – ½ tsp.
- Butter – 4 tbsps. melted
- Black pepper – ½ tsp.
- Cayenne pepper – ½ tsp.
- Garlic paste -1 tsp.
- Broth – ¾ cup
- Salt to taste

Directions:

Melt the butter on Sauté. Add the potatoes and sauté for 9 minutes. Then pierce the potatoes in the middle with a fork. Add everything and cover. Cook for 10 minutes on High. Serve.

Hummus Dip

Cook time: 42 minutes| Serves: 8| Per serving: Calories 206; Carbs 8.8g; Fat 8.1g; Protein 4.6g

Ingredients:

- Dried chickpeas – 1 ½ cups
- Water – 4 cups
- Yellow onion – 1, chopped
- Garlic – 2 cloves, minced
- Tahini paste – 3 tbsps.
- Olive oil – 1 tbsp.
- Fresh lemon juice – 2 tbsps.

Directions:

Add oil and cook onion and garlic in the pot for 2 minutes on Sauté. Clean the pot and add water and chickpeas. Cover and cook 40 minutes on High. Open and drain chickpeas. Reserve the liquid. Add everything in the blender and blend until smooth. Add reserved liquid as needed. Serve.

Artichoke Dip

Cook time: 9 minutes| Serves: 8| Per serving: Calories 190; Carbs 10.3g; Fat 13.2g; Protein 1g

Ingredients:

- Ricotta cheese – 1 cup
- Romano cheese - 1 ¼ cups, grated
- Canned artichoke hearts – 12 ounces, chopped
- Garlic powder – 1 tsp.
- Shallot powder – ½ tsp.
- Gourmet mustard – 1 tsp.
- Salt and pepper to taste
- Cumin powder – ½ tsp.
- Kale – 2 cups, chopped
- Mayonnaise – ½ cup
- Water – 1 cup for the pot

Directions:

Grease a baking pan and add everything in it. Mix well. Add water and trivet to the pot. Pace the baking pan on top of the trivet and cover. Cook 9 minutes on High and serve.

Buttery Mushrooms with Herbs
Cook time: 4 minutes| Serves: 5| Per serving: Calories 88; Carbs 7.6g; Fat 5.5g ; Protein 3.6g

Ingredients:

- Butter – 2 tbsps.
- Button mushrooms – 20 ounces
- Smoked paprika – 1 tsp.
- Salt and pepper to taste
- Dried basil – 1 tsp.
- Broth – 1 cup
- Tomato paste – 2 tbsps.
- Garlic – 2 cloves, minced
- Dried oregano – ½ tsp.
- Dried rosemary – ½ tsp.
- Onion powder – 1 tsp.

Directions:

Place mushrooms, garlic, spices, and broth in the pot. Cover and cook 4 minutes on High. Open and stir in the rest of the ingredients. Serve.

Corn on the Cob with Chips
Cook time: 2 minutes |Serves: 4| Per serving: Calories 260; Carbs 52.5g; Fat 5.2g; Protein 5.7g

Ingredients:

- Barbecue sauce – 1/3 cup
- Corn on the cob – 4 ears, husks removed
- Potato chips – ½ cup, crushed
- Water – 1 cup for the pot

Directions:

Add water and a trivet to the pot. Place the corn on the trivet and cover. Cook on Steam for 2 minutes. Open and brush each corn with sauce and sprinkle with chips. Serve.

Chapter 4 Pasta and Side Dishes

Italian Red Mushroom Fettuccini

Cook time: 14minutes |Serves: 6| Per serving: Calories 465; Carbs 64g; Fat 20.4g; Protein 11g

Ingredients:

- Olive oil – ¼ cup
- Onion – 1, chopped
- Garlic – 3 cloves, minced
- Sun-dried tomatoes – 3 oz., minced
- Mushrooms – 5 oz., chopped
- Fettuccini pasta – 1 lb.
- Vegetable broth – 3 cups
- Pine nuts – ½ cup
- Salt to taste

Directions:

Press Sauté and add oil to the Instant Pot. Add onion, garlic, and a pinch of salt. Sauté for 3 minutes. Add mushrooms, mix and sauté for 2 minutes. Add tomatoes and mix. Place the pasta, mushrooms, and add the broth. Cover the pot. Cook on High for 8 minutes. Open and sprinkle with pine nuts and serve.

Balsamic Pasta Salad

Cook time:10 minutes| Serves: 2 | Per serving: Calories 533; Carbs 79.8g; Fat 18.8g; Protein 15.1g

Ingredients:

- Extra virgin olive oil – 2 tbsps.
- Onion – 1, sliced
- Garlic – 2 tbsps. minced
- Corn – ½ cup, boiled
- Carrot – 1, chopped
- Olives – 6, without kernel
- Dried tomatoes – 2, chopped
- Pasta – ½ lb.
- Honey – 1 tsp.
- Mustard – 1 tsp.
- Balsamic vinegar – 1 tbsp.
- Salt and pepper to taste.

Directions:

Press Sauté on the Instant Pot and add oil. Add onion, salt, and sauté for 3 to 4 minutes. Add carrot, olives, corn, and tomatoes, and sauté for 2 minutes more. Add pasta and remaining ingredients and pour in the water. Season salt and pepper to taste and stir well. Cover the pot and cook on High for 4 minutes. Do a quick release. Open and serve.

Penne Pasta with Tomato Sauce and Cheese
Cook time: 12 minutes |Serves: 5| Per serving: Calories 395; Carbs 51.8g; Fat 15.6g; Protein 14.9g

Ingredients:

- Olive oil – 2 tbsps.
- Scallion stalks – 2, chopped
- Green garlic stalks – 2, minced
- Penne – 10 ounces
- Ground black pepper – 1/3 tsp.
- Sea salt to taste
- Cayenne pepper – ¼ tsp.
- Dried marjoram – ¼ tsp.
- Dried oregano – ½ tsp.
- Dried basil – ½ tsp.
- Marinara sauce – ½ cup
- Vegetable broth – 2 cups
- Tomatoes -2, pureed
- Mizithra cheese – 1 cup, grated

Directions:

Press Sauté and heat the oil in the Instant Pot. Add scallions, and garlic and stir-fry until tender, about 3 to 4 minutes. Stir in spices, pasta, marinara sauce, broth, and pureed tomatoes. Do not stir, but the pasta should be covered with liquid. Cover the pot. Cook on High for 7 minutes. Open and fold in the cheese and cover, so the cheese melts. Serve.

Tuna Pasta and Cherry Tomatoes
Cook time:12 minutes| Serves: 4| Per serving: Calories 665; Carbs 79g; Fat 23g; Protein 37g

Ingredients:

- Tuna steaks – 8 ounces
- Penne pasta – 12 ounces
- Cherry tomatoes – 2 cups, halved
- Olives – 1/3 cup, pitted and halved
- Sweet onion – 1 cup, chopped
- Minced garlic – 2 tsps.
- Salt – ½ tsp.
- Ground black pepper – ½ tsp.

- Red chili flakes – ¼ tsp.
- Basil leaves – ½ cup, chopped
- Grated lemon zest – 1 ½ tsps.
- Lemon juice – 2 tbsps.
- Olive oil – 3 tbsps.
- Water – 2 ¾ cups

Directions:

Add onion, tomatoes, olives, garlic, red chili flakes, and pasta in the Instant Pot. Season with salt and black pepper and mix. Pour in water, stir to combine, then add tuna on top and cover. Cook on High for 6 minutes. Then do a quick release. Open and add remaining ingredients. Stir well and cover. Let pasta stand for 5 minutes, then serve.

Pasta e Fagioli
Cook time: 15 minutes| Serves: 4| Per serving: Calories 486; Carbs 95g ; Fat 8.3g ; Protein 12.4g

Ingredients:

- Olive oil – 2 tbsps.
- Garlic – 1 tsp. pressed
- Small-sized potatoes – 4, peeled and diced
- Parsnip – 1, chopped
- Carrot – 1, chopped
- Celery rib – 1, chopped
- Leek – 1, chopped
- Tomato paste – 6 ounces
- Water – 4 cups
- Vegetable bouillon cubes – 2
- Cannellini beans – 8 ounces, soaked overnight
- Elbow pasta – 6 ounces
- Oregano – ½ tsp.
- Basil – ½ tsp.
- Fennel seeds – ½ tsp.
- Sea salt, to taste
- Freshly cracked black pepper – ¼ tsp.
- Italian parsley – 2 tbsps. chopped

Directions:

Heat the oil on Sauté in the Instant Pot. Add garlic, potatoes, parsnip, carrot, celery, and leek and sauté until softened, about 5 to 7 minutes. Now add in the tomato paste, water, bouillon cubes, beans, pasta, oregano, basil, fennel seeds, black pepper, and salt. Cover and cook on High for 9 minutes. Do a quick release and open. Serve topped with parsley.

Tuscan Pasta

Cook time: 10 minutes| Serves: 4| Per serving: Calories 322; Carbs 52.2g; Fat 7.6g; Protein 13g

Ingredients:

- Penne pasta – 8 ounces
- Bell pepper – 1, chopped
- Fresh spinach – 1 cup, chopped
- Onion – ½ chopped
- Broccoli florets – 1 cup
- Water – 2 cups
- Mozzarella – ½ cup, grated
- Tomato sauce – ½ cup
- Olive oil – 1 tbsp.
- Cremini mushrooms – 3 ½ ounces
- Parmesan cheese – 1 tbsp. grated
- Salt and pepper to taste

Directions:

Press Sauté and add oil in the Instant Pot. Add onion, mushroom, and bell pepper. Cook for 3 to 4 minutes. Add pasta, broccoli, spinach, tomato sauce, water, salt, and pepper. Cover the pot. Cook on High for 5 minutes. Do a quick release and open. Add mozzarella. Press Sauté and stir well until melted. Serve topped with parmesan cheese.

Sausage Penne Pasta

Cook time: 15 minutes |Serves: 6| Per serving: Calories 413; Carbs 48g ; Fat 18g ; Protein 21g

Ingredients:

- Penne pasta – 18 ounces
- Sausage – 16 ounces
- Tomato paste – 2 cups
- Olive oil – 1 Tbsp.
- Garlic – 2 tsps. minced
- Oregano – 1 tsp.
- Parmesan cheese – ¼ cup, grated
- Water as needed

Directions:

Heat oil on Sauté in the Instant Pot. Add sausage and cook for 4 to 5 minutes. Add garlic and cook for 1 minute more. Stir in the remaining ingredients, except for parmesan and oregano. Cover with water and cook for 10 minutes on High. Open and top with grated parmesan and sprinkle with oregano. Serve.

Chicken Enchilada Pasta

Cook time: 14 minutes| Serves: 6| Per serving: Calories 567; Carbs 49g; Fat 25g; Protein 31g

Ingredients:

- Chicken breast – 2, diced
- Dry pasta – 3 cups
- Canned tomatoes – 10 ounces
- Canned Enchilada sauce – 20 ounces
- Water – 1 ¼ cups
- Diced onion – 1 cup
- Garlic – 1 tsp. minced
- Taco seasoning – 1 tsp.
- Olive oil – 1 tbsp.
- Cheddar cheese – 2 cups, shredded

Directions:

Heat oil in the Instant Pot on Sauté. Add onions and cook for 3 minutes. Add the rest of the ingredients except for the cheese. Cover and cook on High for 8 minutes. Open and stir in cheese and cook for 2 minutes, lid off, on Sauté. Serve.

Tagliatelle Pasta Bolognese

Cook time: 16 minutes| Serves: 6| Per serving: Calories 523; Carbs 56g; Fat 23g; Protein 31g

Ingredients:

- Olive oil – 2 tsps.
- Tagliatelle – 20 ounces
- Mixed ground meat – 1 ½ pounds
- Tomato pasta sauce – 1 ½ pounds
- Oregano – 1 tsp.
- Onion – 1 cup, chopped
- Garlic – 2 tsps. minced
- Bacon – 6 ounces, diced
- White wine – ½ cup
- Heavy cream – 1 cup
- Parmesan cheese – 1 cup, grated
- Water as needed
- Salt and pepper to taste

Directions:

Heat the oil on Sauté in the Instant Pot. Add garlic and onion. Cook for 3 minutes. Add meat and cook for 4 minutes. Add everything except for the heavy cream and parmesan cheese. Pour in water to cover entirely. Cover and cook on High for 10 minutes. Open and stir in heavy cream and serve with grated parmesan cheese.

Chicken Pasta
Cook time: 12 minutes| Serves: 4| Per serving: Calories 510; Carbs 46.5g; Fat 17g; Protein 40.9g

Ingredients:

- Penne pasta – 8 oz. dry
- Chicken breast – 1 lb. boneless, skinless, chopped
- Fajita seasoning – 3 tbsps. divided into half
- Tomatoes – 7 oz., chopped
- Garlic – 4 cloves, minced
- Onion – 1, diced
- Chicken stock – 1 cup
- Bell peppers – 2, chopped
- Olive oil – 2 tbsps.

Directions:

Add olive oil in the Instant Pot and press Sauté. Add chicken and half fajita seasoning. Stir well and sauté until chicken looks white. Add garlic, bell pepper, onion, and remaining fajitas seasoning. Stir well and sauté for 2 minutes. Add tomatoes, stock, and pasta in the pot. Mix. Cover and cook on High for 6 minutes. Do a quick release, open, and serve.

Pasta Puttanesca
Cook time: 15 minutes| Serves: 2|Per serving: Calories 606; Carbs 77.9g; Fat 25.6g; Protein 16.5g

Ingredients:

- Penne pasta - 1 cup
- Pasta sauce – 2 cups
- Water – 1 cup
- Chili flakes – 1/3 tsp.
- Salt – ½ tsp.
- Minced garlic – ½ tsp.
- Capers - 1 tsp.

Directions:

Preheat the Instant Pot on Sauté. Place minced garlic inside. Add chili flakes, salt, and pasta sauce. Add water and caper. Mix and cook on Sauté for 10 minutes. Then add penne pasta and stir gently. Close and cook pasta on High for 5 minutes. Open and mix. Serve.

Arrabiatta Pasta
Cook time:16 minutes| Serves: 3| Per serving: Calories 362; Carbs 62.4g; Fat 7.2g; Protein 11.7g

Ingredients:

- Italian seasoning – 1 tbsp.
- Minced garlic – 1 tsp.
- Tomato – 1, chopped
- Yellow onion – 3 oz. diced
- Pasta – 1 cup
- Water – 1 cup
- Pasta sauce – 1 cup
- Sesame oil – 1 tsp.

Directions:

Pour sesame oil in the Instant Pot. Press Sauté. Add minced garlic, chopped tomato, yellow onion, and sauté for 7 minutes. Add pasta sauce and water. Add pasta and cook on High for 7 minutes. Open and chill the cooked pasta for a few minutes and serve.

Italian Style Pasta

Cook time: 5 minutes| Serves: 4| Per serving: Calories 393; Carbs 55.4g; Fat 4.2g; Protein 26.8g

Ingredients:

- Penne pasta – 9 oz.
- Marinara sauce – 1 cup
- Coconut yogurt – ¼ cup
- Ground black pepper – 1 tsp.
- Paprika – 1 tsp.
- Water - 1 cup
- Parmesan – 6 oz. shredded
- Dried oregano – 1 tbsp.

Directions:

Place marinara sauce in the Instant Pot. Add penne pasta. Then pour yogurt and water. Sprinkle the mixture with ground black pepper, paprika, and dried oregano. Close and cook on High for 5 minutes. Then do a quick release. Transfer the cooked pasta in the serving bowls and sprinkle with parmesan. Serve.

Italian Pasta Bolognese

Cook time: 25 minutes| Serves:4| Per serving: Calories 677; Carbs 43.3g; Fat 39.5g; Protein 43.3g

Ingredients:

- Penne rigate – 2 pounds
- Chopped jalapeno – 1
- Heavy cream – ¼ cup
- Garlic – 2 cloves, minced

- Celery – 1, diced small
- Sweet pepper – 1, finely chopped
- Broth – 1 ½ cups
- Italian tomatoes – 1 (28-ounce) can, chopped
- Leeks – 1 cup, chopped
- Olive oil -1 ½ tbsps.
- Ground pork – 1 pound
- Ground beef – ½ pound

Directions:

Add oil in the pot and cook leeks for 4 minutes on Sauté. Add garlic and cook for 1 minute more. Add ground meat and cook for 5 minutes. Add everything, except for the heavy cream. Cover and cook on High for 15 minutes. Open and stir in the cream. Serve.

Bucatini with Olives and Capers
Cook time: 20 minutes| Serves: 4| Per serving: Calories 374; Carbs 72.7g; Fat 7.1g; Protein 7.3g

Ingredients:

- Bucatini pasta – ¾ pound
- Olive oil – 1 tbsp.
- Italian seasoning blend – 1 tbsp.
- Black olives – ½ cup, pitted and sliced
- Garlic – 2 cloves, pressed
- Salt to taste
- Capers – 2 tbsps. soaked and rinsed
- Ripe tomatoes – 2, pureed
- Water – 1 cup

Directions:

Heat oil on Sauté. Cook garlic for 1 minute. Then add olives, capers, tomatoes, seasoning blend and salt. Bring to a boil and simmer for 10 minutes. Stir in the pasta and water. Cover and cook on High for 8 minutes. Serve.

Creamed Ziti with Mozzarella
Cook time: 10 minutes |Serves: 4| Per serving: Calories 459; Carbs 74.9g; Fat 8.2g; Protein 19.8g

Ingredients:

- Dry ziti pasta – 9 ounces
- Shredded mozzarella cheese – 1 cup
- Garlic – 2 cloves, minced
- Tomato sauce – 1 ½ cups
- Double cream – ½ cup
- Broth – 2 cups
- Salt and pepper to taste

Directions:

Add everything in the pot except for the mozzarella. Cover and cook on High for 8 minutes. Do a quick release and open. Add mozzarella and cover. Set aside until cheese melts. Serve.

Chicken and Pasta Casserole
Cook time: 11 minutes |Serves: 4 | Per serving: Calories 756; Carbs 66g; Fat 34.9g; Protein 45.2g

Ingredients:

- Boneless chicken breasts – 1 pound, chopped
- Spiral pasta – 2 cups
- Breadcrumbs - 1 cup
- Queso fresco – 1 cup, crumbled
- Salsa – 1 cup
- Olive oil – 2 tbsps.
- Cotija cheese – 1 cup, crumbled
- Cream of celery soup – 2 cups

Directions:

Heat oil on Sauté. Brown the chicken on Sauté for 5 minutes. Add everything and cover. Cook for 6 minutes at High. Open and serve.

Onion Penne Pasta
Cook time: 11 minutes |Serves: 6 | Per serving: Calories 264; Carbs 46g; Fat 2g; Protein 11g

Ingredients:

- Skimmed milk – 1 cup
- Small onion – 1, chopped
- Olive oil – 1 tsp.
- Water as needed
- Penne pasta – 12 ounces

Directions:

Add 3 cups water and pasta in the Instant Pot. Cover and cook on High for 6 minutes. Drain the pasta and transfer pasta in a bowl. Heat oil on Sauté and cook onions for 2 minutes. Add milk and cook for 3 minutes. Mix in pasta and serve.

Shrimp Pasta Meal
Cook time: 3 minutes| Serves: 2 | Per serving: Calories 468; Carbs 36g; Fat 17.5g; Protein 41g

Ingredients:

- Shrimp – 1 pound
- Olive oil – 1 tbsp.
- Butter - 1 tbsp.
- Garlic – ½ tbsp. minced
- Chicken broth – ¼ cup

- Salt and pepper to taste
- Cooked pasta – 2 cups
- Chicken stock – ¼ cup
- Lemon juice – ½ tbsp.
- Chopped parsley – 1 tbsp.

Directions:

Heat butter and oil on Sauté. Add garlic and cook for 1 minute. Add broth, stock, shrimp and parsley. Cover and cook for 2 minutes. Open and serve with cooked pasta.

Mushroom Zucchini Pasta
Cook time: 20 minutes| Serves: 5| Per serving: Calories 248; Carbs 12g; Fat 12.5g; Protein 3.5g

Ingredients:

- Mushrooms – 12, sliced
- Zucchini – 1, sliced
- Sherry wine – a few drops
- Shallot – 1, chopped
- Penne pasta – 15 ounces
- Tomato paste – 5 ounces
- Soy sauce – 2 tbsps.
- Yellow onion – 1, chopped
- Garlic – 2 cloves, minced
- Olive oil – 1 tbsp.
- Vegetable stock – 1 cup
- Water – 2 cups
- Basil – 1 pinch, dried
- Dried oregano – 1 pinch, dried
- Salt and black pepper to taste

Directions:

Add oil, onion, shallot, pepper, and salt and cook for 3 minutes on Sauté. Add garlic and cook 1 minute more. Add mushrooms, zucchini, basil, and oregano. Cook for 1 minute more. Mix in the stock, water, wine, and soy sauce. Add pasta and tomato sauce. Season and cover. Cook on High for 5 minutes. Open and serve.

Pasta Primavera
Cook time: 4 minutes| Serves: 3| Per serving: Calories 283; Carbs 33g; Fat 12g; Protein 10g

Ingredients:

- Penne pasta – 1 pound
- Water – 4 cups
- Zucchini – 2, julienned
- Red bell pepper – 1, julienned
- Onion – 1, sliced

- Garlic – 2 cloves, minced
- Large tomato – 1, diced
- Fresh basil – ¼ cup, chopped
- Olive oil - 2 tbsps.
- Grated parmesan – ½ cup
- Salt and pepper to taste

Directions:

Combine water and pasta in the Instant Pot. Place a steamer basket over the water and arrange tomato, garlic, onion, pepper, and zucchini. Close and cook for 4 minutes on High. Do a quick release and drain the pasta. Pour the contents from the basket into the pasta and mix with Parmesan, basil and olive oil. Season with salt and pepper and serve.

Spinach Pasta
Cook time: 12 minutes| Serves: 3| Per serving: Calories 198; Carbs 26.5g; Fat 1g; Protein 7g

Ingredients:

- Garlic – 2 cloves, crushed
- Spinach – 1 pound
- Fusilli pasta – 1 pound
- Olive oil – 1 tbsp.
- Pine nuts – ¼ cup, chopped
- Salt and pepper to taste

Directions:

Add oil and cook garlic and spinach for 6 minutes on Sauté. Add pasta, salt, pepper and water to cover the pasta. Close and cook 6 minutes on High. Do a quick release open and add pine nuts. Serve.

Cheesy Meat Pasta
Cook time: 10 minutes |Serves: 2| Per serving: Calories 588; Carbs 52.5g; Fat 24g; Protein 61g

Ingredients:

- Mozzarella cheese – 4 ounces
- Pasta sauce – 1 cup
- Water – 1 cup
- Ground beef – ¼ pound
- Ground pork – ¼ pound
- Ruffles pasta – 6 ounces
- Ricotta cheese – 4 ounces
- Oil for cooking

Directions:

Add oil, pork and beef in the pot. Cook on Sauté for 4 minutes. Add water, pasta and sauce. Cover and cook on High for 5 minutes. Do a quick release and serve with cheese.

Minestrone Pasta Soup

Cook time: 8 minutes| Serves: 2| Per serving: Calories 394; Carbs 58g; Fat 3g; Protein 20.5g

Ingredients:

- Chicken broth – 2 cups
- Elbow pasta – ½ cup
- Tomatoes – 14 ounces, diced
- Cooked white beans – 1 cup
- Carrot – 1, diced
- Dried basil – 1 tsp.
- Olive oil – 1 tbsp.
- Dried oregano – 1 tsp.
- Garlic – 2 cloves, minced
- Bay leaf – 1
- Onion – 1, diced
- Fresh spinach – ¼ cup
- Salt and pepper to taste

Directions:

Add oil in the instant pot. Cook carrot, onion, garlic, and celery for 5 minutes on Sauté. Add basil, oregano, pepper, salt and mix. Mix the spinach, tomatoes, broth, pasta and bay leaf. Close and cook on High for 6 minutes. Open and add the beans. Serve.

American Chop Suey

Cook time: 15 minutes| Serves: 3| Per serving: Calories 495; Carbs 48g; Fat 19g; Protein 29g

Ingredients:

- Olive oil – 1 tbsp.
- Ground beef – ½ pound
- Onion – 1, diced
- Garlic – 2 cloves, minced
- Whole tomatoes with juice – 1 can, crushed
- Beef stock – ½ cup
- Worcestershire sauce – 1 tbsp.
- Salt and pepper to taste
- Uncooked macaroni – ½ pound
- Shredded mozzarella cheese – 1 cup

Directions:

Heat oil on Sauté. Brown the beef for 5 minutes. Add onions and garlic. Pour in tomatoes, stock, sauce, salt and pepper. Add pasta and half of the cheese. Close and cook on High for 8 minutes. Do a quick release and open. Add the remaining cheese and cover until melted. Serve.

Lemon Artichoke

Cook time: 10 minutes| Serves: 4 | Per serving: Calories 142; Carbs 4g; Fat 12g; Protein 5g

Ingredients:

- Bone broth – 2 cups
- Tarragon leaves – 1 tbsp.
- Artichokes – 4, rinsed and trimmed
- Juice from 2 small lemons, freshly squeezed

Directions:

Add the ingredients in the Instant Pot and mix well. Close and cook on High for 10 minutes. Do a quick release when done. Serve.

Avocado and Coconut Pudding
Cook time: 5 minutes |Serves: 4| Per serving: Calories 190; Carbs 6g; Fat 6g; Protein 1g

Ingredients:

- Avocado – 2, chopped
- Vanilla extract – 2 tsps.
- Erythritol – 1 tsp.
- Lime juice – 1 tbsp.
- Coconut milk – 14 ounces
- Water – 1 ½ cup

Directions:

In a bowl, add lime juice, erythritol, vanilla extract, avocado, and milk. Blend well. Pour the mix into a ramekin. Add water to the Instant Pot. Add a steamer basket and place the ramekin in the Pot. Close and cook on High for 5 minutes. Serve.

Casserole
Cook time: 20 minutes| Serves: 8| Per serving: Calories 195; Carbs 1g; Fat 14g; Protein 11g

Ingredients:

- Eggs – 6
- Heavy cream – ½ cup
- Salt and freshly ground black pepper to taste
- Shredded cheddar cheese – 1 cup
- Fresh kale – 2 ½ cups, trimmed and chopped
- Small yellow onion – 1 chopped
- Herbs de Provence – 1 tsp.
- Water – 1 cup for the pot

Directions:

Add heavy cream, eggs, salt, and black pepper in a bowl and beat until mixed. Add remaining ingredients and mix well. Place the mixture into a baking dish evenly. Arrange a steamer trivet in the bottom of the Instant Pot and pour 1-cup water. Place the dish on top of the trivet. Cover and cook on High for 20 minutes. Serve.

Sweet and Sour Kale

Cook time: 10 minutes| Serves: 4| Per serving: Calories 96; Carbs 3.5g; Fat 4.2g; Protein 4.5g

Ingredients:

- Olive oil – 1 tbsp.
- Small yellow onion – 1, thinly sliced
- Garlic cloves – 4, crushed
- Kale – 1 (10 ounces) bag
- Chicken broth – 1 ½ cups
- Fresh lemon juice – 2 tbsps.
- Erythritol – 1 tbsp.
- Crushed red pepper flakes – 1 tsp.
- Salt and black pepper to taste

Directions:

Add oil in the Instant Pot and press Sauté. Add the onion and cook for 3 to 4 minutes. Add the garlic and cook for 1 minute. Stir in remaining ingredients. Cover cook on High for 5 minutes. Serve.

Cheesy Broccoli

Cook time: 10 minutes| Serves: 2 | Per serving: Calories 536; Carbs 5g; Fat 47g; Protein 19g

Ingredients for the broccoli:

- Broccoli florets – 2 cups
- Olive oil – 1 tbsp.
- Garlic powder – 2 tsps.
- Smoked paprika – ½ tbsp.
- Salt and freshly ground black pepper
- Water – 1 cup for the pot

For Cheese Sauce

- Butter – 3 tbsps.
- Almond flour – 2 tbsps.
- Unsweetened almond milk – ½ cups
- Shredded cheddar cheese – 1 cup
- Garlic powder – 1 tsp.
- Salt to taste

Directions:

For the broccoli: in a bowl, add all the ingredients and toss to coat well. Arrange a steamer basket in the bottom of the Instant Pot and pour 1 cup of water. Place the broccoli on top of the steamer basket. Cover and cook on Low for 10 minutes. Meanwhile, for cheese sauce: in a pan melt butter over medium heat. Add flour and beat well. Slowly add almond milk and beat continuously. Cook until thickened, about 2 to 3 minutes. Stirring continuously. Add garlic powder, cheese, and salt and stir until smooth. Top the broccoli with the cheese sauce and serve.

Cheesy Cauliflower Rice
Cook time: 1 minute |Serves: 4| Per serving: Calories 241; Carbs 5g ; Fat 17.9g ; Protein 9.8g

Ingredients:

- Cauliflower – 1 head, chopped into florets
- Water – 1 cup
- Butter – 3 tbsp.
- Heavy cream – 1 tbsp.
- Shredded sharp cheddar cheese – 1 cup
- Salt – ½ tsp.
- Pepper – ¼ tsp.
- Garlic powder – ¼ tsp.

Directions:

Add water into the Instant Pot and place a steamer basket. Place cauliflower on top of the basket and close. Press Steam and cook for 1 minute. Do a quick release. Pulse the cauliflower in a food processor until broken into small pearls. Place the cauliflower in a bowl. Add remaining ingredients and gently fold. Serve.

Zesty Brussels Sprouts
Cook time: 4 minutes |Serves: 4| Per serving: Calories 157; Carbs 9g; Fat 3g; Protein 7.9g

Ingredients:

- Brussels sprouts – 2 pounds, trimmed
- Fresh lemon juice – ¼ cup
- Maple syrup – 2 tbsps.
- Butter – 1 tbsp.
- Lemon zest – 1 tsp. grated
- Black pepper to taste
- Salt to taste

Directions:

Stir the Brussels sprouts with maple syrup, lemon zest, lemon juice, butter, a pinch of salt and pepper into the Instant Pot. Cover and cook 4 minutes on High. Serve.

Buttery Cabbage

Cook time: 5 minutes| Serves: 4| Per serving: Calories 158; Carbs 7.6g; Fat 10g; Protein 3g

Ingredients:

- White cabbage – 1 head, sliced
- Butter – 4 tbsps.
- Salt – ½ tsp.
- Pepper – ¼ tsp.
- Water – 1 cup

Directions:

Place butter, cabbage, salt and pepper in a bowl. Mix. Pour water in the Instant Pot and place in the steam rack. Place the bowl on the rack. Close and cook for 5 minutes. Do a quick release and serve.

Steamed Artichokes

Cook time:10 minutes Serves: 4| Per serving: Calories 60; Carbs 6.6g; Fat 0.2g; Protein 4.2g

Ingredients:

- Medium artichokes – 4
- Lemon wedge – 1
- Water – 1 cup

Directions:

Wash the artichokes and cut off the stem. Rub the cut on top with the lemon, to prevent browning. Gently spread the leaves a bit. Place the artichokes in a steamer insert in the Instant Pot and pour in a cup of water. Cook for 10 minutes on High. Serve.

Vegetable Stir-Fry

Cook time: 15 minutes| Serves: 3| Per serving: Calories 115; Carbs 4.3g; Fat 7.8g; Protein 6.1g

Ingredients:

- Cauliflower – 2 cups, chopped
- Broccoli – 1 cup, chopped
- Garlic – 3 cloves, finely chopped
- Olive oil – 1 tbsp.
- Eggs – 2
- Salt – ½ tsp.
- Black pepper – ¼ tsp. ground
- Red pepper flakes – ¼ tsp.
- Onion powder – ¼ tsp.

Directions:

Grease the pot with olive oil and press Sauté. Add garlic and stir-fry for 2 minutes. Add broccoli and cauliflower. Sprinkle with onion powder, red pepper flakes, salt, and pepper. Stir and cook for 5 minutes. Add ¼ cup of water and cook for 5 more minutes. Stirring occasionally. Poach the eggs on top and season with salt. Cook for 2 to 3 minutes and turn off the pot. Transfer to a serving plate. Serve.

Cheesy Spinach
Cook time: 10 minutes| Serves: 3 | Per serving: Calories 169; Carbs 4.7g; Fat 8.7g; Protein 16.8g

Ingredients:

- Spinach – 2 lbs. chopped
- Eggs – 3
- Vegetable stock – 1 cup
- Parmesan cheese – ¼ cup, grated
- Chili pepper – 1 small, finely chopped
- Onion powder – 1 tsp.
- Garlic powder – ¼ tsp.
- Chili powder – ¼ tsp.
- Salt – 1 tsp.
- Cayenne pepper – ¼ tsp.
- Water - 1 cup

Directions:

Place the spinach in the Instant Pot. Add the vegetable broth and 1 cup of water. Sprinkle with salt and close the lid. Cook on High for 5 minutes. Open and press Sauté and add chili pepper. Sprinkle with cayenne pepper, salt, chili powder, onion powder, and garlic powder. Give it a good stir and cook until the liquid is reduced by half, about 5 minutes. Poach the eggs on top of the spinach and sprinkle all with Parmesan cheese. Serve.

Vegetable Curry
Cook time: 27 minutes| Serves: 4| Per serving: Calories 93; Carbs 2.22g; Fat 7.6g; Protein 3.3g

Ingredients:

- Sliced fresh mushrooms – 3 cups
- Minced garlic – ½ tsp.
- Salt to taste
- Ground coriander – ¼ tsp.
- Ground cumin – ¼ tsp.
- Ground turmeric – ¼ tsp.
- Red chili powder – ¼ tsp.
- Coconut milk – ½ cup
- Plain Greek yogurt – ¼ cup

Directions:

Add all the ingredients in a dish and stir to combine. In the pot, arrange the steamer trivet and pour 1 cup of water. Place the dish on top of the trivet. Cover and cook on High for 27 minutes. Serve.

Spinach Celery Stew
Cook time: 10 minutes| Serves: 4| Per serving: Calories 278; Carbs 4.3g; Fat 28.2g; Protein 2.3g

Ingredients:

- Fresh spinach – 2 cups, chopped
- Celery leaves – 1 cup, chopped
- Celery stalks – 1 cup, chopped
- Garlic – 2 cloves, minced
- Small onion – 1, chopped
- Heavy cream – 2 cups
- Lemon juice – 1 tbsp.
- Butter – 2 tbsps.
- Fresh mint – 1 tbsp. torn
- Salt – 1 tsp.
- Black pepper – ½ tsp. ground

Directions:

Press Sauté, add butter and constantly stir until melts. Add onions, garlic, and celery stalks. Cook for 2 minutes and add spinach and celery leaves. Sprinkle with salt and pepper. Cook for 2 to 3 minutes and pour in heavy cream. Cover and cook 5 minutes on High. Open and stir in the mint and lemon juice. Chill for 5 minutes and serve.

Green Frittata
Cook time: 12 minutes| Serves: 4| Per serving: Calories 338; Carbs 5.1g; Fat 26.7g; Protein 18.2g

Ingredients:

- Celery stalks – 1 lb. chopped
- Fresh spinach – 1 cup, chopped
- Fresh kale – 1 cup, chopped
- Eggs – 6
- Cheddar cheese – 1 cup, grated
- Butter – 2 tbsps.
- Extra virgin olive oil – 1 tbsp.
- Garlic cloves – 2, minced
- Sea salt – 1 tsp.
- Black pepper – 1 tsp. freshly ground
- Italian seasoning – 1 tsp.

- Onion powder – ½ tsp.

Directions:

Add butter and press Sauté. Add garlic and cook for 2 minutes. Now, add spinach, celery, and kale. Cook for 5 minutes. Crack the eggs on top and stir once to combine with greens. Sprinkle with onion powder, Italian seasoning, salt, and pepper. Top with cheddar cheese and cook until the eggs are set, about 3 to 4 minutes. Turn off the pot and transfer the frittata to a serving plate. Drizzle with olive oil and serve.

Cabbage Stew
Cook time: 25 minutes| Serves: 4| Per serving: Calories 338; Carbs 5.7g; Fat 28.8g; Protein 13.3g

Ingredients:

- Purple cabbage – 2 cups, shredded
- Bacon slices – 5, chopped
- Medium celery stalks – 2, chopped
- Medium red bell pepper – 1, chopped
- Vegetable stock – 2 cups
- Heavy cream – 1 cup
- Feta cheese – ½ cup, cubed
- Olive oil – 1 tbsp.
- Balsamic vinegar – 1 tsp.
- Sea salt – 1 tsp.
- Cayenne pepper – ½ tsp. ground
- Diced thyme – ½ tsp. ground
- Garlic powder – ½ tsp.

Directions:

Press sauté, add bacon and cook until crisp. Add red bell pepper, celery, and cabbage. Sprinkle with garlic powder, thyme, cayenne pepper, and salt. Pour in the vegetable stock and heavy cream. Cover and cook 15 minutes on High. Open the pot and stir in the feta cheese, vinegar, and olive oil. Press Sauté and cook for 5 minutes more. Serve.

Glazed Bok Choy
Cook time: 4 minutes| Serves: 4| Per serving: Calories 76; Carbs 7.1g; Fat 4.9g; Protein 2.3g

Ingredients:

- Bok choy – 1 pound
- Maple syrup – 1 tbsp.
- Sesame oil - 1 tbsp.
- Ground cumin – 1 tsp.
- Minced garlic – ½ tsp.

- Ground ginger – 1 tsp.
- Apple cider vinegar – 1 tbsp.
- Sesame seeds – 1 tbsp.
- Water – ½ cup

Directions:

Chop bok choy roughly and sprinkle with maple syrup, ground cumin, sesame oil, minced garlic, ground ginger, and apple cider vinegar. Mix the vegetables and marinate for 10 minutes. Transfer the bok choy and all the liquid into the Instant Pot. Add water, cover, and cook on High for 4 minutes. Open and transfer bok choy to the serving bowls and sprinkle with sesame seeds. Serve.

Lemon Potatoes
Cook time: 8 minutes| Serves: 2| Per serving: Calories 185; Carbs 34g ; Fat 3.9g ; Protein 4.2g

Ingredients:

- White potatoes – 4
- Lemon zest – 1 tsp.
- Pink salt – 1 tsp.
- Fresh dill – 1 tbsp. chopped
- Dried oregano – 1 tsp.
- Lemon juice – 2 tbsps.
- Vegetable broth – ¼ cup
- Olive oil – 1 tbsp.

Directions:

Chop the potatoes. Whisk together lemon juice, olive oil, dried oregano, and fresh dill. Pour olive oil mixture over the potatoes and sprinkle with salt. Shake well and transfer in the Instant Pot. Add vegetable broth and cook on High for 8 minutes. Serve.

Quinoa Patties
Cook time: 15 minutes | Serves: 3| Per serving: Calories 259; Carbs 38.4g; Fat 7.1g; Protein 10.8g

Ingredients:

- Quinoa – 1 cup
- Vegetable broth - 1 cup
- Lemongrass – 1 tbsp. chopped
- Dried basil – 1 tsp.
- Butter - 1 tbsp.
- Ground nutmeg – ¾ tsp.
- Pink salt – 1/3 tsp.

Directions:

Put quinoa in the Instant Pot. Add broth, ground nutmeg, and salt. Close the lid. Cook quinoa on High for 3 minutes. Open and add butter, lemongrass, and dried basil. Mix and serve.

Mashed Potato
Cook time: 10 minutes |Serves: 6| Per serving: Calories 171; Carbs 34.2g; Fat 2.6g; Protein 3.9g

Ingredients:

- Potatoes – 6, peeled, chopped
- Water – 1 cup
- Coconut milk – ¼ cup
- Coconut yogurt – 1 tbsp.
- Salt – 1 tsp.
- Chives - 1 tbsp. chopped

Directions:

Place potato and water in the Instant Pot. Add salt and close the lid. Cook on High for 10 minutes. Open the lid, drain water from the potatoes and mash them. Add yogurt, coconut milk, and chopped chives. Mix until smooth and serve.

Broccoli Rice
Cook time: 1 minute |Serves: 4| Per serving: Calories 32; Carbs 4.4g; Fat 1.4g; Protein 1.7g

Ingredients:

- Broccoli florets – 2 ½ cup
- Salt – 1 tsp.
- Ground peppercorn – 1 tsp.
- Water – ½ cup
- Olive oil – 1 tsp.
- Minced garlic – 1 tsp.

Directions:

Put broccoli florets in a food processor and blend until rice. Pour water in the Instant Pot. Then place broccoli rice in the Instant Pot. Add peppercorns, salt, olive oil, and minced garlic. Mix. Transfer the pan in the Instant Pot and close the lid. Cook on High for 1 minute. Serve.

Sweet Potato Mash
Cook time: 9 minutes| Serves: 6| Per serving: Calories 67; Carbs 14.4g; Fat 0.3g; Protein 1.6g

Ingredients:

- Sweet potatoes – 2 cups, peeled, and chopped
- Salt – 1 tsp.
- Ground black pepper – 1 tsp.
- Vegetable broth – 1 cup

- Fresh parsley – 1 tbsp. chopped

Directions:

Put the potatoes, salt, and vegetable broth in the Instant Pot. Close the lid and cook on High for 9 minutes. Do a quick release and strain the sweet potatoes. Mash until smooth. Add chopped parsley and ground black pepper. Mix and serve.

Red Cabbage with Apples

Cook time: 7 minutes| Serves: 3| Per serving: Calories 123; Carbs 20.2g; Fat 5.1g; Protein 2.6g

Ingredients:

- Red cabbage – 1 pound
- Apple – 1, chopped
- Salt – 1 tsp.
- Coconut milk – ¼ cup
- Almond milk – ¾ cup
- Chili flakes – ½ tsp.

Directions:

Shred red cabbage and mix it with salt. Transfer this mixture in the Instant Pot. Add coconut milk, almond milk, and chili flakes. Then add apple and cook on High for 7 minutes. Do a natural release. Serve.

Butter Corn

Cook time: 2 minutes | Serves: 4 | Per serving: Calories 229; Carbs 34.7g; Fat 9g; Protein 8.1g

Ingredients:

- Corn on the cob – 4
- Butter – 4 tsps.
- Salt – 1 tsp.
- Minced garlic – ½ tsp.
- Water – ½ cup

Directions:

Pour water in the Instant Pot and insert trivet. Place corn on the cobs on the trivet and close the lid. Cook on High for 2 minutes. Do a natural release. Churn together butter, salt, and minced garlic. Spread the corn on the cobs with the churned mixture and serve.

Cooked Beets

Cook time: 17 minutes| Serves: 4 | Per serving: Calories 131; Carbs 22.9g ; Fat 3.9g ; Protein 3.9g

Ingredients:

- Beets – 2 pounds, peeled

- Ground black pepper – 1 tsp.
- Olive oil – 1 tbsp.
- Water – 1 cup, for cooking

Directions:

Cut the beets into medium cubes. Pour water in the Instant Pot and add the trivet. Place beets on the trivet and close the lid. Cook for 17 minutes on High. Then do a quick release. Transfer beets to a bowl and sprinkle with ground black pepper and olive oil. Serve.

Tender Sweet Peppers
Cook time: 13 minutes| Serves: 4| Per serving: Calories 110; Carbs 11.5g; Fat 7.3g; Protein 2g

Ingredients:

- Red sweet peppers – 2
- Green bell pepper – 1
- Yellow sweet pepper – 1
- Garlic clove – 1, peeled
- Tomato – 1, chopped
- Fresh dill – ¼ cup, chopped
- Sesame oil - 2 tbsps.
- Water – ½ cup

Directions:

Cut the peppers into strips. Preheat the Instant Pot on Sauté. Add olive oil, garlic clove, and chopped tomato. Sauté the ingredients for 3 minutes. Mix. Add pepper strips and water. Close and cook on Sauté for 10 minutes. Serve.

Chapter 5 Rice, Grains, Beans

Mexican Rice

Cook time: 8 minutes |Serves: 4| Per serving: Calories 267; Carbs 41.8g; Fat 8.2g; Protein 6.4g

Ingredients:

- Long grain rice – 1 cup
- Tomato paste – 1 tbsp.
- Corn kernels – ¼ cup, canned
- Smoked paprika – 1 tsp.
- Chili flakes - 1 tsp.
- Salt – 1 tsp.
- Vegetable broth – 2 cups
- Carrot – 1, chopped
- Olive oil – 2 tbsps.

Directions:

Press Sauté and pour the olive oil in the Instant Pot. Add rice and start to cook it. Add chili flakes, salt, and ¼-cup vegetable broth. Stir it. Add tomato paste and stir until the rice gets the red color. Then add corn kernels, smoked paprika, carrot, and all the remaining vegetable broth. Close and cook on High for 4 minutes. Open and serve.

Polenta

Cook time: 8 minutes| Serves: 5| Per serving: Calories 156; Carbs 25.5g; Fat 2.8g; Protein 6.3g

Ingredients:

- Polenta – 1 cup
- Vegetable broth – 4 cups
- Coconut milk – 2 tbsps.
- Ground black pepper – ½ tsp.
- Salt – 1 tsp.

Directions:

Whisk together polenta and vegetable broth. Pour mixture in the Instant Pot. Add salt. Close and cook on High for 8 minutes. Do a quick release. Transfer cooked polenta in a bowl and stir well. Add ground black pepper and coconut milk. Stir and serve.

Japgokbap

Cook time: 8 minutes| Serves: 6| Per serving: Calories 175; Carbs 35.9g; Fat 1.1g; Protein 5.7g

Ingredients:

- White rice – ¼ cup

- Red beans – 1/3 cup
- Sorghum – ¼ cup
- Millet – 1/3 cup
- Chickpea – ¼ cup
- Water – 3 cups
- Sea salt – ¼ tsp.

Directions:

Put the red beans, white rice, sorghum, millet, chickpea, and sea salt in the Instant Pot. Mix. Add water and close. Cook on High for 20 minutes. Do a quick release. Mix and serve.

Proso Millet
Cook time: 15 minutes| Serves: 2| Per serving: Calories 436; Carbs 73.8g; Fat 7.9g; Protein 15.9g

Ingredients:

- Proso millet – 1 cup
- Vegetable broth – 2 cups
- Salt – 1 tsp.
- Chili flakes – ¼ tsp.
- Coconut oil – 1 tsp.

Directions:

Press Sauté and add the oil in the Instant Pot. Add salt, chili flakes, and proso millet. Stir it gently and cook for 3 minutes. Then add vegetable broth, and close. Cook on High for 10 minutes. Do a quick release. Open and serve.

Sweet Rice
Cook time: 13 minutes| Serves: 3| Per serving: Calories 440; Carbs 59.4g; Fat 20.4g; Protein 6.6g

Ingredients:

- White rice - 1 cup
- Mango puree – 2 tbsps.
- Water – 1 cup
- Coconut milk - 1 cup
- Brown sugar – 1 tbsp.
- Ground cinnamon – ½ tsp.
- Butter – 1 tsp.

Directions:

Place the rice in the Instant Pot. Add water, coconut milk, and sugar. Close and cook on Rice mode for 13 minutes. Do a quick release. Open and add the butter and ground cinnamon. Mix and serve.

Basmati Ragu

Cook time: 6 minutes| Serves: 4| Per serving: Calories 192; Carbs 42.4g; Fat 0.5g; Protein 4g

Ingredients:

- Basmati rice - 1 cup
- Water – 2 cups
- Sweet pepper – 1, chopped
- Red onion – 1, diced
- Salt – 1 tsp.
- Tomato paste – 1 tsp.
- Turmeric – 1 tsp.

Directions:

Mix together tomato paste, turmeric, salt, and water. Mix well. Pour it in the Instant Pot and add basmati rice. Close and cook on High for 3 minutes. Do a quick release and open the lid. Add sweet pepper and onion and mix well. Close and cook on High for 3 minutes more. Do a quick release. Open, stir, and serve.

Arborio Rice

Cook time: 6 minutes| Serves: 5 | Per serving: Calories 355; Carbs 66.1g; Fat 1.3g; Protein 14.4g

Ingredients:

- Arborio rice – 2 cups
- Water – 4 cups
- Salt – 1 tsp.
- Coconut oil – 1 tsp.
- Onion – ½, diced
- Parmesan – 4 oz. grated

Directions:

Preheat the Instant Pot on Sauté and add coconut oil. Add diced onion and sauté for 3 minutes. Add rice and salt. Mix and toast until light brown. Add water and close the lid. Cook on Rice mode for 6 minutes. Do a quick release and open. Transfer the rice into serving bowls and sprinkle with grated Parmesan. Serve.

Oatmeal with Onions

Cook time: 5 minutes| Serves: 5| Per serving: Calories 99; Carbs 13.4 g ; Fat 4.2g ; Protein 2.6g

Ingredients:

- Steel-cut oats – 2 cups
- Red onion – 1, sliced
- Coconut oil – 1 tbsp.

- Salt – ½ tsp.
- Water – 2 cups
- White pepper – ½ tsp.

Directions:

Preheat the Instant Pot on Sauté and add oil. Melt it and add onions, salt, and white pepper. Stir-fry for 2 minutes. Then add oats and water. Close the lid and cook on High for 3 minutes. Then do a natural release. Open, mix, and serve.

Popcorn

Cook time: 10 minutes| Serves: 2| Per serving: Calories 53; Carbs 7.3g; Fat 2.8g; Protein 1.3g

Ingredients:

- Corn – ½ cup
- Olive oil - 1 tsp.
- Salt – 1 tsp.

Directions:

Press Sauté and add olive oil in the Instant Pot. Preheat and add corn. Sprinkle corn with salt and stir. Close and cook on Sauté for 7 to 10 minutes. Serve.

Teff in Tomato Paste

Cook time: 6 minutes| Serves: 3| Per serving: Calories 255; Carbs 45g ; Fat 3.2g ; Protein 11.3g

Ingredients:

- Teff - 1 cup
- Vegetable broth – 2 cups
- Salt – 1 tsp.
- Tomato paste – 1 tsp.
- Coconut oil – 1 tsp.

Directions:

Press Sauté and add oil. Add tomato paste and salt. Stir. Add teff and stir well. Sauté for 3 minutes. Add vegetable broth and close. Cook on High for 3 minutes. Then do a quick release. Open, mix, and serve.

Amaranth Banana Porridge

Cook time: 6 minutes| Serves: 4| Per serving: Calories 526; Carbs 75g; Fat 21.1g; Protein 13.4g

Ingredients:

- Amaranth – 1 ½ cups
- Almond milk – 1 cup
- Water – 2 cups

- Bananas – 2, sliced
- Brown sugar – ¼ cup
- Vanilla extract – 1 tsp.
- Butter – 1 tsp.

Directions:

Place amaranth, almond milk, and water in the Instant Pot. Add sugar, and butter. Close the lid. Cook amaranth on High for 6 minutes. Do a quick release and open. Add vanilla extract and mix. Transfer the porridge into the serving bowls and garnish with sliced bananas. Serve.

Bean and Rice Casserole
Cook time: 30 minutes| Serves: 4| Per serving: Calories 192; Carbs 37.6g; Fat 1g; Protein 8.7g

Ingredients:

- Red beans – ¼ cup, soaked
- Black beans – 1/3 cup, soaked
- Brown rice – 1/3 cup
- Salt – 1 tsp.
- Barley – ¼ cup
- Water – 4 cups

Directions:

Place black and red beans in the Instant Pot. Add rice, salt, barley, and water. Close the lid and cook on Chili mode for 30 minutes. Do a natural release, open, and serve.

Green Buckwheat
Cook time: 9 minutes |Serves: 4| Per serving: Calories 122; Carbs 17g; Fat 3.6g; Protein 5.8g

Ingredients:

- Green buckwheat – 2 cups
- Butter – 1 tbsp.
- Turmeric – ½ tsp.
- Paprika – 1 tsp.
- Vegetable broth – 2 cups
- Salt - 1 tsp.

Directions:

Press Sauté and place the butter in the Instant Pot. Add green buckwheat and sprinkle it with turmeric, paprika, and stir. Stir gently. Sauté the buckwheat for 5 minutes. Add vegetable broth and close the lid. Set IP to Rice mode and cook on High for 4 minutes. Do a quick release, open, and serve.

Rosemary Creamed Polenta

Cook time: 15 minutes| Serves: 5| Per serving: Calories 357; Carbs 51.7 g; Fat 14.8g; Protein 5.8g

Ingredients:

- Polenta – 2 cups
- Coconut cream – 1 cup
- Water – 3 cups
- Dried rosemary – 1 tsp.
- Pink salt – 1 tsp.
- Minced garlic - 1 tsp.
- Coconut oil - 1 tbsp.

Directions:

Place coconut oil in the Instant Pot and melt on Sauté. Add pink salt, minced garlic, and dried rosemary. Sauté for 3 minutes. Then add the coconut cream and bring the mixture to boil. Then add water and polenta. Mix. Close and cook on High for 8 minutes. Open and serve.

Fennel Jasmine Rice

Cook time: 15 minutes| Serves: 4 | Per serving: Calories 241; Carbs 34g; Fat 14g; Protein 10g

Ingredients:

- Jasmine rice – 1 ½ cups
- Fennel bulb – 1 cup, chopped
- Spring onion – 2, chopped
- Parsnips – 1 cup, chopped
- Carrot - 1, chopped
- Chicken stock – 2 cups
- Water – 1 cup
- Sage – 1 tsp.
- Olive oil – 1 tbsp.
- Salt and pepper, to taste

Directions:

Heat oil on Sauté in the Instant Pot. Add onions and cook for 3 minutes. Add carrots, parsnip, and fennel and cook for 2 minutes more. Stir in the remaining ingredients. Cover and cook for 10 minutes on Rice, at High. Do a quick release and serve.

Shrimp Risotto

Cook time: 14 minutes| Serves: 4 | Per serving: Calories 476; Carbs 59g; Fat 12g; Protein 32g

Ingredients:

- Shrimp – 1 pound, peeled and deveined

- Brown rice – 1 ½ cups
- Olive oil – 3 tbsps.
- Fish stock – 3 cups
- Garlic – 2 tsps. minced
- Shallots – 2, chopped
- White wine – 4 tbsps.
- Salt and pepper, to taste

Directions:

Heat oil on Sauté in the Instant Pot. Add garlic and onion. Cook for 3 minutes. Add shrimp and cook for 3 minutes or until lightly browned. Stir in the remaining ingredients and cover. Cook on 8 minutes on Rice at High. Do a quick release, open, and serve.

Colorful Risotto
Cook time: 24 minutes| Serves: 4| Per serving: Calories 324; Carbs 58g; Fat 5g; Protein 11g

Ingredients:

- Brown rice – 1 ½ cups
- Veggie broth – 2 ½ cups
- Carrots – ½ cup, chopped
- Yellow bell pepper – ½, chopped
- Green bell pepper – ½, chopped
- Tomato – 1, chopped
- Red onion – 1/2, chopped
- Olive oil – 1 tbsp.
- Green peas – ½ cup
- Salt and pepper to taste

Directions:

Heat oil in Instant Pot on Sauté. Add onion and stir-fry for 2 minutes. Add peppers and carrots and cook for 2 minutes more. Stir in the remaining ingredients. Cover the pot. Cook on High for 20 minutes. Do a quick release, open, and serve.

Spinach Vermouth Risotto
Cook time: 13 minutes| Serves: 4| Per serving: Calories 327; Carbs 44g; Fat 8g; Protein 10g

Ingredients:

- Mushrooms – 1 cup, sliced
- Spinach – 2 cups, chopped
- Vermouth – ½ cup
- Rice – 1 cup
- Zucchini – 1, sliced

- Parmesan cheese – ½ cup, shredded
- Shallot - 1, chopped
- Garlic – 1 tsp. minced
- Olive oil – 1 tbsp.
- Chicken stock – 2 cups

Directions:

Heat oil on Sauté in the Instant Pot. Cook the shallot and garlic for two minutes. Add mushrooms and cook for 3 minutes more. Stir in the rest of the ingredients, except the cheese. Cover and cook on 8 minutes on Rice at High. Do a quick release. Open and stir in the cheese. Serve.

Rice Pilaf with Chicken
Cook time: 30 minutes| Serves: 4| Per serving: Calories 341; Carbs 41g; Fat 9g; Protein 21g

Ingredients:

- Rice – 1 cup
- Chicken breast – 1, diced
- Garlic – ½ tsp. minced
- Onion – ½, chopped
- Bell peppers – 1, chopped
- Olive oil – 1 tbsp.
- Chicken broth – 2 cups
- Rosemary – ½ tsp.
- Salt and pepper to taste

Directions:

Add oil in the Instant Pot and heat on Sauté. Add onions and cook for 2 minutes. Stir in garlic and cook for 1 minute more. Add peppers and cook for 2 minutes. Stir in the remaining ingredients. Cover and cook for 25 minutes on Meat/Stew mode at High. Do a quick release and serve.

Tomato Risotto
Cook time: 10 minutes |Serves: 4| Per serving: Calories 348; Carbs 61.4g; Fat 7.1g; Protein 8.5g

Ingredients:

- Olive oil – 2 tbsps.
- Onion – 1, chopped
- Rice – 1 ½ cups
- Vegetable broth – 2 cups
- Tomato sauce – ¾ cup
- Cumin – 1 tsp.
- Garlic powder – 1 tsp.
- Salt – ¼ tsp.

Directions:

Heat the oil on Sauté in the Instant Pot. Add onion and salt and cook for 3 minutes. Add broth and tomato sauce and simmer for 2 minutes. Add rice and season with salt, pepper, garlic powder, and cumin. Cover and cook on Rice mode for 6 minutes. Do a quick release, open, and serve.

Apricot Wild Rice
Cook time: 25 minutes| Serves: 4| Per serving: Calories 246; Carbs 50g; Fat 3g; Protein 8g

Ingredients:

- Wild rice – 1 cup
- Maple syrup – 2 tbsps.
- Dried apricots – ¼ cup chopped, soaked overnight
- Apple juice – ¾ cup
- Milk – ¼ cup
- Egg yolks – 2
- Ground ginger – ¼ tsp.
- Cinnamon – ¼ tsp.
- Salt to taste
- Water – 2 cups

Directions:

Combine all ingredients except the apricots in the Instant Pot. Cover and cook on High for 25 minutes. Do a quick release and open. Stir in the apricots and serve.

Baked Beans
Cook time: 55 minutes| Serves: 4| Per serving: Calories 238; Carbs 46g; Fat 1g; Protein 13g

Ingredients:

- White beans - 1 cup
- Water – 5 cups
- Tomato paste – 2 tbsps.
- Salt – 1 tsp.
- Dried dill - 1 tsp.
- Brown sugar – 1 tsp.
- Barbecue sauce - ½ cup
- Vegetable broth – ½ cup
- Carrot – 1, chopped
- Ground black pepper – ½ tsp.

Directions:

Place the white beans and water into the Instant Pot. Close and cook on High for 30 minutes. Do a quick release, open and drain water from beans. Add tomato paste, salt, dried dill, barbecue sauce, broth, chopped carrot, and ground black pepper. Mix and close the lid. Press Sauté and cook for 25 minutes more. Open and serve.

Mexican Pinto Beans

Cook time: 50 minutes |Serves: 5| Per serving: Calories 300; Carbs 51.3g; Fat 3g; Protein 17.8g

Ingredients:

- Pinto beans – 2 cups
- Water – 6 cups
- Salt – 1 tsp.
- Ground black pepper - 1 tsp.
- Fresh cilantro – ½ cup, chopped
- Jalapeno pepper – 1, chopped
- Onion powder – 1 tsp.
- Garlic powder – 1 tsp.
- Vegan butter – 1 tbsp.
- Coconut yogurt – 3 tbsps.
- Tomato paste – 1 tbsp.

Directions:

Put all the ingredients in the Instant Pot. Mix well and close. Cook on High for 50 minutes. Do a quick release. Open and mix. Serve.

Black Beans

Cook time: 45 minutes| Serves: 4| Per serving: Calories 278; Carbs 45.5g; Fat 4.4g; Protein 15.8g

Ingredients:

- Black beans – 1 ½ cups
- Water – 3 cups
- Salt – 1 tsp.
- Peppercorn – ¼ tsp.
- Chives – 1 tbsp. chopped
- Coconut oil – 1 tbsp.
- Chili flakes – 1 tsp.

Directions:

Add water, black beans, salt, and peppercorn into the Instant Pot. Close and cook on High for 30 minutes. Open and add chili flakes, chives, coconut oil, and mix well. Close and press Sauté. Sauté for 15 minutes. Serve.

Lebanese Lemon and Beans Salad

Cook time: 6 minutes| Serves: 4| Per serving: Calories 110; Carbs 11.3g; Fat 7.4g; Protein 2.6g

Ingredients:

- Green beans – 2 cups
- Chili pepper – 1 tsp.
- Lemon – ½, sliced
- Tomatoes – 1 cup, chopped
- White onion – 1, chopped
- Tomato sauce – 2 tbsps.
- Salt – ½ tsp.
- Ground coriander – 1 tsp.
- Cayenne pepper – ½ tsp.
- Coconut milk - ½ cup

Directions:

Chop the green beans and place them in the Instant Pot. Add chopped tomatoes, chili pepper, onion, tomato sauce, salt, ground coriander, cayenne pepper, and coconut milk. Mix and top with sliced lemon. Close and cook on High for 6 minutes. Open and discard the sliced lemon. Serve.

Red Kidney Beans Burrito
Cook time:15 minutes| Serves: 2| Per serving: Calories 352; Carbs 40.3g; Fat 17.6g; Protein 12.4g

Ingredients:

- Avocado – ½, sliced
- Bell pepper – 1, sliced
- Onion – ½, chopped
- Olive oil - 1 tbsp.
- Tomato paste – 1 tsp.
- Chili flakes – ½ tsp.
- Red kidney beans – ½ cup, canned
- Ground cumin – ½ tsp.
- Ground coriander - ½ tsp.
- Fresh cilantro – ½ cup, chopped
- Flour tortillas – 2

Directions:

Preheat the Instant Pot on Sauté for 3 minutes. Pour olive oil and add sliced bell pepper. Stir-fry for 2 to 3 minutes. Add chopped onion, chili flakes, ground cumin, coriander, and tomato paste. Stir and add red kidney beans. Mix it up. Close and Sauté for 10 minutes. Open and fill the tortillas with the bean mixture, add cilantro, avocado, and roll. Serve.

Quinoa Bowl
Cook time: 7 minutes| Serves: 2| Per serving: Calories 662; Carbs 83.7g; Fat 23g; Protein 24.8g

Ingredients:

- Water – 1 cup
- Quinoa – 1 cup
- Salt – 1 tsp.
- Ground cumin – 1 tsp.
- Red beans – ½ cup, cooked
- Bell pepper – 1, chopped
- Avocado – ½, sliced
- Coconut milk – ¼ cup

Directions:

Transfer quinoa and water in the Instant Pot. Add salt, bell pepper, and close. Cook on High for 7 minutes. Then do a quick release. Transfer the cooked quinoa mixture in the bowl. Add red beans and ground cumin. Mix and add avocado slices. Sprinkle the meal with the coconut milk. Serve.

Cowboy Caviar
Cook time: 6 minutes| Serves: 4| Per serving: Calories 99; Carbs 7.6g; Fat 7.5g; Protein 2.1g

Ingredients:

- Black-eyed peas – ½ cup
- Water – 1 cup
- Tomatoes – 4, chopped
- Apple cider vinegar – 1 tbsp.
- Lemon juice – 1 tbsp.
- Jalapeno pepper – 1, chopped
- Fresh parsley - ½ cup, chopped
- Olive oil – 2 tbsps.
- Salt – ½ tsp.

Directions:

Add the water and peas in the Instant Pot and close. Cook on High for 6 minutes. Then do a quick release. In a bowl, mix tomatoes, jalapeno pepper, parsley, and apple cider vinegar. Add chilled black-eyed peas to the mixture. Add olive oil, salt, and lemon juice. Mix and serve.

Chipotle Chili with Hot Sauce
Cook time: 15 minutes| Serves: 4| Per serving: Calories 223; Carbs 38.2g; Fat 3.3g; Protein 13g

Ingredients:

- Butter – 1 tbsp.
- Mushrooms – ½ cup, chopped
- Chipotle powder – 1 tsp.
- Canned black beans – 1 cup

- Hot sauce – ¼ cup
- Tomato sauce – 1 cup
- Water – ½ cup
- Garlic – 2 cloves, diced
- Tomato – 1, chopped
- Red bell pepper – 1, chopped

Directions:

Melt the butter in the Instant Pot on Sauté. Add garlic, mushrooms, tomato, and bell pepper. Sauté the vegetables for 10 minutes. Then sprinkle the mixture with chipotle powder. Add tomato sauce, hot sauce, water, and black beans. Mix and close. Cook on High for 5 minutes. Then do a quick release. Chill and serve.

Creamy Kidney Beans
Cook time: 25 minutes| Serves: 4| Per serving: Calories 620; Carbs 64 g; Fat 33g; Protein 23.7g

Ingredients:

- Kidney beans – 2 cups
- Water – 2 cups
- Almond milk – 2 cups
- Coconut oil – 1 tbsp.
- Salt – 1 tsp.
- Tomato paste – 1 tbsp.
- Garlic – 1 clove, peeled
- Taco seasoning – 1 tbsp.

Directions:

Place water, kidney beans, almond milk, coconut oil, salt, tomato paste, garlic clove, and taco seasoning in the Instant Pot. Mix and close. Cook on High for 25 minutes. Then do a quick release. Mix and serve.

Mung Beans Croquettes
Cook time: 10 minutes |Serves: 6 | Per serving: Calories 148; Carbs 23.5g; Fat 2.7g; Protein 8.5g

Ingredients:

- Mung beans – 1 cup, soaked
- Green bell pepper – 1, chopped
- Chipotle pepper – ½, chopped
- Minced garlic – ½ tsp.
- Sesame oil – 1 tbsp.

Directions:

Place the mung beans in the food processor and blend well. Add chipotle, bell pepper, and minced garlic. Blend the mixture until smooth. Transfer the mixture in a bowl and make small croquettes with wet hands. Set Sauté mode and preheat Instant Pot. Add sesame oil and croquettes. Cook them for 2 minutes on each side. Serve.

Green Bean and Lentil Stew
Cook time: 20 minutes| Serves: 5| Per serving: Calories 410; Carbs 64.4g ; Fat 7.7g ; Protein 28.8g

Ingredients:

- Olive oil – 2 tbsps.
- Celery stalks – ½ cup, chopped
- Parsnips – ½ cup, chopped
- Green bell pepper – 1, chopped
- Red bell pepper – 1, chopped
- Poblano pepper – 1, chopped
- Leeks – ½ cup, chopped
- Ginger-garlic paste – 1 tsp.
- Dried basil – ½ tsp.
- Dried oregano – ½ tsp.
- Dried rosemary – ½ tsp.
- Curry paste – ½ tsp.
- Brown lentils – 2 cups
- Vegetable broth – 3 cups
- Tomato paste – ½ cup
- Salt and pepper to taste
- Green beans – 2 cups, trimmed and halved

Directions:

Heat the oil in the Instant Pot on Sauté. Add the celery, parsnip, peppers, and leeks and stir-fry for 5 minutes. Stir in aromatics, curry paste, lentils, broth, and tomato paste. Season with salt and pepper. Cover the pot. Cook on High for 10 minutes. Open and the green beans and press Sauté. Sauté for 5 minutes. Serve.

Turkish Bean Stew
Cook time: 35 minutes| Serves: 6| Per serving: Calories 335; Carbs 54.2g; Fat 5.6g; Protein 19.6g

Ingredients:

- Olive oil – 2 tbsps.
- Bell pepper – 1, chopped
- Leeks – ½ cup, chopped
- Parsnip – 1, sliced
- Celery – 1 stalk, sliced

- Fresh garlic – 1 tsp. minced
- White beans – 1 lb. soaked for 6 hours
- Red pepper paste – 2 tbsps.
- Canned tomatoes – 10 ounces, crushed
- Ground black pepper and sea salt, to taste
- Vegetable broth – 1 cup
- Dry bay laurel leaf - 1

Directions:

Heat oil in the Instant Pot on Sauté. Add pepper, leeks, parsnip, celery, and stir-fry for 5 minutes. Add the garlic and cook for one minute more. Add in the beans, red pepper paste, tomatoes, salt, black pepper, broth, and bay laurel leaf. Cover and cook 30 minutes on High. Open and serve.

Biryani Rice

Cook time: 27 minutes| Serves: 2| Per serving: Calories 420; Carbs 92g; Fat 3g; Protein 8.3g

Ingredients:

- Red onion – ¼ cup, diced
- Garlic clove – 1, minced
- Turmeric powder – ½ tsp.
- Cumin seeds – 1 tsp.
- Cinnamon stick – 1
- Salt – ¼ tsp.
- Brown rice – 1 cup, soaked 10 minutes, then drained
- Water – 1 ½ cups
- Raisins – ¼ cup
- Mint – ¼ cup, chopped
- Raw cashew, chopped
- Fresh mint leaves
- Fresh cilantro

Directions:

Press Sauté on your Instant Pot. Add cumin seeds, diced red onion, minced garlic, turmeric powder, cinnamon, and salt to the Instant Pot. Stir-fry for 1 minute. Add brown rice and stir. Cover and cook on Multigrain for 25 minutes. Do a quick release and open. Add raisins and chopped mint. Mix. Serve the rice garnished with fresh mint leaves and chopped cashews.

Spanish Rice

Cook time: 5 to 7 minutes| Serves: 4| Per serving: Calories 394; Carbs 80g; Fat 4.2g; Protein 7.7g

Ingredients:

- White rice – 2 cups
- Vegetable oil – 1 tbsp.

- Green onions – 6
- Diced tomatoes – 1 can
- Red onion – 1
- Cilantro – 1 tsp.
- Lemon zest – 1 tsp.
- Water – 3 cups

Directions:

Add tomatoes to the Instant Pot. Add chopped onion and rest of the ingredients. Cover and cook for 5 minutes on High. Open and check. If the rice isn't done, then cook for 2 minutes more. Stir the rice and serve.

Potato and Green Bean Salad
Cook time: 7 minutes| Serves: 6| Per serving: Calories 218; Carbs 40.4g; Fat 5.1g; Protein 6.3g

Ingredients:

- Large potatoes – 3, skinned and chopped
- Frozen green beans – 2 large bags (about 2 pounds)
- Mushrooms – 1 cup
- Water – 1 ½ cup
- Olive oil – 2 tbsps.
- Dash of sea salt
- Splash of lemon juice
- Pepper to taste

Directions:

Add lemon juice, water, salt, pepper, mushrooms, and potatoes to the Instant Pot. Place a steamer basket. Place green beans on top of the steamer basket and drizzle with oil. Cover and cook on High 7 minutes. Open and pour the beans into a strainer, then place on a large bowl. Mix the green beans and the rest of the ingredients from the Instant Pot. Serve.

Three Bean Delight
Cook time: 10 minutes| Serves: 4| Per serving: Calories 676; Carbs 100g; Fat 19g; Protein 30.6g

Ingredients:

- Chickpeas – 1 can
- Black beans – 1 can
- Green beans – 2 cups
- Garlic powder – 1 tbsp.
- Celery – 2 stalks, sliced
- Small red onion – 1, chopped
- Coconut oil – 4 tbsps.

- Sugar – 2 tbsps.
- Apple cider vinegar – 5 tbsps.
- Salt and pepper

Directions:

Place everything except for the green beans in the Instant Pot. Place a steamer and add the green beans on top. Cover and cook on High for 10 minutes. Do a natural release. Open and add the green beans with the rest of the salad. Serve.

Green Chili Baked Beans

Cook time: 30 minutes| Serves: 4| Per serving: Calories 435; Carbs 89g; Fat 4g; Protein 21g

Ingredients:

- Blackstrap molasses – ¼ cup
- Maple syrup – ¼ cup
- Packed light brown sugar – ¼ cup
- Ketchup – 2 tbsps.
- Worcestershire sauce – 1 tbsp.
- Olive oil – 1 tbsp.
- Sweet onion – 1 small, chopped
- Garlic – 3 to 4, minced
- Salt – 1 tsp.
- Dried navy beans – 1 pound, soaked in water overnight, rinsed and drained
- Diced roasted green chilies – 1 ½ cups
- Apple cider vinegar – 1 tsp.

Directions:

In a bowl, whisk the sauce, ketchup, brown sugar, maple syrup, and molasses. Press Sauté on the Instant Pot and add oil. Add onion and garlic. Stir-fry for 2 minutes. Add molasses mix, beans, and salt and mix. Cover the Instant Pot. Cook on High for 30 minutes. Open the lid and press Sauté. Stir in green chilies and simmer until thickens about 5 to 10 minutes. Serve.

Mexican Black Beans

Cook time: 30 minutes| Serves: 6| Per serving: Calories 287; Carbs 50g; Fat 5g; Protein 17g

Ingredients:

- Olive oil - 2 tbsps.
- Small onion – 1, diced
- Garlic – 3 to 4 cloves, diced
- Ground cumin – 1 tbsp.
- Dried oregano – 1 tsp.
- Chili powder – 1 tsp.

- Diced roasted green chillies – 1 cup
- Vegetable stock - 3 cups
- Dried black beans – 2 cups, rinsed but not soaked
- Salt – 1 tsp. plus more to taste
- Lime juice – 2 tbsps.
- Fresh cilantro leaves – ¼ cup, chopped

Directions:

Press Sauté on the Instant Pot. Add oil. Add onion and stir-fry for 2 minutes. Add garlic and stir-fry for 30 seconds. Stir in chili powder, oregano, and cumin — Cook for 30 seconds. Add the black beans, stock, green chillies, and mix. Cover and cook on High for 30 minutes. Do a natural release. Open and add cilantro, lime juice, and salt. Serve.

Refried Pinto Beans
Cook time: 32 minutes| Serves: 6| Per serving: Calories 310; Carbs 53g; Fat 6g; Protein 17g

Ingredients:

- Olive oil - 1 tbsp.
- Onion – 1, quartered
- Garlic – 3 cloves, peeled
- Dried pinto beans – 1 pound, rinsed
- Vegetable stock – 2 quarts
- Ground cumin – 1 tsp.
- Dried Mexican oregano – 1 tsp.
- Chili powder – ½ tsp.
- Ground black pepper – ¼ tsp.
- Lime juice – 1 tbsp.
- Salt to taste

Directions:

In the Instant Pot, combine pepper, chili powder, oregano, cumin, stock, beans, garlic, onion, and oil. Cover and cook on High for 32 minutes. Do a natural release and open. Remove most of the remaining liquid. Blend with a hand mixer until smooth. Add cooking water as needed. Stir in salt and lime juice. Serve.

Red Beans and Rice
Cook time: 34 minutes| Serves: 4| Per serving: Calories 609; Carbs 116g; Fat 5g; Protein 26g

Ingredients:

- Olive oil – 1 tbsp.
- Red onion – 1, diced
- Bell pepper – 1, diced

- Celery stalks – 2, sliced
- Garlic cloves – 4, minced
- Bay leaves – 2
- Cajun seasoning – 2 tsps.
- Dried oregano – ½ tsp.
- Dried parsley – ½ tsp.
- Dried red beans – 2 cups
- Vegetable stock – 4 cups
- Salt and ground black pepper
- Cooked white rice – 4 cups
- Chopped parsley and hot sauce for garnishing

Directions:

Press Sauté and add oil. Add celery, bell pepper, and red onion. Stir-fry for 4 minutes. Add dried parsley, oregano, seasoning, bay leaves, and garlic. Cook for 1 minute. Stir in beans and stock. Cover and cook on High for 34 minutes. Do a natural release and open. Discard the bay leaves. Garnish and serve with rice.

Chickpea Basil Salad

Cook time: 38 minutes| Serves: 2 | Per serving: Calories 396; Carbs 67g; Fat 6g; Protein 21g

Ingredients:

- Dried chickpeas – 1 cup, rinsed
- Enough water to cover chickpeas by 3 to 4 inches
- Fresh basil leaves – 1 cup, chopped
- Grape tomatoes – 1 ½ cups, halved
- Balsamic vinegar – 2 tbsps.
- Garlic powder – ½ tsp.
- Salt – to taste

Directions:

Combine the water and chickpeas in the Instant Pot. Cover and cook on High for 38 minutes. Do a natural release and open. Drain the chickpeas. Cool. Stir together the salt, garlic powder, vinegar, tomatoes, and basil in a bowl. Add the beans and mix. Serve.

Green Chili Chickpeas

Cook time: 43 minutes |Serves: 4| Per serving: Calories 416; Carbs 71g; Fat 6g; Protein 24g

Ingredients:

- Dried chickpeas – 2 cups, rinsed
- Water – 6 cups
- Small tomato – 1, diced

- Diced roasted green chillies – 1 cup
- Lemon juice – 2 tsps.
- Ground cumin – 1 tsp.
- Chili powder – ½ tsp. plus more as needed
- Salt – to taste
- Garlic powder – ½ tsp.
- Red pepper flakes – ½ tsp.
- Smoked paprika – ½ tsp.
- Onion powder – ½ tsp.
- Dried oregano – ¼ tsp.
- Ground black pepper – ¼ tsp.

Directions:

In the Instant Pot, combine water and chickpeas. Cover and cook on High for 38 minutes. Drain the chickpeas when cooked. Reserve 2 tbsps. of the cooking water. Return the chickpeas to the Instant Pot. Add rest of the ingredients. Add the reserved cooking water if the mixture is too dry. Press Sauté on the Instant Pot and sauté for 4 minutes. Press Cancel and cover. Let the chickpeas sit for 5 minutes. Serve.

Cilantro Lime Brown Rice
Cook time: 19 minutes| Serves: 4| Per serving: Calories 344; Carbs 72g; Fat 3g; Protein 7g

Ingredients:

- Brown rice – 2 cups, rinsed and drained
- Water – 2 ½ cups
- Fresh cilantro – 1/3 cup, chopped
- Juice of 1 lime
- Zest of 1 lime
- Dash ground cumin
- Salt to taste

Directions:

In the Instant Pot, combine the water and rice. Cover and cook on High for 19 minutes. Open and stir in cumin, lime juice, zest, and cilantro. Season with salt. Serve.

Garlic Butter Rice
Cook time: 23 minutes| Serves: 4| Per serving: Calories 450; Carbs 77g; Fat 13g; Protein 8g

Ingredients:

- Butter-infused olive oil – 2 tbsps.
- Sweet onion – 1 small, diced
- Garlic – 2 to 4 cloves, minced

- Long-grain brown rice – 2 cups, rinsed and drained
- Vegetable stock – 2 ½ cups
- Salt to taste
- Ground black pepper to taste
- Lemon juice – 1 tsp.
- Butter – 1 tbsp.
- Fresh herbs for garnishing

Directions:

Press Sauté and add oil. Add onion and stir-fry for 3 minutes. Add the garlic. Cook for 1 minute. Add the salt, pepper, stock, and rice. Mix. Cover and cook on High for 23 minutes. Do a natural release. Open and stir in butter and lemon juice. Taste and adjust seasoning. Serve garnished with herbs.

Chapter 6 Soups and Stews

Carrot Ginger Soup
Cook time: 3 minutes| Serves: 2 | Per serving: Calories 112; Carbs 26g; Fat 1g; Protein 2g

Ingredients:

- Carrots – 7, chopped
- Fresh ginger – 1-inch, peeled and chopped
- Sweet onion – ½, chopped
- Vegetable stock – 1 ¼ cups
- Salt – ½ tsp.
- Sweet paprika – ½ tsp.
- Ground black pepper
- Sour cream for garnish
- Fresh herbs for garnish

Directions:

In the Instant Pot, combine the paprika, salt, stock, onion, ginger, and carrots. Season with pepper. Cover and cook on High for 3 minutes. Open and blend with a hand mixer until smooth. Garnish and serve.

Lamb Stew
Cook time:1 hour 25 minutes |Serves: 8|Per serving: Calories 462; Carbs1.2g; Fat 37g; Protein 30g

Ingredients:

- Lamb tallow – ½ cup
- Garlic – 3 cloves, crushed
- Onion – 1 large, diced
- Rosemary – ¼ cup, chopped
- Celery – 3 sticks, diced
- Salt – 1 tsp.
- Ground black pepper – 1 tsp.
- Red wine vinegar – ½ cup
- Tomato puree – 1 cup
- Beef broth – 4 cups
- Lamb shoulder – 4 lbs. (cut into 1 ½ inch chunks)
- Mushrooms – ½ lbs. (cut into ½ inch slices)
- Sour cream – 1 cup
- Parmesan cheese – ½ cup
- Water as needed

Directions:

Place the tallow, celery, rosemary, onions, and garlic in the instant pot. Press Sauté and cook for 5 minutes. Stirring occasionally. Add the tomato puree, vinegar, salt and pepper and cook for 5 more minutes. Add the beef broth, mix and then add the lamb chunks. Add water until the lamb is just covered. Cover and cook on Meat/Stew for 60 minutes. When done, do a natural release. Press Sauté and add sliced mushrooms. Cook for 15 minutes. Serve hot, topped with 1 tbsp. grated parmesan cheese and 2 tbsps. of sour cream.

Classic Fish Stew
Cook time: 20 minutes |Serves: 6| Per serving: Calories 503; Carbs 5.8g; Fat 23.9g; Protein 62g

Ingredients:

- Trout fillets – 2 lbs.
- Shrimps – 1 lb. peeled
- Large onions – 2, finely chopped
- Extra virgin olive oil – ¼ cup
- Cauliflower – 1 cup, chopped
- Fresh parsley – ¼ cup, finely chopped
- Garlic cloves – 3, crushed
- Fish stock – 4 cups
- Sea salt – 1 tsp.
- Dried thyme – ½ tsp.

Directions:

Add three tbsps. of olive oil in the instant pot and press Sauté. Add onions and garlic. Stir-fry for 4 minutes. Now add shrimps and cook for 5 more minutes. Add the remaining ingredients and cover. Cook for 10 minutes on High. Open and sprinkle with a few drops of freshly squeezed lemon juice and serve.

Rabbit Cabbage Stew
Cook time: 35 minutes| Serves: 4| Per serving: Calories 543; Carbs 1.8g; Fat 24.3g; Protein 74g

Ingredients:

- Whole rabbit – 1, cleaned
- Cabbage – 1 cup, shredded
- Beef broth – 4 cups
- Butter – 3 tbsps.
- Salt – 1 tsp.
- Freshly ground white pepper – ½ tsp.
- Cayenne pepper – 1 tsp.

Directions:

Combine all the ingredients in instant pot and season with spices. Stir to mix well. Cover and cook 35 minutes on High. Serve warm.

Chicken, Turkey and Mushroom Stew
Cook time: 38 minutes |Serves: 4| Per serving: Calories 436; Carbs 2.8g; Fat 20.5g; Protein 57g

Ingredients:

- Turkey breast – 1 lb. boneless, skinless and chopped into bite-sized pieces
- Chicken breast – 1 lb. boneless, skinless and chopped into bite-sized pieces
- Button mushrooms – 12 oz. sliced
- Butter – 2 tbsps. softened
- Olive oil – 1 tbsp.
- A bunch of celery leaves, finely chopped
- Salt – 1 tsp.
- Freshly ground pepper – ½ tsp.
- Cayenne pepper – 1 tbsp.
- Water – 3 cups

Directions:

Grease the bottom of the IP with one tbsp. olive oil. Add turkey breast, cayenne pepper, salt, and pepper. Mix and add two cups of water. Close the lid. Press the Meat button and cook for 13 minutes. Open and add the chicken breast, butter, and one cup water. Simmer until the meat is fully cooked and tender, about 15 minutes. Add the celery leaves and the mushrooms. Cook for 10 minutes and serve.

Pork Meatball Stew
Cook time: 30 minutes |Serves: 10 | Per serving: Calories 530; Carbs 11g; Fat 29g; Protein 42g

Ingredients:

- Minced pork – 3 lbs.
- Almond meal – 2 cups
- Vegetable broth – 1 cup
- Tomato passata – 1 cup
- Celeriac – 1, cubed
- Onion – 1, chopped
- Collards – 2 lbs. chopped
- Eggs – 4
- Olive oil– 1 tbsp.

Directions:

In a bowl, mix the eggs, almonds, and meat. Make the meat into balls. Add oil in the instant pot and brown the meatballs for 5 minutes. Add broth and sauce. Cover and cook on Stew for 5 minutes. Open and add the vegetables. Seal and cook on Stew for 20 minutes more. Serve.

White Chili
Cook time: 30 minutes| Serves: 6 | Per serving: Calories 265; Carbs 4g; Fat 16g; Protein 35g

Ingredients:

- Turkey – 1 ½ lbs. ground
- Chicken stock – 20 oz.
- Chopped cauliflower – 16 oz.

- White onions – 2, chopped
- Italian herbs – 2 tbsps.
- Paprika – 2 tbsps.
- Oil – 2 tbsps.

Directions:

Mix all the ingredients in the instant pot. Cover and cook on Stew for 30 minutes. Serve.

Worcestershire Chili
Cook time: 38 minutes |Serves: 4 | Per serving: Calories 304; Carbs 9.3g; Fat 10g; Protein 37g

Ingredients:

- Ground beef – 1 pound
- Carrot – 1, diced
- Canned diced tomatoes – 26 ounces
- Chili powder – 1 tbsp.
- Garlic powder – 1 tsp.
- Onion powder – 1 tsp.
- Paprika – 1 tsp.
- Onion – 1, diced
- Parsley – 1 tbsp.
- Salt – 1 tsp.
- Worcestershire chili – 1 tbsp.
- Oil – 1 tbsp.
- Cauliflower rice – 1 cup

Directions:

Heat the oil in the instant pot on Sauté setting. Add the beef and cook for 5 minutes. Add onion and all to the spices and cook for 3 minutes. Except for the cauliflower, stir in the remaining ingredients. Cook for 20 minutes on Meat/Stew. Add cauliflower rice and cook for 10 minutes. Release the pressure naturally. Serve.

Creamy Chicken Chili
Cook time: 3 minutes |Serves: 8| Per serving: Calories 357; Carbs 5g; Fat 20.6g; Protein 38g

Ingredients:

- Chicken breasts – 2 pounds
- Diced tomatoes with green chilies – 1 (10-ounce) can
- Green chilies – 1 (4 ½ ounce) can
- Ground cumin – ½ tsp.
- Red chili powder – ½ tsp.
- Salt and freshly ground black pepper to taste
- Chicken broth – 4 cups
- Softened cream cheese – 8 ounces
- Sour cream – ¼ cup

Directions:

Except for the cream cheese and sour cream, add all the ingredients in the instant pot. Cover and press Soup and use the default time. Then remove the lid, add cheese and stir the mixture well. Serve with sour cream.

Spiced Chili

Cook time: 40 minutes| Serves: 10 | Per serving: Calories 305; Carbs 1g; Fat 10.7g; Protein 43.7g

Ingredients:

- Olive oil – 1 tbsp.
- Ground beef – 3 pounds
- Chopped yellow onion – ½
- Ground cumin – 2 tbsps.
- Smoked paprika – 1 tbsp.
- Ground chipotle – 1 tbsp.
- Salt and freshly ground black pepper to taste
- Sugar-free tomato paste – 1 (6-ounce)
- Green chiles – 1 (4-ounce) can
- Homemade beef broth – 2 cups
- Soy sauce – 2 tbsps.
- Fresh lemon juice – 1 tbsp.
- Xanthan gum – ½ tsp.

Directions:

Add oil in the instant pot and press Sauté. Then add onion and beef and cook for 9 minutes. Add the spices and cook for 1 minute. Stir in tomato paste, green chiles, and broth. Cook on High for 25 minutes. Open and press Sauté. Stir in the lemon juice and soy sauce. Slowly add the xanthan gum. Stir continuously. Serve.

Pork Chili

Cook time: 30 minutes |Serves: 10 | Per serving: Calories 554; Carbs 1g; Fat 39.43g; Protein 43g

Ingredients:

- Boneless pork shoulder – 4 pounds, cut into 2-inch chunks
- Tomatillos – ¾ pound, husk removed
- Chopped Serrano peppers – 6
- Medium yellow onion – 1, chopped
- Garlic cloves – 6, peeled
- Ground cumin – 1 tbsp.
- Salt and black pepper to taste
- Water – ½ cup
- Fresh cilantro leaves – ½ cup
- Fresh lemon juice – 2 tbsps.

Directions:

Except for cilantro and lemon juice, add all ingredients in the instant pot and stir to combine. Cover and cook 30 minutes on High. Open and transfer pork into a bowl. Stir lemon juice and cilantro in the pot and blend the mixture with an immersion blender until pureed. Add the pork pieces and serve.

Italian Sausage and Kale Soup

Cook time: 5 minutes| Serves: 6 | Per serving: Calories 400; Carbs 7g; Fat 33g; Protein 16g

Ingredients:

- Hot Italian sausage stuffing – 1 lbs.
- Onion – 1 cup, diced
- Garlic – 6 cloves, minced
- Cauliflower – 12 oz. frozen
- Kale – 12 oz. frozen
- Water – 3 cups
- Heavy cream – ½ cup
- Parmesan cheese – ½ cup, grated

Directions:

Press Sauté add the sausage and lightly brown for 2 minutes. Constantly stir and break into smaller pieces. Add the garlic and onions and mix thoroughly to combine. Add the kale, cauliflower and three cups of water. Cover and cook 3 minutes on High. Open and slowly stir in the cream. Serve sprinkled with parmesan. Serve.

Creamy Spinach Soup

Cook time: 10 minutes |Serves: 2| Per serving: Calories 286; Carbs 4.3g; Fat 24.9g; Protein 10.3g

Ingredients:

- Spinach – 3 cups, chopped
- Cauliflower – 1 cup, chopped
- Beef broth – 3 cups
- Heavy cream – ½ cup
- Butter – 2 tbsps.
- Sea salt – ¼ tsp.
- Black pepper – ½ tsp. freshly ground
- Garlic powder – 1 tsp.

Directions:

In a bowl, add chopped spinach and cauliflower. Season with salt, pepper, and garlic. Stir well and pour in the broth. Cook for 10 minutes on High. Open the lid and stir in two tbsps. of butter. Chill for a while. Blend with a hand mixer. Stir in the heavy cream and serve.

Broccoli and Cauliflower Soup

Cook time: 25 minutes| Serves: 4 | Per serving: Calories 172; Carbs 10.9g; Fat 8.9g; Protein 10.7g

Ingredients:

- Broccoli – 1 lb. chopped
- Cauliflower – 2 cups, chopped into florets
- Vegetables broth – 3 cups
- Milk – 1 cup
- Sour cream – ½ cup
- Salt – ½ tsp.
- Dried rosemary – ½ tsp.

Directions:

Add broccoli, cauliflower, and broth into the Instant Pot and cover. Cook for 20 minutes on High. Open and chill for a while, then transfer to a food processor and process until smooth. Pour the soup back into the pot and press Sauté. Bring the mixture to a boil and add milk. Sprinkle with salt and dried rosemary. Stir well and cook for 2 to 3 minutes. Stir in the sour cream and cook for 1 minute. Serve.

Creamy Bacon Soup

Cook time: 15 minutes |Serves: 4| Per serving: Calories 404; Carbs 5.8g; Fat 67.7g; Protein 37.2g

Ingredients:

- Bacon – 10 slices
- Bone broth – 6 cups
- Full-fat cream cheese – 6 ounces, softened
- Sugar-free tomato paste – 5 tbsps.
- Butter – 4 tbsps. softened
- Cumin – 2 tsps. ground
- Chili powder- 2 tsps.
- Garlic – 1 clove, chopped
- Dried basil – ½ tsp.
- Dried parsley – ½ tsp.
- Cayenne pepper – ½ tsp. ground
- Black pepper – ½ tsp.
- Heavy whipping cream – 1 cup
- Full-fat cheddar cheese – 1 cup, shredded

Directions:

Press Sauté on your Instant Pot. Add bacon and cook until slightly crispy. Remove. Add butter, tomato paste, cream cheese, broth, black pepper, cayenne pepper, parsley, basil, garlic, chili powder, and cumin to the IP. Mix well. Close and cook for 10 minutes on High. Open the pot and add whipping cream. Let the soup sit for 10 minutes. Serve topped with crumbled bacon and cheddar cheese.

Italian Chicken Soup

Cook time: 10 minutes| Serves: 6| Per serving: Calories 183; Carbs 3.3g; Fat 6.9g; Protein 25.3g

Ingredients:

- Bone broth – 4 cups
- Chicken – 1 pound, ground
- Hot peppers – ½ tsp. chopped
- Dried basil – ½ tsp.
- Rosemary – ½ tsp. ground
- Dried oregano – ½ tsp.
- Salt – ½ tsp.
- Ground black pepper – ½ tsp.
- Coconut oil – 2 tbsps.
- Fire roasted tomatoes – 1 (14-ounce) can

Directions:

Add everything in the Instant Pot. Close and cook on High for 10 minutes. Open and serve.

Classic Chicken Noodle Soup
Cook time: 5 minutes| Serves: 6 | Per serving: Calories 200; Carbs 6.1g; Fat 6.4g; Protein 28.6g

Ingredients:

- Chicken bone broth – 7 cups
- Chicken breasts – 1 pound, cubed, and cooked
- Avocado oil – 2 tbsps.
- Dried oregano – 1 tsp.
- Chopped carrot – 1
- Dried basil – ½ tsp.
- Dried parsley - ½ tsp.
- Salt – ½ tsp.
- Black pepper – ½ tsp.
- Zucchinis – 2, spiralized

Directions:

Add the broth into the Instant Pot. Add in oil, black pepper, salt, parsley, basil, carrot, oregano, and chicken. Stir to mix. Close and cook 5 minutes on High. Open and stir in the zucchini noodles. Serve.

Butternut Squash Soup
Cook time: 10 minutes| Serves: 6| Per serving: Calories 278; Carbs 9g; Fat 23.7g; Protein 7.4g

Ingredients:

- Coconut oil – 2 tbsps.
- Garlic – 4 cloves, minced
- Bone broth – 6 cups

- Butternut squash – 2 cups, cubed
- Curry powder – ½ tsp.
- Ginger – ½ tsp. grated
- Salt – ½ tsp.
- Ground black pepper – ½ tsp.
- Full-fat coconut milk – 2 cups

Directions:

Press Sauté and add oil. Add the garlic and sauté for 2 minutes. Add squash, salt, pepper, ginger, curry powder, and bone broth to the Instant Pot. Close and cook 10 minutes on High. Open and pour in the coconut milk and blend with a hand mixer. Serve.

Hearty Hamburger Soup
Cook time: 25 minutes |Serves: 4| Per serving: Calories 514; Carbs 9g; Fat 30.2g; Protein 49.4g

Ingredients:

- Coconut oil – 2 tbsps.
- Ground beef – 1 pound
- Bone broth – 4 cups
- Bacon – 3 slices, cooked and chopped
- Full-fat cheddar cheese – 1 cup, shredded
- Carrot – 1, chopped
- Celery – 1 stalk, chopped
- Dried parsley - ½ tsp.
- Crushed red pepper – ½ tsp.
- Dried basil – ½ tsp.
- Salt – ½ tsp.
- Freshly ground black pepper – ½ tsp.
- Diced tomatoes – 1 (14-ounce) can

Directions:

Add the oil in the Instant Pot and melt on Sauté. Add the beef and brown for 2 to 5 minutes. Add tomatoes, black pepper, salt, basil, red pepper, parsley, celery, carrot, cheese, bacon, and broth. Close and cook on High for 25 minutes. Do a natural release and serve.

Pumpkin and Bacon Soup
Cook time: 10 minutes |Serves: 4| Per serving: Calories 578; Carbs 8.3g; Fat 51.2g; Protein 17.4g

Ingredients:

- Coconut oil – 2 tbsps.
- Bacon – 4 slices, cooked and chopped
- Bone broth – 2 cups

- Pumpkin puree – 2 cups
- Full-fat coconut milk – 2 cups
- Full-fat cheddar cheese – ½ cup, shredded
- Crushed red pepper – ½ tsp.
- Salt – ½ tsp.
- Freshly ground black pepper – ½ tsp.
- Heavy whipping cream – ¼ cup

Directions:

Add all the ingredients to the Instant Pot and mix well. Close and cook 10 minutes on Low. Serve.

Traditional Egg Drop Soup
Cook time: 6 minutes| Serves: 6| Per serving: Calories 177; Carbs 3.3g; Fat 12.4g; Protein 12.2g

Ingredients:

- Bone broth – 8 cups
- Butter – 4 tbsps. softened
- Scallion – 1, thinly sliced
- Dried basil – ½ tsp.
- Cayenne pepper – ½ tsp. ground
- Dried parsley – ½ tsp.
- Salt – ½ tsp.
- Eggs – 6, whisked

Directions:

Add the butter, broth, salt, parsley, pepper, basil, and scallion into the Instant Pot. Close and cook 5 minutes on High.   Open and pour in the eggs. Let sit for 1 minute. Serve.

Clam Chowder
Cook time: 8 minutes| Serves: 6| Per serving: Calories 314; Carbs 7.8g; Fat 26.7g; Protein 5.2g

Ingredients:

- Full-fat coconut milk – 2 cups
- Bay leaves – 2
- Bone broth – 1 cup
- Cauliflower – 1 pound, chopped
- Celery – 1 cup, chopped
- Ground black pepper – ½ tsp.
- Salt – ½ tsp.
- Small onion – ¼, thinly sliced
- Clams – 2 (7-ounce) cans, chopped and drained
- Heavy whipping cream – 1 cup

Directions:

Add the onion, salt, black pepper, celery, cauliflower, bone broth, bay leaves, and coconut milk to the Instant Pot. Mix well. Close and cook 5 minutes on high. Open and remove bay leaves and stir in the clams and whipping cream. Press Sauté and cook for 2 to 3 minutes. Serve.

Lasagna Soup
Cook time: 5 minutes |Serves: 2 | Per serving: Calories 545; Carbs 8.3g; Fat 41.9g; Protein 34g

Ingredients:

- Full-fat cheddar cheese – 1 cup, shredded
- Full-fat Parmesan cheese – ½ cup, grated
- Heavy whipping cream – ½ cup
- Dried basil – ½ tsp.
- Dried oregano – ½ tsp.
- Grated zucchini – ¼ cup
- Fire roasted tomatoes – 1 (14-ounce) can
- Water – 1 ½ cups

Directions:

Add everything and mix well. Press Sauté and cook for 5 minutes. Stirring occasionally. Serve.

Mexican Soup
Cook time: 17 minutes |Serves: 8| Per serving: Calories 395; Carbs 1.6g; Fat 20.5g; Protein 40g

Ingredients:

- Boneless, skinless chicken breasts – 2 pounds
- Salsa – 1 (15-ounce) jar
- Diced green chilies – 1 (4-ounce) can
- Ground cumin – 2 tbsps.
- Red chili powder – 1 tbsp.
- Garlic powder – 1 tsp.
- Salt and freshly ground black pepper to taste
- Chicken broth – 5 cups
- Water – 1 cup
- Softened and chopped cream cheese – 1 (8-ounce) block

Directions:

In the pot, add all ingredients except cream cheese. Mix to combine. Cook on High for 15 minutes. Remove the lid and transfer the chicken breasts into a bowl. Shred chicken breasts with two forks, and then return to the pot. Press Sauté and stir in cream cheese. Cook for 1 to 2 minutes, stirring continuously. Serve.

Chicken, Spinach and Mushroom Soup

Cook time: 30 minutes| Serves: 6| Per serving: Calories 513; Carbs 1g; Fat 45.1g; Protein 22.1g

Ingredients:

- Boneless, skinless chicken thighs – 6, cubed
- Sliced fresh mushrooms – 6 ounces
- Chopped frozen onion – ½ cup
- Chopped frozen celery – ½ cup
- Garlic – 4 cloves, minced
- Softened cream cheese – 8 ounces
- Softened butter – ¼ cup
- Dried thyme – 1 tsp.
- Salt and pepper to taste
- Homemade chicken broth – 3 cups
- Heavy cream – 1 cup
- Fresh spinach – 2 cups
- Chopped cooked bacon – 1 cup

Directions:

Except for the cream, spinach, and bacon, add all the ingredients in the Instant Pot. Stir to combine. Cover and cook 30 minutes on Soup. Remove the lid and stir in the spinach and cream. Immediately, cover the lid and let stand for 10 minutes. Top with bacon and serve.

Cheesy Pepper Soup

Cook time: 22 minutes| Serves: 6| Per serving: Calories 504; Carbs 1g; Fat 23g; Protein 56g

Ingredients:

- Butter – 3 tbsps.
- Seeded and chopped green bell pepper - ½
- Yellow onion – ½, chopped
- Seeded and chopped jalapeno peppers – 2
- Garlic cloves – 2, minced
- Ground cumin – 1 tsp.
- Paprika – ¼ tsp.
- Salt and black pepper to taste
- Cubed boneless, skinless chicken breasts – 1 ½ pound
- Cream cheese – 6 ounces
- Chicken broth – 3 cups
- Heavy whipping cream – ½ cup
- Cheddar cheese – ¾ cup
- Monterrey Jack Cheese – ¾ cup

- Cooked and crumbled bacon - ½ pound
- Xanthan gum – ½ tsp.

Directions:

Press Sauté and add the bell pepper, onion, jalapenos, garlic, and spices and cook for 5 minutes. Stir in chicken, cream cheese and bacon. Cover and cook on High for 15 minutes. Then open and press Sauté. Add bacon, cheeses, and cream and stir until smooth. Sprinkle xanthan gum on top of soup and cook for 1 to 2 minutes. Serve hot.

Chicken Fajita Soup
Cook time: 30 minutes |Serves: 8| Per serving: Calories 165; Carbs 7g; Fat 3g; Protein 25g

Ingredients:

- Chicken breasts – 2 lbs. boneless, skinless
- Diced tomatoes – 2 (10-oz.) cans
- Chicken broth – 2 cups
- Taco seasoning – 2 tbsps.
- Minced garlic – 2 tsps.
- Onion – ½ cup, chopped
- Green bell pepper – 1, chopped
- Red bell pepper – 1, chopped

Directions:

In the Instant Pot, combine all the ingredients. Close and cook 30 minutes on High. Do a quick release. Remove chicken and shred. Return chicken to the pot and serve.

Cheddar Chicken Soup
Cook time: 15 minutes| Serves: 4| Per serving: Calories 513; Carbs 4g; Fat 31g; Protein 39g

Ingredients:

- Chopped yellow onion – ¼ cup
- Garlic clove – 1, minced
- Hot sauce – ¼ cup
- Boneless, skinless chicken thighs – 2 (6-ounces, each)
- Chopped celery – ½ cup
- Butter – 2 tbsps.
- Chicken broth – 3 cups
- Shredded cheddar cheese – 2 cups
- Heavy cream – 1 cup

Directions:

Except for the cheese and cream, add the rest of the ingredients in the Instant Pot and mix. Close and cook on High for 15 minutes. Then open and remove the cooked meat and shred it. Add the shredded meat back in the potting mix. Mix in the cream and cheese. Stir to mix well. Enjoy.

Cream Zucchini Soup
Cook time: 10 minutes| Serves: 4| Per serving: Calories 264; Carbs 7g; Fat 26g; Protein 4g

Ingredients:

- Vegetable stock – 2 cups
- Garlic – 2 cloves, crushed
- Butter- 1 tbsp.
- Medium zucchinis – 4, peeled and chopped
- Small onion – 1, chopped
- Heavy cream – 2 cups
- Dried oregano – ½ tsp. ground
- Black pepper – ½ tsp. ground
- Dried parsley – 1 tsp. ground
- Sea salt – 1 tsp.
- Lemon juice to taste

Directions:

Press Sauté add the butter and melt it. Add the garlic, onions, and zucchini and cook for 2 to 3 minutes. Add the vegetable broth and sprinkle with parsley, pepper, oregano, and salt. Mix well. Close and cook on High for 5 minutes. Open add the cream and mix. Serve in bowls. Drizzle with lemon juice and serve.

Beef Cabbage Soup
Cook time: 20 minutes |Serves: 4| Per serving: Calories 246; Carbs 8g; Fat 17g; Protein 19g

Ingredients:

- Garlic – 1 clove, minced
- Finely ground beef – 1 pound
- Water – 2 cups
- Coconut oil – 1 tbsp.
- Onion - ½ diced
- Black pepper and salt to taste
- Cabbage – ½ head, chopped

Directions:

Press Sauté and add oil to the Instant Pot. Add the onion and garlic and stir-fry for 2 minutes. Add the meat and brown for 3 minutes. Pour in water and season to taste. Mix. Close and press Poultry. Cook 10 minutes on High. Open and mix in the cabbage. Press Sauté and cook 5 minutes. Serve.

Chicken Curry Soup

Cook time: 11 minutes| Serves: 3| Per serving: Calories 108; Carbs 3g; Fat 8g; Protein 15g

Ingredients:

- Coconut milk – ½ cup; plus ¼ cup
- Chicken thighs – ½ pound, skinless
- Garlic – 2 cloves, crushed
- Onion – ¼, chopped
- Ginger – 1 inch, chopped
- Mushrooms – ½ cup, sliced
- Baby spinach – 2 ounces
- Cayenne pepper – ¼ tsp.
- Salt – ½ tsp.
- Turmeric – ¼ tsp.
- Garam masala – ½ tsp.
- Cilantro – 2 tbsps. chopped

Directions:

Add the listed ingredients to the Instant Pot. Cover and cook on High for 10 minutes. Open and remove meat and shred it. Return the shredded meat to the pot. Press Sauté and stir for 1 minute. Serve.

Summer Vegetable Soup

Cook time: 6 minutes| Serves: 6| Per serving: Calories 210; Carbs 10g; Fat 14g; Protein 10g

Ingredients:

- Finely sliced leeks – 3 cups
- Chopped rainbow chard – 6 cups, stems and leaves
- Chopped celery – 1 cup
- Minced garlic – 2 tbsps. divided
- Dried oregano – 1 tsp.
- Salt – 1 tsp.
- Black pepper – 2 tsps.
- Chicken broth – 3 cups, plus more as needed
- Sliced yellow summer squash – 2 cups
- Chopped fresh parsley – ¼ cup
- Heavy whipping cream – ¾ cup
- Grated Parmesan cheese – 6 tbsps.

Directions:

Put the chard, leeks, celery, 1 tbsp. garlic, oregano, salt, pepper, and broth into the Instant Pot. Cover and cook on High for 3 minutes. Open and press Sauté. Add the remaining 1 tbsp. garlic, parsley, and squash. Cook for 3 minutes. Stir in the cream. Sprinkle with Parmesan and serve.

Chili Lime Chicken Soup

Cook time: 30 minutes| Serves: 5| Per serving: Calories 285; Carbs 3g; Fat 16g; Protein 25g

Ingredients:

- Olive oil – 2 tbsps.
- Boneless, skinless chicken thighs – 1 lb. cut into bite-sized pieces
- Medium yellow onion – ½, diced
- Garlic cloves – 4, minced
- Jalapeno peppers – 2, chopped
- Diced fresh tomato – ½ cup
- Chicken broth – 5 cups
- Juice of 2 limes
- Fine grind sea salt – 2 tsps.
- Chili powder – 1 tsp.
- Garlic powder – ½ tsp.
- Ground black pepper – ¼ tsp.
- Avocado – 1 medium, chopped
- Shredded pepper Jack cheese – 1/3 cup
- Chopped fresh cilantro – 2 tbsps.

Directions:

Press Sauté and add olive oil to the Instant Pot. Add the chicken and sauté for 3 minutes per side. Add the jalapenos, garlic, and onions to the pot. Stir-fry until the vegetables begin to soften. Add the chicken broth, diced tomatoes, lime juice, sea salt, chili powder, garlic powder, and black pepper. Stir to combine. Cover and cook on High for 20 minutes. Open and serve in bowls. Top each serving with chopped cilantro, avocado, and pepper jack. Serve.

Creamy Tomato Basil Soup

Cook time: 4 minutes| Serves: 4 | Per serving: Calories 265; Carbs 20,9g ; Fat 12g ; Protein 9g

Ingredients:

- Butter – 2 tbsps.
- Small sweet onion – 1, chopped
- Garlic – 2 cloves, minced
- Carrot – 1, chopped
- Celery – 1 stalk, chopped
- Vegetable stock – 3 cups
- Tomatoes – 3 pounds, quartered

- Fresh basil – ¼ cup, plus more for garnishing
- Salt and ground black pepper
- Milk – 1 cup

Directions:

Press Sauté on the Instant Pot add butter and melt. Add the garlic and onion and stir-fry for 4 minutes. Add celery and carrot and cook 2 minutes more. Stir continuously. Add the stock and deglaze the pot. Add salt, basil, and tomatoes. Stir to mix. Cover and cook on High for 4 minutes. Open and blend with a hand mixer until smooth. Stir in milk. Taste and adjust seasoning. Garnish and serve.

Cream of Mushroom Soup
Cook time: 5 minutes |Serves: 4| Per serving: Calories 111; Carbs 10g; Fat 8g; Protein 7g

Ingredients:

- Butter – 2 tbsps.
- Small sweet onion – 1, chopped
- White button mushrooms – 1 ½ pound, sliced
- Garlic – 2 cloves, minced
- Dried thyme – 2 tsps.
- Sea salt -1 tsp.
- Vegetable stock – 1 ¾ cups
- Silken tofu – ½ cup
- Chopped fresh thyme for garnishing

Directions:

Press Sauté on the Instant Pot. Melt the butter and add the onion. Stir-fry for 2 minutes. Add the salt, dried thyme, garlic, and mushrooms. Stir-fry for 2 minutes more. Stir in the stock. Cover and cook on High for 5 minutes. Meanwhile, process the tofu in a food processor until smooth. Set aside. Open the pot and blend with a hand mixer until smooth. Add tofu, garnish and serve.

Split Pea Soup
Cook time: 15 minutes| Serves: 4| Per serving: Calories 224; Carbs 35g; Fat 5g; Protein 13g

Ingredients:

- Roasted walnut oil – 1 tbsp.
- Carrots – 2, diced
- Celery – 1 stalk, diced
- Dried thyme – 1 tsp.
- Smoked paprika – 1 tsp.
- Bay leaf – 1
- Salt – ½ to 1 tsp. plus more as needed

- Garlic – 2 cloves, minced
- Green split peas – 1 cup
- Vegetable stock – 2 ½ cups
- Ground black pepper

Directions:

Press Sauté on the Instant Pot. Add oil. Add salt, bay leaf, paprika, thyme, celery, and carrots. Stir-fry for 3 minutes, then add garlic and cook for 30 seconds more. Stir in the split peas and stock. Cover and cook on High for 15 minutes. Open and discard the bay leaf. Taste and adjust seasoning and serve.

Potato Leek Soup
Cook time: 4 minutes |Serves: 4| Per serving: Calories 360; Carbs 29g; Fat 28g; Protein 4g

Ingredients:

- Butter – 3 tbsps.
- Large leeks – 2, white and light green parts only, chopped
- Garlic – 2 cloves, minced
- Vegetable stock – 4 cups
- Yukon Gold potatoes – 1 pound, cubed
- Bay leaf - 1
- Salt – ½ tsp. plus more as needed
- Soy milk – 2/3 cup
- Extra-virgin olive oil – 1/3 cup
- Ground black pepper

Directions:

Press Sauté on the Instant Pot. Add butter and leeks. Stir-fry for 3 minutes. Add the garlic. Cook for 30 seconds more. Add stock, salt, bay leaf, and potatoes. Mix. Cover and cook on High for 4 minutes. Meanwhile, in a blender, combine olive oil and soymilk. Blend until smooth. Open and discard the bay leaf. Stir in the soymilk-olive oil mixture. Blend with a hand mixer until smooth. Taste and adjust seasoning. Serve.

Sweet Potato Stew
Cook time: 10 minutes| Serves: 4| Per serving: Calories 224; Carbs 26g; Fat 13g; Protein 5g

Ingredients:

- Avocado oil – 2 tbsps.
- Sweet onion – ½, diced
- Sweet potatoes – 2, peeled and cubed
- Garlic – 2 cloves, minced
- Salt – 1 to 1 ½ tsp.

- Ground turmeric – 1 tsp.
- Paprika – 1 tsp.
- Ground cumin – ½ tsp.
- Dried oregano – ½ tsp.
- Chili powder – 1 to 2 dashes
- Roma tomatoes – 2, chopped
- Lite coconut milk – 1 (14-ounce) can, shaken well
- Water – 1 ¼ cups, plus more as needed
- Chopped kale – 1 to 2 cups

Directions:

Press Sauté on the Instant pot and add oil. Add onion and stir-fry for 3 minutes. Stir in chili powder, oregano, cumin, paprika, turmeric, salt, garlic, and sweet potatoes. Stir-fry for 1 minute. Add the water, tomatoes, and coconut milk and mix. Cover and cook on High for 4 minutes. Open and stir in the kale. Mix. Serve.

Italian Vegetable Stew
Cook time: 10 minutes| Serves: 4 | Per serving: Calories 285; Carbs 51g; Fat 8g; Protein 8g

Ingredients:

- Olive oil – 2 tbsps.
- Leeks – 2, white and very light green parts only, chopped
- Sweet onion – 1, chopped
- Carrot – 1, chopped
- Celery – 1, sliced
- White mushrooms – 1 cup, sliced
- Small eggplant – 1, chopped
- Garlic – 3, cloves, minced
- Yukon gold potatoes – 3, chopped
- Roma tomatoes – 3, chopped
- Vegetable stock – 4 cups
- Dried oregano – 1 tsp.
- Salt – ½ tsp. plus more as needed
- Torn kale leaves – 2 cups
- Ground black pepper
- Fresh basil for garnishing

Directions:

Press Sauté on the Instant Pot and add oil. Add eggplant, mushrooms, celery, carrot, onion, and leeks. Stir-fry for 2 minutes. Add the garlic. Cook for 30 seconds more. Add the salt, oregano, stock, tomatoes, and potatoes. Cover and cook on High for 7 minutes. Open and stir in the kale. Taste and adjust seasoning. Serve.

White Bean & Swiss Chard Stew

Cook time: 7 minutes| Serves: 4| Per serving: Calories 174; Carbs 29g; Fat4g; Protein 9g

Ingredients:

- Olive oil – 1 tbsp.
- Carrots – 2, chopped
- Celery – 1 stalk, sliced
- Onion – ½, chopped
- Garlic – 2 to 3 cloves, minced
- Tomatoes – 3, chopped
- Red pepper flakes – ¼ to ½ tsp.
- Dried rosemary – ½ tsp.
- Dried oregano – ½ tsp.
- Dried basil – ¼ tsp.
- Salt – ½ tsp. plus more as needed
- Ground black pepper to taste
- Cooked great northern beans – 2 cups
- Swiss chard leaves – 1 small bunch, chopped

Directions:

Press Sauté on the Instant Pot and add oil. Add onion, celery, and carrots and stir-fry for 3 minutes. Add garlic and cook for 30 seconds. Stir in beans, pepper, salt, basil, oregano, rosemary, red pepper flakes, and tomatoes. Cover and cook on High for 3 minutes. Open and stir in Swiss chard. Wilt for 3 minutes. Taste and adjust seasoning. Serve.

Peanut Stew

Cook time: 8 minutes| Serves: 4| Per serving: Calories 602; Carbs 33g; Fat 46g; Protein 22g

Ingredients:

- Roasted walnut oil – 1 tbsp.
- Small onion – 1, chopped
- Red bell pepper – 1, chopped
- Jalapeno pepper – 1, chopped
- Garlic – 3 cloves, minced
- Tomatoes – 3, chopped
- Sweet potato – 1, chopped
- Minced peeled fresh ginger – 2 tbsps.
- Ground cumin – 1 ½ tsps.
- Chili powder – ½ tsp.

- Salt – ½ tsp. plus more as needed
- All-natural peanut butter – ½ cup, not sweetened
- Vegetable stock – 2 cups, divided
- Collard green leaves – 1 small bunch, chopped
- Ground black pepper to taste
- Chopped roasted peanuts – ½ cup

Directions:

Press Sauté and add oil. Add jalapeno, bell pepper, and onion and stir-fry for 3 minutes. Now add garlic. Cook another 30 seconds. Stir in salt, chili powder, cumin, ginger, sweet potatoes, and tomatoes. Let rest for a few minutes. Meanwhile, in a bowl, whisk 1 cup stock and peanut butter until smooth. Pour this mixture into the Instant Pot. Use the remaining 1 cup of stock to rinse out the mixture cup. Add to the Instant Pot. Cover the Instant Pot. Cook on High for 3 minutes. Open and stir in the collard greens. Taste and adjust seasoning. Serve topped with chopped peanuts.

Butternut Quinoa Chili
Cook time: 7 minutes| Serves: 4| Per serving: Calories 325; Carbs 61g; Fat 7g; Protein 10g

Ingredients:

- Olive oil –2 tbsps.
- Carrots – 2, sliced
- Sweet onion – 1, chopped
- Red bell pepper – 1, chopped
- Jalapeno pepper – 1, diced
- Garlic cloves – 1, minced
- Butternut squash – 1, peeled and chopped
- Diced tomatoes with juice – 1 (14-ounce) can
- Uncooked quinoa – 1 cup, rinsed
- Vegetable stock – 2 ½ cups
- Bay leaf – 1
- Ground cumin – 1 tsp.
- Salt – ½ to 1 tsp. plus more if needed
- Sweet paprika – ½ tsp.
- Chili powder – ½ tsp. or more to taste
- Ground black pepper to taste
- Lemon juice – 1 tbsp.

Directions:

Press Sauté and add oil. Add jalapeno, bell pepper, onion, and carrots. Stir-fry for 3 minutes. Add garlic and cook for 30 seconds. Add the pepper, chili powder, paprika, salt, cumin, bay leaf, stock, quinoa, tomatoes, and squash. Cover and cook for 7 minutes on High. Open and discard the bay leaf. Stir in the lemon juice. Taste and adjust seasoning. Serve.

Wild Rice Soup
Cook time: 33 minutes| Serves: 4| Per serving: Calories 480; Carbs 57g; Fat 26g; Protein 10g

Ingredients:

- Butter – 8 tbsps. divided
- Carrots – 5, sliced
- Celery stalks – 5, diced
- Small sweet onion – 1, diced
- Garlic – 4 cloves, minced
- Baby Bella mushrooms – 8 ounces, sliced
- Bay leaves – 2
- Paprika – ½ tsp.
- Dried thyme – ½ tsp.
- Salt – ½ tsp. plus more as needed
- Vegetable stock – 4 cups
- Wild rice – 1 cup
- All-purpose flour – ½ cup
- Non-dairy milk – 1 cup
- Ground black pepper

Directions:

Press Sauté on the Instant Pot and add 2 tbsps. butter. Add the salt, thyme, paprika, bay leaves, mushrooms, garlic, onion, celery, and carrots. Cook for 2 to 3 minutes. Stir in the wild rice and stock. Cover and cook on High for 30 minutes. Heat the remaining 6 tbsps. of butter in a saucepan. Add flour and cook for 3 to 4 minutes. Whisk in the milk and mix well. Open the pot and discard the bay leaves. Press Sauté stir in the mixture. Mix and thicken. Taste and adjust seasoning and serve.

Curried Squash Soup
Cook time: 30 minutes| Serves: 4| Per serving: Calories 267; Carbs 50g; Fat 11g; Protein 5g

Ingredients:

- Olive oil - 1 tbsp.
- Onion – 1, chopped
- Garlic – 2 cloves, chopped
- Curry powder – 1 tbsp.
- Butternut squash – 1 (2 to 3-pound), cubed
- Vegetable stock – 4 cups
- Salt – 1 tsp.

- Lite coconut milk – 1 (14-ounce) can

Directions:

Press Sauté on the Instant Pot. Add oil. Add onion and stir-fry for 3 to 4 minutes. Add curry powder and garlic and cook for 1 minute. Add the stock, squash, and salt. Cover and cook on High for 25 minutes. Open the pot and blend with a hand mixer. Stir in the coconut milk and serve.

Smoky White Bean Soup
Cook time: 27 minutes| Serves: 4| Per serving: Calories 183; Carbs 27g; Fat 7g; Protein 6g

Ingredients:

- Dried great northern white beans – 1 cup, rinsed
- Tomato – 1, diced
- Raw millet – ¼ cup
- Vegetable cube – 1
- Smoked paprika – 1 to 1 ½ tsps.
- Salt -1 tsp.
- Water – 4 cups plus more as needed
- Lite coconut milk – 1 (14-ounce) can
- Frozen sweet corn – 1 cup

Directions:

In the Instant Pot, stir together the coconut milk, water, salt, paprika, bouillon cube, millet, tomato, and beans. Cover and cook on High for 27 minutes. Open and stir in the corn. Taste and adjust the seasoning and serve.

Chapter 7 Vegetable Recipes

Minestrone Soup

Cook time: 7 minutes |Serves: 4| Per serving: Calories 332; Carbs 54g; Fat 12g; Protein 13g

Ingredients:

- Olive oil – 2 tbsps.
- Celery stalks – 2, sliced
- Sweet onion – 1, diced
- Large carrot – 1, sliced
- Garlic – 2 cloves, minced
- Dried oregano – 1 tsp.
- Dried basil – 1 tsp.
- Salt – ½ tsp. to 1 tsp. plus more as needed
- Bay leaf – 1
- Zucchini – 1, diced
- Diced tomatoes – 1 (28-ounce) can
- Kidney beans – 1 (16-ounce) can, drained and rinsed
- Dried pasta – 1 cup
- Vegetable stock – 6 cups
- Fresh baby spinach – 2 to 3 cups
- Ground black pepper

Directions:

Press Sauté on your Instant Pot. Add oil, carrot, onion, and celery. Stir-fry for 2 to 3 minutes. Now add garlic and stir-fry for 1 minute. Add bay leaf, salt, basil, and oregano. Stir and let sit for 30 seconds. Add the stock, pasta, kidney beans, tomatoes, and zucchini. Cover the Instant Pot. Cook on High for 3 minutes. Open and discard the bay leaf. Stir in spinach. Taste and adjust seasoning. Serve.

Corn Chowder

Cook time: 12 minutes| Serves: 4 | Per serving: Calories 413; Carbs 49g; Fat 24g; Protein 6g

Ingredients:

- Olive oil – 1 tbsp.
- Small sweet onion – 1, diced
- Celery stalks – 3, sliced
- Garlic – 2 cloves, minced
- Dried thyme – 1 tsp.
- Ground coriander – ½ tsp.
- Salt – ½ to 1 tsp.

- Ground black pepper – ¼ tsp.
- Russet potatoes – 3, peeled and chopped
- Vegetable stock – 3 ½ cups
- Butter – 6 tbsps.
- All-purpose flour – ½ cup
- Milk – 1 cup
- Frozen sweet corn – 12 ounces
- Carrot – 1, grated
- Sliced scallion for garnish

Directions:

Press Sauté on the Instant Pot and add oil. Add onion and stir-fry for 3 minutes. Add salt, pepper, coriander, thyme, garlic, and celery. Cook for 1 minute more. Stir in stock and potato. Cover and cook on High for 5 minutes. Meanwhile, melt the butter in a pan. Add the flour. Cook for 3 minutes. Whisk in the milk and mix well. Do a quick release. Open and press Sauté. Add carrot and corn. Stir in roux and warm through. Thicken the sauce. Taste and adjust seasoning. Garnish and serve.

Chipotle Sweet Potato Chowder

Cook time: 2 minutes| Serves: 4| Per serving: Calories 216; Carbs 35g; Fat 10g; Protein 5g

Ingredients:

- Vegetable stock – 1 ¼ cups
- Lite coconut milk – 1 (14-ounce) can
- Sweet potatoes – 2, peeled and diced
- Canned chipotle peppers – 2 to 4 (in adobo sauce), diced
- Red bell pepper – 1, diced
- Small onion – 1, diced
- Ground cumin – 1 tsp.
- Salt – ½ to 1 tsp.
- Frozen sweet corn – 1 ½ cups
- Adobo sauce from the canned peppers, to taste

Directions:

Whisk the coconut milk and stock in a bowl. Mix well. Pour into the Instant Pot. Add the salt, cumin, onion, bell pepper, chipotles, and sweet potatoes. Cover and cook on High for 2 minutes. Open and add the adobo sauce and frozen corn. Warm the corn and serve.

Pumpkin Soup

Cook time: 20 minutes| Serves: 6| Per serving: Calories 267; Carbs 16g; Fat 22.8g; Protein 3.6g

Ingredients:

- Pumpkin – 1 large can
- Full-fat coconut cream – 1 can
- Small onion – 1, chopped
- Potato – 1, chopped
- Coconut milk – 2 cups
- Salt and pepper
- Parsley - 1 bunch

Directions:

Add everything in the Instant Pot. Mix well. Cover and cook on High for 20 minutes. Open and serve.

Taco Soup
Cook time:11 minutes| Serves: 4| Per serving: Calories 296; Carbs 39.7g; Fat 9.8g; Protein 15.2g

Ingredients:

- Red onion – 1, diced
- Garlic powder – 3 tbsps.
- Black beans – 1 large can, drained
- Diced tomatoes – 1 large can
- Tomato sauce – 1 large can
- Corn – 1 can
- Frozen chopped spinach – 1 cup
- Prepared rice – 1 cup
- Taco seasoning – 1 packet
- Salt and black pepper to taste
- Cilantro -1 tsp.

Directions:

Add everything in the Instant Pot and mix. Cover and cook on High for 3 minutes. Do a quick release. Let simmer uncovered on Sauté for 8 minutes. Serve.

Tomato Soup
Cook time: 3 minutes| Serves: 4 | Per serving: Calories 316; Carbs 25.3g; Fat 24.3g; Protein 6.3g

Ingredients:

- Diced tomatoes – 2 cans, drained
- Full-fat coconut cream – 1 can
- Tomato sauce – 1 large can
- Basil – 1 tbsp.
- Garlic – 2 cloves
- Salt and black pepper to taste

- Coconut milk – 1 cup

Directions:

Combine all ingredients in the Instant Pot. Cover and cook on High for 3 minutes. Open and stir. Serve.

Beans with Jalapenos
Cook time: 45 minutes |Serves: 3 | Per serving: Calories 61; Carbs 12.5g; Fat 1.3g; Protein 3.2g

Ingredients:

- Dry pinto beans – 1 ½ cups, rinsed
- Chili powder – 1 tbsp.
- Cumin – 1 tbsp.
- Salt – 1 tsp.
- Salsa – ¾ cups
- Diced jalapenos – 4 oz.
- Water as needed

Directions:

Place the beans in the Instant Pot. Add enough water, so the beans are submerged by 2-inches of water. Cook on High for 45 minutes. Place the drained beans in a bowl. Add salt, cumin and chili powder. With a hand mixture, blend until it reaches your desired consistency. Add diced jalapenos and salsa to the beans and mix well. Serve.

Candied Carrots
Cook time: 2 minutes| Serves: 4| Per serving: Calories 123; Carbs 16g ; Fat 7g ; Protein 1g

Ingredients:

- Baby carrots – 1 pound
- Water – 1 cup
- Butter – 3 tbsps.
- Light brown sugar – 3 tbsps.
- Salt – ½ tsp.

Directions:

Pour in water into the Instant Pot, then place a steamer basket. Add the carrots on top. Close and cook on High for 2 minutes. Do a quick release. Open and add the butter. Let it melt for 1 minute. Add the salt, and brown sugar and mix to coat. Serve.

Lemon Ginger Asparagus
Cook time: 2 minutes| Serves: 4| Per serving: Calories 84; Carbs 5g; Fat 7g; Protein 3g

Ingredients:

- Asparagus – 1 bunch, tough ends removed

- Water – 1 cup
- Olive oil – 2 tbsps.
- Lemon juice – 1 tbsp.
- Salt – ½ to 1 tsp.
- Grated peeled fresh ginger – ½ tsp

Directions:

Add water to the Instant Pot. Place a steamer basket into the Instant Pot and add asparagus on top. Close and cook for 2 minutes. Do a quick release. In a bowl, stir together ginger, salt, lemon juice, and oil. Add the asparagus to the bowl. Toss and serve.

Garlicky Lemon Broccoli
Cook time: 2 minutes| Serves: 2| Per serving: Calories 108; Carbs 21g; Fat 1g; Protein 8g

Ingredients:

- Water – 1 cup
- Garlic – 4 cloves, roughly chopped
- Chopped broccoli – 6 cups
- Juice of 1 lemon
- Salt – ½ tsp.
- Zest of 1 lemon

Directions:

Combine the water and garlic in the Instant Pot. In a steamer basket, place the broccoli, and place the basket in the Instant Pot. Pour lemon juice over the broccoli. Cover and cook on High for 2 minutes. Do a quick release. Remove the broccoli. Sprinkle the salt and lemon zest over the broccoli. Serve.

Slaw in Cups
Cook time: 8 minutes| Serves: 6| Per serving: Calories 344; Carbs 65g; Fat 5g; Protein 11g

Ingredients:

- Wonton or dumpling wrappers - 12
- Water – 1 cup
- Sliced green cabbage – 2 cups
- Shredded sweet potato – 1 cup
- Sweet onion – ½, sliced
- Lite soy sauce – 2 tbsps.
- Hoisin sauce – 1 tbsp.
- Lemon juice – 1 ½ tbsps.
- Sesame oil – 1 ½ tsps.
- Zest of 1 lime

- Ground ginger – ½ tsp. plus more to taste
- Scallions – 3, green and light green parts, sliced

Directions:

Preheat the oven. Use nonstick spray to coat a muffin tin. Place one wonton wrapper in each well of the prepared tin. Bake for 5 to 6 minutes. Set aside. Pour water into the Instant Pot. Place a steamer basket into the Instant Pot and place onion, sweet potato, and cabbage on the basket. Cover, press Steam and cook for 2 minutes. Meanwhile, in a bowl, stir together the ginger, lime zest, lime juice, hoisin sauce, oil, and soy sauce. Open and stir in the veggies. Coat well. Before serving, fill the cups with the slaw and sprinkle the tops with scallion. Serve.

Perfect Beets
Cook time: 17 minutes| Serves: 4 | Per serving: Calories 66; Carbs 15g; Fat 0g; Protein 3g

Ingredients:

- Beets – 8, roots and leafy greens trimmed
- Water – 1 cup

Directions:

In the Instant Pot, add the water, and place a steamer basket inside. Place the beets in the basket and close. Cook 17 minutes on High. Do a quick release. Remove the beets, season and serve.

Creamy Corn
Cook time: 20 minutes| Serves: 4| Per serving: Calories 395; Carbs 44g; Fat 23g; Protein 12g

Ingredients:

- Raw cashews - 1 cup, soaked overnight and drained
- Vegetable stock – 1 cup
- Lemon juice – 2 tbsps.
- Sugar – 1 tbsp.
- Salt – 1 tsp. plus more for seasoning
- Vegetable oil – ½ tsp.
- Frozen sweet corn – 20 oz.
- Milk – ¾ cup
- Butter – 1 tbsp.
- Smoked paprika – ¼ tsp.
- Ground black pepper

Directions:

In a food processor, combine the oil, salt, sugar, lemon juice, stock, and cashews. Blend until smooth. Pour cashew mixture into the Instant Pot. Add paprika, butter, milk, and corn. Season with salt and pepper. Press Slow Cooker and cook 20 minutes. Remove the lid and stir the corn. Serve.

Cheesy Kale Bake
Cook time: 2 minutes| Serves: 2| Per serving: Calories 126; Carbs 12.6g; Fat 7.4g; Protein 4.4g

Ingredients:

- Kale - 3 cups
- Coconut oil - 1 tbsp.
- Fresh green beans - ½ cup
- Water - 1 cup
- Dash Parmesan cheese

Directions:

Place the water in the Instant Pot then place in a trivet. Top the trivet with vegetables. Then cook on High for 2 minutes. Remove the veggies and garnish with cheese. Serve.

Cauliflower Veggie Mashup
Cook time: 10 minutes |Serves: 4 | Per serving: Calories 119; Carbs 12.7g; Fat 7.5g; Protein 3.5g

Ingredients:

- Carrots – 2
- Yellow zucchini – 1, chopped
- Cauliflower – 2 cups, chopped
- Broccoli – 1 cup, chopped
- Coconut milk – ½ cup
- Salt and pepper
- Red pepper – 1
- Parmesan cheese for garnishing

Directions:

Add everything in the Instant Pot and cover. Cook on High for 10 minutes. Do a natural release. Open and stir. Garnish with parmesan and serve.

Spaghetti
Cook time: 4 minutes| Serves: 4| Per serving: Calories 73; Carbs 9.4g; Fat 4.2g; Protein 1.4g

Ingredients:

- Spaghetti squash – 1 large, sliced in half and seeds removed
- Basil
- Garlic powder
- Coconut cream – ¼ cup
- Water – 1 cup
- Dash of pink sea salt

Directions:

Add the water into the Instant Pot and other ingredients into the water. Cover and cook for 4 minutes at High. Open and pull the squash out. Scoop out the center, then add the centers along back into the Instant Pot. Swirl around with the other ingredients. Serve.

Red Thai Curry Cauliflower

Cook time: 2 minutes| Serves: 4 | Per serving: Calories 349; Carbs 18g; Fat 31g; Protein 5g

Ingredients:

- Full-fat coconut milk – 1 (14-ounce) can
- Water – 1 cup
- Red curry paste – 2 tbsps.
- Garlic powder – 1 tsp.
- Salt – 1 tsp. plus more as needed
- Ground ginger – ½ tsp.
- Onion powder – ½ tsp.
- Chili powder – ¼ tsp.
- Bell pepper – 1, sliced
- Cauliflower – 1 medium head, chopped
- Diced tomatoes and liquid – 1 (14-ounce) can
- Freshly ground black pepper

Directions:

Stir together the chili powder, onion powder, ginger, salt, garlic powder, curry paste, water, and coconut milk in the Instant Pot. Mix. Add tomatoes, cauliflower, and bell pepper and mix. Cover and cook on High for 2 minutes. Open and stir. Taste and adjust seasoning. Serve.

Polenta and Kale

Cook time: 17 minutes| Serves: 4| Per serving: Calories 329; Carbs 46g; Fat 13g; Protein 10g

Ingredients:

- Olive oil – 1 tbsp.
- Kale – 2 bunches, chopped
- Garlic – 4 cloves, minced
- Salt – 1 tsp. divided plus more as needed
- Polenta – 1 cup
- Vegetable stock -1 quart
- Butter – 3 tbsps.
- Ground black pepper

Directions:

Press Sauté on the Instant Pot and add oil. Add garlic, kale, and ½ tsp. salt. Stir-fry for 2 minutes. Transfer to a bowl. In the Instant Pot, add ½ tsp. salt, stock, and polenta. Cover and cook on High for 17 minutes. Do a natural release. Remove the lid and mix. Add butter, and more salt and pepper if needed. Serve.

Butternut Mac 'N' Cheese
Cook time: 2 minutes| Serves: 6| Per serving: Calories 520; Carbs 78g; Fat 14g; Protein 23g

Ingredients:

- Raw cashews – 1 cup, soaked overnight, drained and rinsed
- Cooked cubed butternut squash – 2 cups
- Nutritional yeast – 1/3 cup
- Lemon juice – 2 tbsps.
- Dijon mustard – 1 tsp.
- Salt – 2 tsp
- Ground nutmeg – 1/8 tsp
- Water – 4 ½ cups, divided
- Pasta – 1 (16-ounce) box
- Milk – 1 cup, plus more as needed
- Ground black pepper

Directions:

Combine 2 cups water, cashews, squash, nutritional yeast, lemon juice, mustard, salt, and nutmeg in a food processor and combine until smooth. Pour the mixture into the Instant Pot. Add the rest 2 ½ cups water into the blender and blend to capture any remaining mixture. Add to the Instant Pot, and pasta. Cover and cook on Low for 2 minutes. Do a natural release. Remove the lid and stir in milk. Mix. Serve.

Rice and Veggies
Cook time: 9 minutes |Serves: 4 | Per serving: Calories 418; Carbs 70g; Fat 13g; Protein 10g

Ingredients:

- Jasmin rice – 1 cup, rinsed and drained
- Water – 1 cup
- Salt -1 tsp.
- Ground ginger – ½ tsp.
- Sesame oil – 1 tbsp.
- Carrot – 1, chopped
- Small onion – 1, diced
- Bok choy – 1 cup, chopped
- Sugar snap peas – 1 cup, rinsed, tough ends removed
- Garlic – 2 cloves, minced

- White button mushrooms – 8 ounces, sliced
- Sliced water chestnuts – 1 (8-ounce), drained
- Lite coconut milk – 1 (14-ounce)
- Chinese five-spice – 1 tsp.
- Soy sauce – 1 tsp.

Directions:

Combine ginger, salt, rice, and water in the Instant Pot. Cover and cook on High for 3 minutes. Do a natural release. Open and fluff the rice. Transfer to a bowl and set aside. Press Sauté on the Instant Pot. Stir in cooked rice, soy sauce, five-spice powder, and coconut milk. Cook for 5 to 6 minutes. Serve.

Broccoli Patties
Cook time: 5 minutes| Serves: 6| Per serving: Calories 79; Carbs 14.2g; Fat 1.7g; Protein 3.3g

Ingredients:

- Broccoli florets – 1 pound
- Wheat flour – 3 tbsps.
- Salt – 1 tsp.
- Fresh dill - 1 tbsp. chopped
- Potato – 1, peeled
- Red onion – ½, grated
- Olive oil – 1 tsp.
- Water - 1 cup for cooking

Directions:

Pour water in the Instant Pot and insert steamer rack. Place broccoli and potato on the steamer rack and close. Cook on High for 3 minutes. Then do a natural release. Transfer potato and broccoli to the blender. Add salt, fresh dill, grated onion, and blend until smooth. Then make medium patties from the mixture and coat them in wheat flour. Freeze the patties in the freezer for 10 minutes. Meanwhile, preheat the Instant Pot on Sauté and grease with olive oil. Place the frozen patties in the pot and close the lid. Cook on High for 2 minutes. Serve.

Cauliflower Potato Burgers
Cook time: 7 minutes |Serves: 2| Per serving: Calories 163; Carbs 17g; Fat 9g; Protein 6.6g

Ingredients:

- Cauliflower rice – 7 oz.
- Mashed potato – ¼ cup
- Almond flour – 1 tbsp.
- Salt – 1 tsp.
- White pepper – 1 tsp.

- Coconut yogurt – 1 tbsp.
- Breadcrumbs – 1 tbsp.
- Water – ½ cup, for cooking
- Burger buns – 2, cut into halves

Directions:

In a bowl, combine mashed potato and cauliflower. Add almond flour, salt, white pepper, and coconut yogurt. Make medium size burgers from the mixture. Coat burgers with breadcrumbs and wrap in the foil. Pour water in the Instant Pot and insert steamer rack. Place wrapped burgers on the steamer rack and close the lid. Cook on High for 7 minutes. Do a natural release. Serve with burger buns.

Sweet Potato Burgers
Cook time: 20 minutes| Serves: 2 | Per serving: Calories 139; Carbs 19.7g; Fat 6.4g; Protein 4.3g

Ingredients:

- Sweet potato – 1
- Onion – ½, diced
- Chives – 1 tsp.
- Salt – ½ tsp.
- Cayenne pepper – 1 tsp.
- Flax meal – 3 tbsps.
- Kale – ½ cup
- Olive oil - 1 tsp.
- Water – ½ cup, for cooking
- Burger buns – 2, cut into halves

Directions:

Pour water in the Instant Pot and insert steamer rack. Place sweet potato on the steamer rack and close the lid. Cook on High for 15 minutes and do a quick release. Meanwhile, place, onion, chives, and kale in the blender. Blend until smooth. Transfer the blended mixture into the mixing bowl. When the sweet potato is cooked, cut it into halves and scoop all the flesh into the kale mixture. Mix. Add flax meal, salt, and cayenne pepper. Stir well. Make medium burgers from the mixture. Clean the Instant Pot bowl and add olive oil. Preheat on Sauté for 2 to 3 minutes. Add burgers and cook for 2 minutes on each side. Serve with burger buns.

Lentil Burger
Cook time: 26 minutes| Serves: 7| Per serving: Calories 122; Carbs 20.7g; Fat 1.1g; Protein 7.7g

Ingredients:

- Lentils – 1 cup, soaked overnight
- Water – 1 cup

- Carrot – ½ cup, peeled
- Cayenne pepper - 1 tsp.
- Wheat flour – 4 tbsps.
- Salt – 1 tsp.
- Olive oil – 1 tsp.
- Dried dill - 1 tbsp.
- Burger buns – 7, cut into halves

Directions:

Put the lentils in the Instant Pot along with water, carrot, salt, and cayenne pepper. Close the lid and cook on High for 25 minutes. Then do a natural release. Transfer the cooked ingredients in a blender and blend until smooth. Add dried dill and wheat flour. Mix it up until smooth. Make the burgers. Add olive oil in the Instant Pot and add the burgers. Cook on High for 1 minute. Do a quick release. Serve with burger buns.

Black Bean Burger
Cook time: 5 minutes| Serves: 5| Per serving: Calories 155; Carbs 28.8g; Fat 1g; Protein 9.2g

Ingredients:

- Black beans – 1 cup, cooked
- Breadcrumbs – 2 tbsps.
- Salt – 1 tsp.
- Sweet corn – ¼ cup, cooked
- Turmeric – 1 tsp.
- Fresh parsley – 1 tbsp. chopped
- Yellow sweet pepper – ½, chopped
- Water – ½ cup
- Burger buns – 5, cut into halves

Directions:

Mash the black beans until they are puree and combine with salt, sweet corn, turmeric, parsley, and sweet pepper. Mix and add breadcrumbs. Mix again. Pour water into the Instant Pot and insert seamer rack. Make the burgers from the black bean mixture and freeze for 30 minutes. Wrap burgers in foil and place on the steamer rack. Close the lid and cook on High for 5 minutes. Do a natural release. Remove the foil from the burgers and transfer them to a plate. Serve with burger buns.

Mushroom Burger
Cook time: 14 minutes| Serves: 4| Per serving: Calories 47; Carbs 5.4g; Fat 2.6g; Protein 2.6g

Ingredients:

- Mushrooms – 2 cups, chopped

- Onion – 1, diced
- Silken tofu – ½ cup
- Salt – ½ tsp.
- Chili flakes – ½ tsp.
- Dried parsley – 1 tbsp.
- Dried dill – 1 tsp.
- Flax meal – 3 tbsps.
- Olive oil – ½ tsp.
- Burger buns – 4, cut into halves

Directions:

Put mushrooms in the blender and blend. Then transfer the vegetable to the Instant Pot along with onion and olive oil. Stir gently and close the lid. Cook on Sauté for 10 minutes. Meanwhile, mash silken tofu in a blender until you get a puree. Add salt, chili flakes, dried parsley, and dried dill and blend. Add flax meal and pulse for 10 seconds. When the mushroom mixture is cooked, transfer it in the bowl and combine it together with the silken tofu. Stir well and make the burgers. Line the Instant Pot with baking paper and place burgers on it. Close the lid and cook 4 minutes on High. Then do a quick release. Chill and serve with buns.

Seitan Burger
Cook time: 2 minutes| Serves: 1| Per serving: Calories 303; Carbs 24.9g; Fat 8.8g; Protein 26.8g

Ingredients:

- Burger bun – 1, cut into halves
- Mustard – 1 tsp.
- Soy sauce – 1 tsp.
- Seitan steak – 1
- Onion powder – 1 tsp.
- Olive oil - 1 tsp.
- Apple cider vinegar - 1 tbsp.

Directions:

Make the sauce for the seitan steak: mix up together soy sauce, onion powder, olive oil, and apple cider vinegar. Brush seitan steak with sauce on each side and place in the Instant Pot. Close the lid and cook on Manual for 2 minutes. Then do a quick release. Meanwhile, cut burger buns into halves and spread with mustard. Place seitan steak on the one-half of the burger bun and cover with the second one.

Spinach Patties
Cook time: 10 minutes |Serves: 7| Per serving: Calories 47; Carbs 4.5g; Fat 2.9g; Protein 1.5g

Ingredients:

- Spinach – 3 cups, chopped
- Coconut shred – 2 tbsps.
- Panko breadcrumbs – 4 tbsps.
- Salt – 1 tsp.
- Chili flakes – ½ tsp.
- Flax meal – 2 tbsps.
- Hot water – 6 tbsps.
- Olive oil - 1 tsp.
- Coconut yogurt - 1 tbsp.

Directions:

In a bowl, mix flax meal and hot water. Whisk the mixture. Then add coconut shred, panko breadcrumbs, spinach, chili flakes, coconut yogurt, and salt. Mix well. Press the Sauté on the Instant Pot and preheat. Add oil and make patties from the spinach mixture. Cook the patties 5 minutes on each side. Serve.

Apple Patties
Cook time: 6 minutes| Serves: 4| Per serving: Calories 104; Carbs 23.3g; Fat 1.4g; Protein 1g

Ingredients:

- Granny smith apples – 2
- Wheat flour – 3 tbsps.
- Baking powder – ½ tsp.
- Brown sugar - 1 tbsp.
- Vanilla extract – 1 tsp.
- Olive oil – 1 tsp.

Directions:

Grate the apples and place them in a bowl. Add wheat flour, baking powder, sugar, and vanilla extract. Mix and let it rest. Meanwhile, press Sauté and preheat the Instant Pot. Pour olive oil in the Instant Pot. Make patties from the apple mixture and put in the Instant Pot. Sauté the patties for 3 minutes on each side or until golden brown. Serve.

Onion Patties
Cook time: 6 minutes |Serves: 4| Per serving: Calories 266; Carbs 23.1g; Fat 19.1g; Protein 3.9g

Ingredients:

- Yellow onions – 3, diced
- Wheat flour – 4 tbsps.
- Coconut milk – ¾ cup
- Baking powder – ½ tsp.
- Garlic powder – 1 tsp.

- Turmeric – 1 tsp.
- Sesame oil - 1 tbsp.

Directions:

Mix the diced onions, wheat flour, and coconut milk. Add garlic powder, and turmeric. Mix. and make patties. Heat sesame oil in the Instant Pot on Sauté. Cook in the Instant Pot 3 minutes per side.

Zucchini Patties
Cook time: 5 minutes| Serves: 2 | Per serving: Calories 159; Carbs 26.2g; Fat 5g; Protein 5.6g

Ingredients:

- Zucchini – 1, grated
- Ground black pepper – ½ tsp.
- Smoked paprika – 1 tsp.
- Turmeric – ¼ tsp.
- Salt – 1 tsp.
- Flax meal – 3 Tbsps.
- Sesame seeds - 1 tsp.
- White rice – ¼ cup, boiled

Directions:

In a bowl, mix grated zucchini, ground black pepper, smoked paprika, and turmeric. Add salt, flax meal, sesame seeds, and boiled rice. Mix the mixture and make patties. Freeze the patties in the freezer for 20 minutes. Wrap the frozen patties in the foil and place them on the steamer rack. Insert the rack into the Instant Pot and close the lid. Cook patties for 5 minutes on High. Do a quick release. Remove foil from the patties and serve.

Carrot Patties
Cook time: 8 minutes| Serves: 4| Per serving: Calories 228; Carbs 34.3g; Fat 6.3g; Protein 10.6g

Ingredients:

- Chickpeas – 1 cup, cooked
- Carrots – 2, grated
- Fresh cilantro – 1 tbsp.
- Tahini paste – 1 tbsp.
- Miso paste – ½ tsp.
- Salt – 1 tsp.
- Chili flakes – ½ tsp.
- Olive oil – 1 tsp.

Directions:

Blend the chickpea and cilantro until smooth and transfer to a bowl. Add grated carrot, tahini, and miso paste, salt, and chili flakes. Mix and make patties. Preheat the Instant Pot on Sauté and add oil. Put the patties in the hot oil and Sauté them for 4 minutes on each side.

Pumpkin Burger

Cook time: 3 minutes| Serves: 2| Per serving: Calories 197; Carbs 30.5g; Fat 5.6g; Protein 7.2g

Ingredients:

- Hamburger buns – 2
- Pumpkin seeds – 1 tbsp.
- Pumpkin powder – 1 tbsp.
- Pumpkin pure – 3 tbsps.
- Breadcrumbs – 2 tbsps.
- Chili flakes – ½ tsp.
- Turmeric - 1 tsp.
- Flax meal - 1 tbsp.
- Hot water – 3 tbsps.

Directions:

In a bowl, mix flax meal and water. Whisk the mixture and add the pumpkin powder, pumpkin puree, breadcrumbs, chili flakes, and turmeric. Mix and add pumpkin seeds. Make 2 burgers. Place them in the Instant Pot and close the lid. Cook on High for 3 minutes. Do a quick release and open the lid. Fill the burger buns with pumpkin burgers. Serve.

Butternut Squash Burger

Cook time: 15 minutes| Serves: 4| Per serving: Calories 210; Carbs 30.6g; Fat 7.6g; Protein 8.1g

Ingredients:

- Butternut squash – 10 oz. boiled
- Chickpea – ¼ cup, cooked
- Fresh parsley – 1 tbsp. chopped
- Quinoa – 1/3 cup, soaked
- Vegetable broth – 1 cup
- Flax meal – 3 tbsps.
- Wheat flour – 2 tbsps.
- Salt – 1 tsp.
- Smoked paprika – 1 tsp.
- Ground black pepper - 1 tsp.
- Minced garlic - 1 tsp.
- Olive oil – 1 tbsp.
- Burger buns – 4, cut into halves

Directions:

Pour vegetable broth into the Instant Pot. Add quinoa and close the lid. Cook on High for 8 minutes. Do a quick release. Meanwhile, in a bowl, mix chickpeas, parsley, flax meal, wheat flour, salt, smoked paprika, ground black pepper, butternut squash, and minced garlic. Add cooked quinoa and mix the mixture. Make four burgers and place them in the Instant Pot. Add olive oil and Sauté for 5 minutes. Flip and cook the other side for 2 minutes more. Serve with burger buns.

Pumpkin Cream Soup

Cook time: 20 minutes| Serves: 5| Per serving: Calories 305; Carbs 24.8g; Fat 23.4g; Protein 4.8g

Ingredients:

- Coconut cream - 2 cups
- Water – 2 cups
- Pumpkin – 3 cups, chopped
- Salt – 1 tsp.
- Paprika – 1 tsp.
- Ground cardamom – ¼ tsp.
- Turmeric – ½ tsp.
- Potato – 1, peeled
- Wheat flour – 1 tbsp.

Directions:

Whisk water with wheat flour until smooth and pour mixture in the Instant Pot. Add chopped pumpkin, coconut cream, salt, paprika, ground cardamom, and turmeric. Grate the potato and add it in the Instant Pot. Close and cook on High for 20 minutes. Do a quick release and open. Blend with a hand mixer and serve.

Classic Vegetable Soup

Cook time: 17 minutes| Serves: 4| Per serving: Calories 125; Carbs 26.8g; Fat 1.4g; Protein 4g

Ingredients:

- Water – 2 cups
- Carrot – 1, chopped
- Yellow onion – 1, diced
- Minced garlic - ½ tsp.
- Ground black pepper – 1 tsp.
- Avocado oil - 2 tbsps.
- Salt – 1 tsp.
- Potatoes – 2, chopped
- Tomatoes – 1 cup, chopped
- Fresh dill – ½ cup, chopped

Directions:

Preheat Instant Pot on Sauté and add the avocado oil. Then add the onion and carrot. Stir-fry for 5 minutes. Add garlic, black pepper, salt, and chopped tomatoes. Sauté vegetables for 5 minutes. Add potato, dill, and water. Mix well. Close the lid and cook on High for 7 minutes. Do a natural release. Open and serve.

Cauliflower Soup
Cook time: 15 minutes| Serves: 4| Per serving: Calories 106; Carbs 9.7g; Fat 7.3g; Protein 3g

Ingredients:

- Cauliflower head – 1 pound
- Coconut cream – ¼ cup
- Water – 2 cups
- Lemon juice – 2 tbsps.
- Olive oil – 1 tbsp.
- Onion – 1, diced
- Salt – 1 tsp.
- Ground black pepper – ½ tsp.
- Water – ½ cup, for cooking

Directions:

Pour ½ cup water in the Instant Pot and insert steamer rack. Place cauliflower on the rack and close the lid. Cook on High for 5 minutes, then do a quick release. Remove cauliflower and water from the Instant Pot. Pour water in the Instant Pot. Add diced onion and sauté for 3 to 4 minutes. Sprinkle the onion with salt and ground black pepper. Chop cooked cauliflower and add into the Instant Pot. Then add water and coconut cream. Close and seal the lid. Cook on High for 4 minutes. Do a quick release and open the lid. Blend the soup with a hand mixer. Ladle the soup in the bowls and sprinkle with lemon juice. Serve.

Potato Chowder with Corn
Cook time: 10 minutes |Serves: 2| Per serving: Calories 374; Carbs 23.9g; Fat 31.6g; Protein 5.5g

Ingredients:

- Mushrooms – ¼ cup, chopped
- Onion – ½, diced
- Coconut cream – 1 cup
- Water – 1 cup
- Corn kernels – ½ cup
- Salt – 1 tsp.
- Paprika – 1 tsp.
- Chili flakes – ½ tsp.
- Potato – 1 cup, chopped
- Olive oil – 1 tsp.

Directions:

Add olive oil in the Instant Pot. Add onion and mushrooms and stir-fry for 4 minutes or until golden brown. Then transfer vegetables in the bowl. Add water and coconut cream in the Instant Pot. Then add corn kernels and potato. Sprinkle the mixture with salt, paprika, and chili flakes. Close the lid and cook on High for 5 minutes. Then do a natural release. Ladle chowder in the bowls and sprinkle with cooked onion and mushrooms. Serve.

French Onion Soup

Cook time: 25 minutes |Serves: 2| Per serving: Calories 332; Carbs 27.7g ; Fat 14g ; Protein 19.5g

Ingredients:

- Onion – 3 cups, diced
- Coconut oil – 2 tbsps.
- Water - ¼ cup
- Vegetable broth – 2 cups
- Salt – 1 tsp.
- Ground black pepper – 1 tsp.
- Minced garlic – 1 tsp.
- Ground nutmeg - ½ tsp.
- Parmesan – 3 oz. grated

Directions:

Add oil and onions in the Instant Pot and cook on Sauté for 3 to 4 minutes. Add salt, ground black pepper, minced garlic, and ground nutmeg. Stir well. When the onions start to become tender, add water and mix. Close the lid and cook on High for 12 minutes. Then do a quick release. Add broth and mix. Close the lid and cook on Sauté for 10 minutes more. Top with parmesan and serve.

Quinoa Tomato Soup

Cook time: 15 minutes |Serves: 3| Per serving: Calories 313; Carbs 53.3g; Fat 6.9g; Protein 12.2g

Ingredients:

- Carrot – 1, diced
- Onion – 1/2, diced
- Quinoa – 1 cup
- Tomato puree – 1 cup
- Fresh dill - 1 tbsp.
- Bell pepper – ½, chopped
- Water – 1 cup
- Salt – 1 tsp.
- Cayenne pepper – 1 tsp.
- Green peas – 1/3 cup
- Butter – 1 tsp.

Directions:

Add butter in the Instant Pot and heat on Sauté. Add onion, carrot, and bell pepper. Sauté for 10 minutes. Add green peas, quinoa, cayenne pepper, salt, fresh dill, and water. Add the tomato puree and mix. Close the lid and cook on High for 3 minutes. Do a quick release and serve.

Lentil Soup

Cook time: 15 minutes| Serves: 2| Per serving: Calories 349; Carbs 57.3g; Fat 11g; Protein 27.3g

Ingredients:

- Red lentils – 1 cup
- Potato – 1, chopped
- Onion – ½, chopped
- Water – 5 cups
- Salt – 1 tsp.
- Ground black pepper – 1 tsp.
- Coconut oil – 1 tbsp.
- Chili flakes - 1 tsp.
- Tomato paste – 1 tbsp.

Directions:

Melt coconut oil in the Instant Pot on Sauté. Add onion and potato and sauté for 7 minutes. Add salt, ground black pepper, chili flakes, and tomato paste. Mix and add the lentils. Add the water and mix again. Close the lid. Cook on High for 8 minutes. Do a natural release and serve.

Winter Stew

Cook time: 20 minutes |Serves: 6 | Per serving: Calories 177; Carbs 23.8g; Fat 5.7g; Protein 8.8g

Ingredients:

- Red lentils - ½ cup
- Mushrooms – 1 cup, chopped
- Yellow onion – 1, chopped
- Sweet potatoes – 2, chopped
- Carrot – 1, chopped
- Red kidney beans – ½ cup, canned
- Tomato paste – 1 tbsp.
- Water – 2 cups
- Almond milk – ½ cup
- Salt – 1 tsp.
- Peppercorns - ½ tsp.
- Olive oil - 1 tsp.

Directions:

Add oil in the Instant Pot and cook onions and mushroom on Sauté for 10 minutes. Then add red lentils, sweet potatoes, carrot, red kidney beans, tomato paste, almond milk, water, salt, and peppercorns. Mix and close the lid. Cook on High for 10 minutes. Do a natural release and serve.

Vegetable Stew

Cook time: 45 minutes| Serves: 2| Per serving: Calories 100; Carbs 22.4 g; Fat 1.2g; Protein 3g

Ingredients:

- Yellow onion – ½ chopped
- Celery stalk – 1 oz. chopped
- Carrot – ¼ cup, chopped
- Garlic – 1 clove, chopped
- Tomato sauce – 1 tbsp.
- Green peas – ¼ cup
- Tomato – 1, chopped
- Vegetable stock – 1 cup
- Salt – 1 tsp.
- Thyme – 1 tsp.
- Yukon potatoes – 2, chopped

Directions:

Add the potatoes, celery, yellow onion, carrot, garlic, tomato sauce, green peas, tomato, salt, thyme, and mix. Add the vegetable stock and close the lid. Press Sauté and cook for 45 minutes on High. Open mix and serve.

Egyptian Stew

Cook time: 12 minutes| Serves: 5| Per serving: Calories 451; Carbs 81.1g; Fat 4.4g; Protein 25.1g

Ingredients:

- Tomato paste – 1 tbsp.
- Olive oil – 1 tbsp.
- Red pepper - 1 tbsp.
- Paprika – 1 tsp.
- Potatoes – 4, peeled and chopped
- Lentils – 2 cups
- Water – 6 cups
- Salt – 1 tsp.
- Fresh dill – 1 cup, chopped
- Lemon juice – 3 tbsps.

Directions:

Place the tomato paste, paprika, potatoes, lentils, water, and salt in the Instant Pot. Close the lid and cook for 12 minutes on High. Do a quick release and open the lid. Add lemon juice and mix. Transfer the stew in the serving bowls. Mix together red pepper and olive oil. Pour mixture over the stew. Garnish with fresh dill and serve.

Peas and Carrot Stew
Cook time: 10 minutes |Serves: 5 | Per serving: Calories 125; Carbs 27.5g; Fat 0.3g; Protein 4.1g

Ingredients:

- Potatoes – 3, peeled and chopped
- Carrots – 2, chopped
- Green peas – 1 cup, frozen
- Water – 2 cups
- Tomato paste – 1 tbsp.
- Salt – 1 tsp.
- Cayenne pepper – 1 tsp.

Directions:

Place the potatoes, carrots, and green peas in the Instant Pot. Then in a bowl, combine tomato paste, water, salt, and cayenne pepper. Whisk the liquid and then pour it into the Instant Pot. Close the lid and cook on High for 10 minutes. Do a natural release and serve.

Mediterranean Stew
Cook time: 35 minutes| Serves: 4 | Per serving: Calories 83; Carbs 16.8g; Fat 1.4g; Protein 2.8g

Ingredients:

- White cabbage – ¼ cup, shredded
- Potato – 1, chopped
- Corn kernels – ½ cup
- Sweet pepper – 1, chopped
- Fresh parsley – ½ cup
- Tomatoes – 1 cup, chopped
- Green beans – ¼ cup, chopped
- Water – 1 ½ cup
- Salt – 1 tsp.
- Coconut cream – 1 tbsp.
- White pepper - 1 tsp.

Directions:

Place everything in the Instant Pot and mix. Close the lid and press Sauté. Cook for 35 minutes. Open the lid and mix. Close the lid and rest for 10 to 15 minutes. Serve.

Sweet Potato Stew II

Cook time: 35 minutes |Serves: 2 | Per serving: Calories 165; Carbs 24.7g; Fat 7.4g; Protein 2.6g

Ingredients:

- Tomatoes – ¼ cup, diced
- Wheat flour – 1 tbsp.
- Tomato juice – 1 cup
- Onion – ½, chopped
- Olive oil – 1 tbsp.
- Chives – 1 tbsp. chopped
- Salt – 1 tsp.
- Curry powder – 1 tsp.
- Sweet potatoes – 3, chopped
- Water – ½ cup
- Brown sugar – 1 tsp.

Directions:

Pour olive oil in the Instant Pot. Add onion and sweet potatoes. Add salt, curry powder, and cook on Sauté for 10 minutes. In a bowl, whisk together wheat flour and water until smooth. Pour the liquid in the Instant Pot. Add tomato juice and sugar. Close the lid and cook on Sauté for 35 minutes. Mix the stew every 10 minutes. Serve.

Rainbow Stew

Cook time: 30 minutes| Serves:4 | Per serving: Calories 135; Carbs 22g; Fat 4.3g; Protein 5.6g

Ingredients:

- Eggplant – 1, sliced
- Zucchini – 1, sliced
- Tomatoes – 2, sliced
- Corn kernels – ½ cup
- Red beans – ¼ cup, canned
- Water – 1 cup
- Coconut oil - 1 tbsp.
- Salt – 1 tsp.
- Paprika – 1 tsp.
- Cayenne pepper – 1 tsp.

Directions:

In a bowl, combine eggplant, zucchini, corn kernels, salt, paprika, and cayenne pepper. Mix. Transfer the vegetables in the Instant Pot. Add water, oil, and red beans. Close the lid and cook on Sauté for 30 minutes. Open and stir. Serve.

Turkish Green Beans

Cook time: 15 minutes| Serves: 4| Per serving: Calories 61; Carbs 6.9g; Fat 3.7g; Protein 1.5g

Ingredients:

- Green beans – 1 ½ cup, chopped
- Onion – ½, diced
- Tomatoes – 2, chopped
- Tomato paste – 1 tsp.
- Chili flakes – 1 tsp.
- Salt – 1 tsp.
- Water – 1 cup
- Olive oil – 1 tbsp.

Directions:

Add oil, onion, and green beans in the Instant Pot. Stir-fry on Sauté for 5 minutes. Add salt, chili flakes, tomato paste, and water. Close the lid and cook on High for 8 minutes. Do a natural release and open. Mix and serve.

Lentil Gumbo

Cook time: 23 minutes| Serves: 4| Per serving: Calories 129; Carbs 20.7g; Fat 2.2g; Protein 7.7g

Ingredients:

- Garlic – ½ tbsp. diced
- Coconut oil – ½ tbsp.
- Bell pepper – 1, chopped
- Celery – 1 stalk, chopped
- Thyme – ½ tsp.
- Coriander – 1½ tsps.
- Cajun spices – 1 tsp.
- White pepper – ½ tsp.
- Lentils - ½ cup
- Water – 1 ½ cup
- Okra – ½ cup, chopped
- Tomatoes – ½ cup, diced, canned
- Lemon juice – 1 tsp.
- Cauliflower – 4 oz. chopped
- Salt – 1 tsp.

Directions:

Preheat the Instant Pot on Sauté and add oil. Add bell pepper, garlic, celery stalk, thyme, coriander, and Cajun spices. Mix and cook for 10 minutes. Then add everything except the salt. Close the lid and cook on High for 13 minutes. Do a quick release. Open and add salt. Serve.

Chapter 8 Poultry Recipes

Kung Pao Chicken

Cook time: 17 minutes | Serves: 5| Per serving: Calories 380; Carbs 7g; Fat 25g; Protein 30.6g

Ingredients:

- Coconut oil – 2 tbsps.
- Boneless, skinless chicken breasts – 1 pound, cubed
- Hot sauce – 6 tbsps.
- Cashews – ½ cup, chopped
- Ginger – ½ tsp. finely grated
- Chili powder – ½ tsp.
- Kosher salt – ½ tsp.
- Freshly ground black pepper – ½ tsp.

Directions:

Press Sauté add oil and heat it. Add chicken, salt, pepper, chili powder, ginger, cashews, and hot sauce. Close the lid and Press Manual. Cook on High for 17 minutes.

Whole Roast Chicken

Cook time: 25 minutes| Serves: 6| Per serving: Calories 215; Carbs 1g; Fat 13.4g; Protein 21.6g

Ingredients:

- Butter – 4 tbsps.
- Dried basil – 1 tsp.
- Dried cilantro – 1 tsp.
- Salt – ½ tsp.
- Black pepper – ½ tsp.
- Bone broth – ½ cup
- Whole chicken – 1

Directions:

In a bowl, mix the butter, salt, pepper, basil, and cilantro. Add bone broth into the IP. Baste the chicken with the butter mixture and place into the IP (keep the breast facing the bottom of the pot). Cover and cook 25 minutes on Meat settings. Do a natural pressure release. Remove chicken, carve and enjoy.

Chicken Cacciatore

Cook time: 18 minutes| Serves: 4 | Per serving: Calories 344; Carbs 5g; Fat 24.3g; Protein 26.5g

Ingredients:

- Coconut oil – 6 tbsps.

- Chicken legs – 5
- Bell pepper – 1, diced
- Dried basil – ½ tsp.
- Onion – ½, chopped
- Dried parsley – ½ tsp.
- Salt – ½ tsp.
- Freshly ground black pepper – ½ tsp.
- Diced tomatoes – 1 (14-ounce) can

Directions:

Press Sauté and melt the oil. Add the chicken and sauté until browned. Remove chicken and set aside. Add tomatoes, black pepper, salt, parsley, onion, basil, and pepper and sauté. Add ½-cup water and add the chicken on top. Close the lid and hit Cancel. Press Manual and cook on High for 18 minutes. Do a natural release and serve.

Spicy Mexican Chicken
Cook time: 17 minutes| Serves: 4| Per serving: Calories 269; Carbs 4.2g; Fat 14.7g; Protein 30g

Ingredients:

- Avocado oil – 2 tbsps.
- Chicken – 1 pound, ground
- Finely chopped jalapeno – ½
- Coriander – ½ tsp.
- Crushed red pepper – ½ tsp.
- Curry powder – ½ tsp.
- Chili powder – ½ tsp.
- Salt – ½ tsp.
- Freshly ground black pepper – ½ tsp.
- Poblano chili pepper – ¼ finely chopped
- Tomatoes – 1 (14 ounces) can

Directions:

Press Sauté and heat the oil. Add ½-cup water, then add tomatoes, chili pepper, black pepper, salt, chili powder, curry powder, red pepper, coriander, jalapeno, and chicken. Close the lid and hit Cancel. Press Manual and cook 17 minutes on High. Do a natural release. Open and serve.

Chicken Casserole
Cook time: 20 minutes| Serves: 4|Per serving: Calories 538; Carbs 4.9g; Fat 30.8g; Protein 57.9g

Ingredients:

- Pepperoni – 16 slices, uncured
- Mozzarella cheese – 1 cup, shredded

- Full-fat cheddar cheese – 1 cup, shredded
- Chicken – 1 pound, ground
- Egg – 1
- Garlic – 1 tsp. minced
- Full-fat Parmesan cheese – ½ cup, grated
- Dried parsley – ½ tsp.
- Thyme – ½ tsp.
- Dried basil – ½ tsp.
- Black pepper - ½ tsp.
- Crushed red pepper – ½ tsp.
- Dried oregano – ½ tsp.
- Fire roasted tomatoes – 1 (14 ounces) can

Directions:

Add 1-cup water into the Instant Pot. Insert the trivet. In a bowl, combine tomatoes, oregano, red pepper, black pepper, basil, thyme, parsley, Parmesan, garlic, egg, chicken, cheddar, mozzarella, and pepperoni slices. Mix well and transfer mixture into a greased dish. Place the dish on top of the trivet. Use an aluminum foil to cover loosely. Close the lid and press Manual. Cook 20 minutes on High. Do a natural release and open. Serve.

Turkey Burger with Fries
Cook time: 10 minutes| Serves: 4| Per serving: Calories 429; Carbs 8.1g; Fat 31.5g; Protein 29.4g

Ingredients:

- Coconut oil - 2 tbsps.
- Bacon – 6 slices
- Thinly sliced avocado – 1
- Turkey – ½ pound, ground
- Freshly ground black pepper – ½ tsp.
- Parsley – ½ tsp. dried
- Turmeric – ½ tsp. ground
- Dried basil – ½ tsp.
- Salt – ½ tsp.
- Broccoli – 2 cups, chopped
- Water – ¼ cup

Directions:

Spread an aluminum foil. On top of the foil wrap the bacon around the avocado slices. Fold the foil to make a packet. In a bowl, mix turkey, salt, basil, turmeric, parsley, and black pepper. Combine and make a large and thin patty. Press Sauté and add oil in your IP. Add ¼-cup water into the Instant Pot. Place in the patty and broccoli. Insert the trivet and place the aluminum foil packet on top. Close and press Manual. Cook for 10 minutes on High. Do a natural release. Open and remove the food. Cut the patty in 4 parts. Serve with avocado fries.

Spicy Turkey Meatballs
Cook time: 25 minutes| Serves: 5 |Per serving: Calories 205; Carbs 0.7g; Fat 10.1g; Protein 26.7 g

Ingredients:

- Ground turkey – 1 pound
- Hot sauce – ¼ cup
- Coconut oil – 2 tbsps.
- Grated ginger – 1 tsp.
- Chili powder – ½ tsp.
- Basil – ½ tsp. dried
- Salt – ½ tsp.
- Ground black pepper – ½ tsp.

Directions:

Make 1 ½ inch meatballs with the ground turkey and place in a dish. In a bowl, stir together salt, pepper, basil, chili powder, ginger, oil, and hot sauce. Mix and sprinkle evenly over the meatballs. Add 1 cup water into the Instant Pot and insert the trivet. Gently place the meatball dish on top of the trivet. Close and press Manual. Cook 25 minutes on high. Do a natural pressure release. Open and serve.

Cheesy Chicken with Jalapenos
Cook time: 12 minutes| Serves: 4| Per serving: Calories 310; Carbs 4g; Fat 26g; Protein 20g

Ingredients:

- Chicken breasts – 1 pound
- Cheddar cheese – 8 ounces, grated
- Sour cream – ¾ cup
- Jalapenos – 3, seeded and sliced
- Water – ½ cup
- Cream cheese – 8 ounces
- Salt and pepper to taste

Directions:

In the IP, whisk together the water, sour cream, and cheeses. Stir in the jalapenos and place the chicken inside. Season with salt and pepper. Close the lid and cook on Manual for 12 minutes. Do a quick release. Serve.

Salsa Verde Chicken
Cook time: 25 minutes| Serves: 6| Per serving: Calories 340; Carbs 5g; Fat 6.8g; Protein 55g

Ingredients:

- Salsa Verde – 16 ounces
- Chicken breasts – 2 ½ pounds
- Cumin – 1 tsp.
- Garlic powder – ¼ tsp.
- Salt – 1 tsp.
- Pepper – ¼ tsp.
- Pinch of paprika

Directions:

Whisk together the salsa and spices in the Instant Pot. Add the chicken. Close the lid and press the Manual. Cook for 25 minutes on High. Do a quick pressure release. Serve.

Creamy Bacon Chicken
Cook time: 30 minutes| Serves: 4| Per serving: Calories 620; Carbs 6g; Fat 38g; Protein 48g

Ingredients:

- Cream cheese – 8 ounces
- Bacon slices – 8, cooked and crumbled
- Chicken breasts – 2 pounds
- Ranch seasoning – 1 packet
- Cheddar cheese – 4 ounces, shredded
- Arrowroot – 2 tbsps.
- Water – 1 cup

Directions:

Whisk together the water, cream cheese and seasoning in the Instant Pot. Add the chicken breast. Close the lid and cook on High for 25 minutes. Press Cancel and do a quick pressure release. Transfer the chicken to a cutting board and shred with forks. Press sauté and stir in the arrowroot. Add bacon, shredded chicken, and cheddar. Cook until thickened, about 3 to 4 minutes. Serve.

Italian Duck with Spinach
Cook time: 15 minutes| Serves: 3| Per serving: Calories 455; Carbs 1g; Fat 26g; Protein 57g

Ingredients:

- Duck breasts – 1 pound, halved
- Spinach – ½ cup, chopped
- Chopped Sun-Dried Tomatoes – ¼ cup
- Chicken stock – ½ cup
- Grated Parmesan Cheese – ¼ cup
- Italian seasoning – 1 tsp.
- Heavy cream – 1/3 cup
- Minced garlic – 1 tsp.

- Salt and pepper to taste
- Olive oil – 2 tbsps.

Directions:

Whisk together the seasoning, garlic, oil, and salt and pepper. Rub this mixture into the meat. Place the duck in the IP and cook on Sauté until golden on all sides. Add the stock, close the lid and cook on Manual for 4 minutes. Press Cancel and do a quick release. Stir in the remaining ingredients and cover. Cook on High for 5 minutes more. Release the pressure quickly and serve.

Creamy Mushroom Turkey
Cook time: 30 minutes| Serves: 10 | Per serving: Calories 192; Carbs 4.5g; Fat 15g; Protein 25g

Ingredients:

- Turkey breast – 1 ¼ pounds
- White wine – 1/3 cup
- White button mushrooms – 6 ounces, sliced
- Arrowroot – 1 tbsp.
- Garlic – 1 clove, minced
- Minced shallots – 3 tbsps.
- Olive oil – 2 tbsps.
- Parsley – ½ tsp.
- Chicken stock – 2/3 cup
- Heavy cream – 3 tbsps.

Directions:

Tie the turkey every 2 inches, crosswise. Press Sauté and heat the oil in it. Add the turkey and brown on all sides. Set aside. Add the garlic, mushrooms, shallots, and parsley. Cook for a few minutes. Add the broth and return the turkey to the pot. Cook on High for 15 minutes. Do a quick pressure release. Transfer the turkey to a plate. Untie and slice it. Whisk the cream and arrowroot in the Instant Pot and cook until thickened. Drizzle the sauce over the turkey. Serve.

Soft and Juicy Chicken
Cook time: 30 minutes| Serves: 10| Per serving: Calories 270; Carbs 3g; Fat 20g; Protein 22g

Ingredients:

- Chicken – 1 (4-pound)
- Coconut oil – 1 tbsp.
- Lemon juice – 2 tbsps.
- Garlic – 2 cloves, peeled
- Paprika – 1 tsp.
- Chicken stock – 1 ½ cups
- Salt – ½ tsp.

- Pepper – ¼ tsp.
- Onion powder – 1 tsp.

Directions:

In a bowl, combine all the spices. Rub the mixture into the chicken. Add the coconut oil in the IP and melt on Sauté. Add the chicken and cook until browned on all sides. Pour the stock and lemon juice over. Add the garlic cloves. Close and cook on Manual for 25 minutes. Serve.

Herby Juicy Chicken Fillets
Cook time: 13 minutes| Serves: 4| Per serving: Calories 357; Carbs 1g; Fat 18.4g; Protein 43.2g

Ingredients:

- Olive oil – 2 tbsps.
- Chicken fillets – 4
- Red wine – ¼ cup
- Chicken broth – ¾ cup
- Ground black pepper and salt to taste
- Dried marjoram – ½ tsp.
- Dried sage – 1 tsp.
- Dried parsley flakes – ½ tsp.
- Dried basil – ½ tsp.

Directions:

Press Sauté and add oil to the Instant Pot. Sear chicken for about 8 minutes. Turning once or twice. Add the red wine and deglaze the pot. Add the rest of the ingredients. Cover and cook on Poultry for 5 minutes on High. Do a natural release and serve.

Chicken Bowl with Pine Nuts
Cook time:20 minutes| Serves: 4|Per serving: Calories 328; Carbs 11.1g; Fat 20.6g; Protein 24.7g

Ingredients:

- Chicken legs – 1 pound, skinless and cut into pieces
- Olive oil – 1 tbsp.
- Red wine vinegar – 2 tbsps.
- Watercress – 1-ounce, tough stalks removed and chopped
- Bell pepper – 1, chopped
- Sweet onion – 1, sliced
- Garlic – 2 cloves, minced
- Cucumber – 1, sliced
- Gem lettuce – 2 cups, leaves separated
- Ground black pepper and salt to taste
- Spanish paprika – 1 tsp.

- Marjoram – ½ tsp.
- Oregano – ½ tsp.
- Pine nuts – 4 tbsps.
- Water – 1 cup, for the pot

Directions:

Add 1 cup water and a metal rack to the Instant Pot. Lower the chicken legs onto the metal rack. Cover and cook on Steam mode for 15 minutes on High. Do a quick release and open. Slice the chicken into bite-sized pieces and discard the bones. Place the meat into a bowl. Clean the Instant Pot and add 1 tbsp. oil. Heat on Sauté. Add sweet onion and garlic and sauté for 5 minutes. Add the remaining ingredients except for the pine nuts and lettuce and mix. Add the mixture to the bowl and toss to combine. Garnish with pine nuts and serve with lettuce leaves.

Chicken with Mustard Greens and Olives
Cook time:15 minutes| Serves: 4|Per serving: Calories 336.5; Carbs 4.2g; Fat 23.5g; Protein 26.9g

Ingredients:

- Boneless chicken thighs – 4
- Mustard greens – 1 bunch, rinsed and chopped
- Green olives – ½ cup, pitted
- Cherry tomatoes – ½ cup, washed
- Minced garlic – 1 ½ tsps.
- Salt – ¾ tsp.
- Ground black pepper – ½ tsp.
- Honey – 1 tsp.
- Dijon mustard – 1 tsp.
- Olive oil – 4 tbsps.
- Lemon – 1, juiced
- White wine – 1 cup

Directions:

Add the oil to the Instant Pot. Season chicken with salt, black pepper. Place the chicken in the Instant Pot along with mustard greens, garlic, olives, tomatoes, mustard, and honey. Add the lemon juice and wine and close the lid. Cook on High for 15 minutes. Do a quick release and open. Serve.

Greek Chicken and Rice
Cook time: 4 minutes |Serves: 4| Per serving: Calories 314.3; Carbs 31.4g; Fat 9g; Protein 26.7g

Ingredients:

- Rice – 1 cup
- Chicken breasts – 3, diced

- Red bell pepper – 1, chopped
- Yellow bell pepper – 1, chopped
- Zucchini – 1, sliced
- Red onion – 1, chopped
- Minced garlic – 2 tsps.
- Salt – ½ tsp.
- Ground black pepper – ½ tsp.
- Oregano – 1 tbsp.
- Lemon juice – 3 tbsps.
- Olive oil – 2 tbsps.
- Chicken broth – 1 ½ cups
- Parsley – ¼ cup, chopped
- Feta cheese – ¼ cup, crumbled

Directions:

Add everything in the Instant Pot except for zucchini, peppers, cheese, and parsley. Mix and cover the pot. Cook for 4 minutes on High. Do a natural release and open. Stir in chicken and remaining ingredients. Close and let rest for 10 minutes. Top with cheese and serve.

Maple Mustard Turkey Thighs
Cook time: 30 minutes| Serves: 4| Per serving: Calories 633; Carbs 4.1g; Fat 34g; Protein 44g

Ingredients:

- Turkey thighs – 2 (3 lb.) bone-in, skin on
- Olive oil – ½ cup
- Fresh rosemary – 1 tsp. chopped
- Fresh thyme – 1 tsp. chopped
- Smoked paprika – 1 tbsp.
- Dijon mustard – 2 tbsps.
- Maple syrup – ½ cup
- Onion – 1, chopped
- Celery – 5 stalks, chopped
- Carrots – 5, chopped
- Rosemary – 4 sprigs
- Thyme – 2 sprigs
- Salt – 1 tsp.
- Pepper – ½ tsp.
- Water – 1 cup

Directions:

Add the oil, thyme, rosemary, maple syrup, smoked paprika, and Dijon mustard to the Instant Pot. Cook the mixture on Sauté and stir occasionally. Add the salt, pepper, and half the maple syrup mixture to the turkey thighs. Mix. Add the water, celery, onion, rosemary, thyme, and carrots to the Instant Pot. Place the trivet in the pot. Then place turkey thighs over the trivet. Pour the remaining maple syrup mixture over the thighs. Cover. Cook on High for 30 minutes. Then do a natural release. Remove the lid, then take out the turkey thighs. Cut them into slices, pour maple mustard mixture over the sliced thighs and serve.

Turkey Cheese Gnocchi

Cook time: 25 minutes|Serves:6| Per serving: Calories 533; Carbs 32.6g; Fat 19.9g; Protein 99.2g

Ingredients:

- Turkey boneless pieces – 1 pound
- Fresh spinach – 2 cups, chopped
- Mozzarella cheese – 2 cups, shredded
- Parmesan cheese – ½ cup, shredded
- Olive oil – 2 tbsps.
- Black pepper – ½ tsp.
- Shallots – ¼ cup, chopped
- Garlic minced – 2 cloves
- Sun-dried tomatoes – ¼ cup, chopped
- Cream – 1 cup
- Chicken broth – 2 cups
- Gnocchi – 2 lbs.
- Salt – ½ tsp.

Directions:

Press Sauté and then add the oil. Add the turkey with salt and pepper. Cook 3 minutes on each side. Add the garlic, tomatoes, and shallots to the pot. Cook and stir for 2 minutes. Add the cream and chicken broth to the pot. Cover the pot. Cook on High for 10 minutes, then do a natural release. Add gnocchi to the mixture and press Sauté. Cook for 5 minutes, or until gnocchi is tender. Add cheese and serve.

Orange Spice Chicken

Cook time:15 minutes| Serves:6|Per serving: Calories 618; Carbs 23.7g; Fat 19.6g; Protein 128.2g

Ingredients:

- Chicken breast – 2 lb. chopped
- Olive oil – 2 tbsps.
- Garlic – 2 heads, minced
- Granulated sugar – ¼ cup
- Brown sugar – ¼ cup

- Soy sauce – ¼ cup
- Tomato sauce – 1 cup
- Orange juice – 1 cup
- Corn starch – 4 tbsps.
- Green onions – 4, chopped
- Orange zest – 2 tbsps.
- Salt and pepper to taste

Directions:

Add oil and press Sauté. Add the chicken and cook for 3 minutes. Then add the rest of the ingredients to the pot, except for the corn starch, orange juice, green onions, and orange zest. Mix and cover. Cook for 7 minutes on Poultry on High. Do a natural release and open. Mix corn-starch with orange juice in a bowl and add to the pot. Press Sauté and cook the chicken in the sauce for 5 minutes. Stir constantly until it thickens. Garnish with chopped green onions and orange zest and serve.

Chicken with Smoked Paprika

Cook time:20 minutes|Serves:6 |Per serving: Calories 524; Carbs 29.3g; Fat 10.3g; Protein 68.5g

Ingredients:

- Chicken breasts – 1 ½ lb. cut into small pieces
- Smoked paprika – 2 tsps.
- Olive oil – 1 tsp.
- Bacon – 3 strips, chopped
- Onion – 1, chopped
- Garlic – 2 cloves, minced
- Red bell pepper – 1, chopped
- Salt – ½ tsp.
- Beer – 1 (12 oz.) can
- White rice – 1 cup
- Bacon – 2 strips, cooked (topping)

Directions:

Put the oil and bacon in the pot. Sauté for 3 minutes. Add the bell pepper and stir-fry for 3 minutes more. Add chopped onion and cook for 2 minutes. Add garlic and cook for 1 minute. Add all the seasoning to the pot and add the beer. Mix. Add the chicken and rice and cover the pot. Cook on High for 10 minutes. Do a quick release and open. Serve dish topped with bacon.

Green Chili Adobo Chicken

Cook time: 25 minutes| Serves: 6 | Per serving: Calories 204; Carbs 7.6g; Fat 4.2g; Protein 32.9g

Ingredients:

- Boneless, skinless chicken breasts – 6
- Adobo all-purpose seasoning with pepper – 1 tbsp.
- Diced tomatoes – 2 cups
- Water – ½ cup
- Turmeric – 1 tbsp.
- Diced green chilies – 1 cup

Directions:

Place the chicken breasts in the Instant Pot. Add seasoning pepper to the chicken and sprinkle on both sides. Add diced tomatoes to the chicken. Pour half cup of water over the chicken. Cover and cook on High for 25 minutes. Do a natural release and open. Shred the chicken and serve.

Turkey Noodle Soup

Cook time: 40 minutes| Serves: 4| Per serving: Calories 358; Carbs 9.4g; Fat 11.6g; Protein 56.7g

Ingredients:

For the broth

- Shredded turkey – 1 cup
- Turkey carcass – 1, left over from a carved turkey
- Water – 14 cups
- Onion – 1, chopped
- Carrots -3, chopped
- Celery – 2 stalks, chopped
- Salt and pepper to taste

Soup

- Cooked turkey meat – 3 cups, chopped
- Cooked egg noodles – 8 oz.
- Scallions – 4, chopped
- Salt and pepper to taste

Directions:

Put the water, onion, celery, carrots, salt, pepper, and turkey pieces into the Instant Pot. Cover and cook on Soup function, on High for 35 minutes. Do a natural release and open. Strain the broth and put the broth back into the pot. Add the shredded turkey, carrots, and celery. Press Sauté and boil the soup. Add the cooked noodles and cook for 1 minute more. Serve with scallions for garnishing.

Chicken Curry

Cook time: 20 minutes| Serves: 2 | Per serving: Calories 178; Carbs 8g; Fat 3.6g; Protein 26g

Ingredients:

- Chicken breast – 7 oz. chopped into bite-sized pieces
- Cherry tomatoes – 1 cup, chopped
- Cauliflower – 1 cup
- Liquid aminos – ¼ cup
- Garlic – 2 cloves, crushed
- Chicken stock – 3 cups

Spices

- Chili powder – 2 tbsps.
- Coriander powder – 2 tsps.
- Turmeric powder – 3 tsps.
- Onion powder – 2 tsps.
- Garlic powder – ½ tsp.

Directions:

Combine all ingredients in the Instant Pot. Cover and cook 20 minutes on High. Once cooked, open the lid, chill and serve.

Duck Breast with Prosciutto
Cook time: 27 minutes| Serves:4 |Per serving: Calories 496; Carbs 3.5g; Fat 34.3g; Protein 40.9g

Ingredients:

- Duck breasts – 1 lb.
- Shallot – 1, finely chopped
- Garlic cloves – 2, crushed
- Duck fat – ½ cup
- Chicken broth – 4 cups
- Prosciutto – 7 oz. chopped
- Fresh parsley – 2 tbsps. finely chopped
- Apple cider vinegar – 3 tbsps.
- Cremini mushrooms – 1 cup
- Orange zest – 1 tbsp.
- Sea salt – 1 tsp.
- White pepper – ½ tsp. freshly ground

Directions:

Press Sauté and add duck fat. Stir constantly and slowly melt the fat. Add the garlic and shallots. Cook and stir for 2 to 3 minutes. Add the mushrooms and continue to cook until the liquid has evaporated. Add the prosciutto and stir well. Briefly brown on all sides and press Cancel. Add the meat in the pot and pour in the broth. Sprinkle with orange zest and spices. Pour in the cider and seal the lid. Press Manual and cook 20 minutes on High pressure. Once cooked release pressure naturally and open the lid. Sprinkle with parsley and cover for 10 minutes before serving.

Turkey with Broccoli
Cook time: 35 minutes |Serves:3 |Per serving: Calories 327; Carbs 1.3g; Fat 24.5g; Protein 29.8g

Ingredients:

- Ground turkey – 10 oz.
- Broccoli – 1 cup, chopped
- Olive oil – 2 tbsps.
- Spring onion – 1, finely chopped
- Chicken stock – ¼ cup
- Shredded mozzarella – 1 cup
- Sour cream – 3 tbsps.
- Parmesan cheese – ¼ cup, grated
- Salt – ½ tsp.
- White pepper – ¼ tsp. freshly ground
- Dried thyme – ½ tsp.
- Dried oregano – ¼ tsp.

Directions:

Press the Sauté button and add olive oil. Now add the spring onions in the hot oil. Cook and stir for 1 minute. Add broccoli and turkey. Pour in the stock and cook for 12 to 15 minutes. Stirring occasionally. Season with thyme, oregano, salt and pepper and stir in the cheese. Press Cancel and remove from the pot. Transfer the mixture to a baking dish and set aside. Preheat the oven to 350F and bake for 15 to 20 minutes. Remove from the oven and chill for a while. Top with sour cream and serve.

Salsa Verde Turkey Breast
Cook time: 30 minutes| Serves: 4| Per serving: Calories 342; Carbs 5.5g; Fat 17.7g; Protein 37.8g

Ingredients:

- Medium sized turkey breast – 2, cut in half
- Onion – 1, sliced
- Chicken broth – 3 cups

For the salsa Verde

- Tomatillos – 1 cup, chopped
- Fresh parsley – ¼ cup, finely chopped
- Green chili – 1, finely chopped
- Onion powder – 1 tsp.
- Garlic cloves – 2, crushed
- Olive oil – 3 tbsps.
- Salt – 1 tsp.
- Chili powder – ¼ tsp.

For the rub

- Chili powder – 1 tsp.
- Garlic powder – 2 tsps.
- Onion powder – 1 tsp.
- Salt – 1 tsp.
- Cumin powder – ½ tsp.

Directions:

Combine garlic powder, chili powder, onion powder, salt and cumin in a bowl. Mix well and set aside. Rub the meat with the spices. Place at the bottom of the IP and pour in the chicken broth. Add onions and seal the lid. Press Poultry and cook on High for 15 minutes. When cooked, remove the meat from the pot and set aside. Remove broth and press Sauté. Grease the inner pot with olive oil and heat up. Add garlic and green chili. Cook for 2 to 3 minutes and then add the tomatillos along with the remaining ingredients for the salsa. Pour in about 3 tbsps. of the broth and simmer for 10 to 12 minutes. Stirring occasionally. Press Cancel and remove the mixture from the pot. Transfer to a food processor and process until smooth. Drizzle over the meat and serve.

Thai Basil Goose Cubes

Cook time: 15 minutes |Serves: 4| Per serving: Calories 192; Carbs 1g ; Fat 9g ; Protein 27g

Ingredients:

- Chopped basil leaves – ¼ cup
- Cubed goose breasts – 2 cups
- Fish sauce – 2 tbsps.
- Minced chilies – 2 tbsps.
- Minced garlic – 2 tsps.
- Minced ginger – 1 tsp.
- Avocado oil – 2 tbsps.
- Granulated sweetener – 1 tsp.
- Water – 1 ½ cups
- Salt and pepper to taste

Directions:

Heat half of the oil in the IP on Sauté. Add goose and cook until golden. Transfer to a baking dish. Whisk together the remaining oil, fish sauce, chilies, ginger, garlic, and sweetener. Pour over the goose. Add the basil and season with salt and pepper. Pour the water into the IP and lower the rack. Place the baking dish inside the IP and close the lid. Cook on Manual for 10 minutes. Do a quick pressure release. Serve.

Italian Chicken Thighs

Cook time: 17 minutes |Serves: 6| Per serving: Calories 245; Carbs 7g; Fat 25g; Protein 35g

Ingredients:

- Chicken thighs – 6
- Cherry tomatoes – 2 cups
- Basil – ½ cup
- Garlic – 3 cloves, minced
- Onion – 1, chopped
- Cremini mushrooms – ½ pound, sliced
- Olives – ½ cup
- Tomato paste – 1 tbsp.
- Olive oil – 1 tbsp.
- Parsley – ¼ cup
- Chicken broth – 1 cup

Directions:

Heat the olive oil in your IP on Sauté. Sear the chicken until golden. Set aside. Add onions and mushrooms and cook for a few minutes. Add garlic and cook for 30 seconds. Stir in the remaining ingredients including the chicken and close the lid. Cook on High for 10 minutes. Do a quick pressure release. Serve.

Turkey and Cauliflower Casserole

Cook time: 15 minutes| Serves: 6| Per serving: Calories 311; Carbs 4g; Fat 18g; Protein 33g

Ingredients:

- Cauliflower florets – 20 ounces, chopped
- Shredded Cheddar Cheese – 1 cup
- Cooked and shredded turkey – 2 cups
- Cream cheese – 4 ounces
- Sour cream – ¼ cup
- Salsa Verde – ½ cup
- Salt and pepper to taste
- Water – 1 ½ cups

Directions:

Pour the water into the IP and lower the rack. Combine all the ingredients in a greased baking dish. Place the dish in the IP and close the lid. Cook on High for 15 minutes. Do a quick pressure release. Serve.

Glazed Duck Breast

Cook time: 25 minutes |Serves: 2| Per serving: Calories 398; Carbs 4.7g; Fat 15g; Protein 55.7g

Ingredients:

- Duck breast – 1 lb. chopped into bite-sized pieces, thaw if frozen
- Olive oil – 1 tbsp.
- Chicken broth – 3 cups
- Dijon mustard – 1 tbsp.
- Erythritol – 1 tsp. powdered
- Apple cider vinegar – ¼ cup

- Salt – 1 tsp.
- Pepper – ½ tsp.
- Garlic powder – 1 tsp.

Directions:

Rub the meat with garlic powder and place in the IP along with chicken broth. Seal the lid and press the Meat button. Once cooked, do a quick release and open the lid. Remove the meat from the pot along with the broth. Press the Sauté button and grease the insert with oil. Add erythritol, Dijon, and apple cider. Sprinkle with salt and pepper and cook for 3 to 4 minutes. Add the meat and coat well. Serve.

Roast Goose
Cook time: 30 minutes| Serves: 5| Per serving: Calories 441; Carbs 2.4g; Fat 22.9g; Protein 53.2g

Ingredients:

- Goose fillets – 2 lbs. sliced into one-inch thick slices
- Onions – 1 cup, finely chopped
- Butter – 4 tbsps.
- Garlic cloves – 2, crushed
- Chicken stock – 2 cups
- Bay leaves – 2
- Dried thyme – 1 tsp.
- Sea salt – 1 tsp.
- White pepper – ¼ tsp.
- Water for the pot

Directions:

Rinse the meat and pat dry and season with salt and white pepper. Place at the bottom of the IP and dried thyme and bay leaves. Pour in two cups of water and seal the lid. Press the Meat button. Do a quick release and open the lid. Remove the meat from the pot along with the liquid. Add the butter and press the Sauté button. Allow it to melt and add onions and garlic. Stir-fry for 3 to 4 minutes. One at a time, add the fillets and brown on both sides for 2 minutes. Remove from the pot and serve.

Chicken and Corn Soup
Cook time: 15 minutes| Serves: 4| Per serving: Calories 273; Carbs 6g; Fat 14g; Protein 18g

Ingredients:

- Oil – 2 tbsps.
- Yellow onion – ¼ cup, chopped
- Garlic – 1 tsp. minced
- Red bell pepper – ½ cup, chopped
- Chicken stock – 30 ounces, low sodium
- Chicken breasts – 1 ½ pounds, skinless, boneless and cubed
- Canned corn – 20 ounces, drained
- Tomatoes – 1 cup, chopped

- Chili powder – 1 tbsp.
- Coconut cream - 1 cup

Directions:

Heat the oil on Sauté. Add meat, onion, bell pepper and garlic. Cook for 3 minutes. Add the rest of the ingredients except the cream. Mix and cover. Cook on High for 10 minutes. Open and press Sauté. Add cream, stir and cook for 2 minutes. Serve.

Zucchini and Chicken Soup
Cook time: 15minutes| Serves: 4 | Per serving: Calories 192; Carbs 9g; Fat 8g; Protein 12g

Ingredients:

- Zucchinis – 2, cubed
- Green onions – ½ cup, chopped
- Celery – ½ cup, chopped
- Canned chicken stock – 29 ounces
- Garlic – 1 clove, minced
- Tomatoes – 2 cups, cubed
- Chicken breasts – 2, skinless, boneless and cubed
- Parsley – 1 tbsp. chopped
- Oil – ½ tbsp.

Directions:

Press Sauté and add oil, green onions, garlic, celery, and tomatoes. Cook for 3 minutes. Add the rest of the ingredients except the parsley. Cover and cook on High for 12 minutes. Open and serve, topped with parsley.

Chicken and Pea Soup
Cook time: 20 minutes |Serves: 4| Per serving: Calories 192; Carbs 7g; Fat 5g; Protein 16g

Ingredients:

- Olive oil – 2 tbsps.
- Chicken breasts – 1 pound, skinless, boneless, and cubed
- Yellow onion – 1, chopped
- Carrots – ½ cup, chopped
- Garlic – 2 cloves, chopped
- Chicken stock – 28 ounces
- Salt and pepper to taste
- Fresh peas – 1 pounds
- Coconut cream – ½ cup
- Dill – 1 tbsp. chopped

Directions:

Heat oil on Sauté. Add chicken, onion, and garlic and brown for 4 minutes. add the rest of the ingredients except the cream and dill. Cover and cook on High for 12 minutes. Open and press Sauté. Add the cream and dill. Cook for 4 minutes and serve.

Chicken and Eggplant Soup
Cook time: 15 minutes |Serves: 4| Per serving: Calories 200; Carbs 6g; Fat 4g; Protein 12g

Ingredients:

- Yellow onion – 1, chopped
- Olive oil – 1 tbsp.
- Celery rib – 1, chopped
- Eggplant – 1, cubed
- Salt and pepper to taste
- Chicken stock – 6 cups
- Chicken breasts – 2, skinless, boneless and cubes
- Parsley – 1 tbsp. chopped

Directions:

Press Sauté and heat the oil. Add onion and celery and cook for 3 minutes. Add the rest of the ingredients except the parsley and cover. Cook on High for 12 minutes. Open and add the parsley. Serve.

Chicken and Rice Soup
Cook time: 15 minutes| Serves: 4| Per serving: Calories 200; Carbs 6g; Fat 8g; Protein 12g

Ingredients:

- Yellow onion – 1, chopped
- Olive oil – 2 tbsps.
- Carrots – 1 cup, chopped
- Chicken stock – 28 ounces
- Chicken breasts – 2, skinless, boneless and cubed
- Wild rice – 6 ounces
- Salt and pepper to taste
- Parsley – 1 tbsp. chopped

Directions:

Heat oil on Sauté. Add chicken, onion, and carrots. Cook for 3 minutes. Add the rest of the ingredients except the parsley. Cover and cook on High for 12 minutes. Open and add parsley. Serve.

Turkey and Brussels Sprouts Stew
Cook time: 25 minutes |Serves: 4| Per serving: Calories 239; Carbs 9g; Fat 14g; Protein 16g

Ingredients:

- Turkey breast – 1 pound, skinless, boneless and cubed

- Brussels sprouts – 1 pound, halved
- Shallot – 1, chopped
- Garlic – 2 cloves, minced
- Olive oil – 1 tbsp.
- Salt and pepper to taste
- Thyme – 1 tbsp. chopped
- Tarragon – ½ tbsp. chopped
- Parsley – 1 tbsp. chopped
- Chicken stock – 1 cup
- Tomato sauce – ½ cup

Directions:

Heat oil on Sauté. Add meat, sprouts, shallot and garlic and cook for 5 minutes. add rest of the ingredients and covers. Cook on Low for 20 minutes. Open and serve.

Turkey Salad

Cook time: 15 minutes| Serves: 4| Per serving: Calories 181; Carbs 7g; Fat 4g; Protein 15g

Ingredients:

- Turkey breast – 1 ½ pounds, skinless, boneless and cubed
- Tomatoes – 2, cubed
- Red bell peppers – 2, cut into strips
- Olive oil – 1 tbsp.
- Red onions – 2, chopped
- Parsley – ½ cup, chopped
- Canned tomatoes – 20 ounces, chopped
- Basil – 1 tbsp. chopped
- Salt and pepper to taste
- Baby arugula – 1 cup
- Baby spinach – ½ cup

Directions:

Heat oil on Sauté. Add onions and turkey and cook for 5 minutes. Add rest of the ingredients except for the basil, arugula and spinach and cover. Cook on High for 10 minutes. Open and add spinach, basil and arugula. Serve.

Cumin and Cardamom Turkey

Cook time: 20 minutes |Serves: 4 | Per serving: Calories 231; Carbs 6g; Fat 7g; Protein 12g

Ingredients:

- Turkey breast – 1, skinless, boneless and cubed
- Salt and pepper to taste
- Chicken stock – 1 cup
- Yellow onion – 1, chopped
- Garlic – 3 cloves, minced

- Cumin – 1 and ½ tsps. ground
- Cardamom – 1 tsp. ground
- Chives – 1 tbsp. chopped

Directions:

Add everything in the pot except the chives and cover. Cook on High for 20 minutes. Top with chives and serve.

Turkey and Eggplant Mix
Cook time: 20 minutes |Serves: 4| Per serving: Calories 252; Carbs 7g; Fat 12g; Protein 13g

Ingredients:

- Big turkey breast – 1, skinless, boneless and cubed
- Salt and pepper to taste
- Big eggplant – 1, chopped
- Oil – 2 tbsps.
- Red onion – 1, chopped
- Tomato sauce – 10 ounces
- Oregano – 1 tbsp. dried
- Basil – 1 tsp. dried

Directions:

Heat oil on Sauté. Add onion and turkey and cook for 5 minutes. Add the rest of the ingredients and cover. Cook 15 minutes on High. Serve.

Creamy Turkey
Cook time: 20 minutes| Serves: 4| Per serving: Calories 234; Carbs 7g; Fat 14g; Protein 15g

Ingredients:

- Turkey – 1 big breast, skinless, boneless and cubed
- Yellow onion – 1, chopped
- Garlic – 4, cloves, minced
- Parsley – ¼ cup, chopped
- Salt and pepper to taste
- Oregano – 1 tsp. dried
- Coconut milk – 1 cup
- Chicken stock – 1 cup
- Olive oil – 2 tbsps.

Directions:

Heat oil on Saute. Add onion, garlic, and turkey and cook for 5 minutes. Add remaining ingredients and mix. Cover and cook on High for 15 minutes. Open and serve.

Lemongrass Turkey
Cook time: 25 minutes |Serves: 4| Per serving: Calories 263; Carbs 6g; Fat 12g; Protein 14g

Ingredients:

- Lemongrass – 1 bunch, chopped
- Garlic – 4 cloves, minced
- Balsamic vinegar – 2 tbsps.
- Oregano – 1 tbsp. chopped
- Coconut milk – 1 cup
- Turkey breasts – 2, skinless, boneless and cubed
- Salt and pepper to taste
- Cilantro – ¼ cup, chopped

Directions:

In a food processor, add everything except the turkey and milk and mix well. In the IP, combine the turkey with the lemongrass mix, and milk. Cover and cook on High for 25 minutes. Open and serve topped with cilantro.

Turkey and Mushroom Sauce
Cook time: 25 minutes |Serves:4 | Per serving: Calories 262; Carbs 8g; Fat 16g; Protein 16g

Ingredients:

- Big turkey breast – 1, skinless and boneless, chopped
- Coconut cream – ½ cup
- Yellow onion – 1, chopped
- Olive oil – 1 tbsp.
- White mushrooms -1 pound, sliced
- Chicken stock – ½ cup
- Cilantro – ¼ cup, chopped

Directions:

Heat oil on Sauté. Add onion and mushrooms and cook for 3 minutes. Add the turkey and brown for 2 minutes. Add remaining ingredients and cover. Cook on High for 20 minutes. Serve.

Duck Curry
Cook time: 30 minutes| Serves: 4 | Per serving: Calories 231; Carbs 7g; Fat 12g; Protein 15g

Ingredients:

- Duck breasts – 1 ½ pounds, skinless, boneless and cubed
- Olive oil – 1 tbsp.
- Yellow onion – 1, sliced
- Canned coconut milk – 5 ounces
- Green curry paste – 1 tbsp.
- Coriander – ½ bunch, chopped

Directions:

Heat oil on Sauté. Add onion, curry paste and duck and cook for 5 minutes. Add the resto of the ingredients and cover. Cook on High for 25 minutes. Open and serve.

Duck and Brown Onions Mix

Cook time: 30 minutes| Serves: 4| Per serving: Calories 263; Carbs 7g; Fat 12g; Protein 16g

Ingredients:

- Duck pieces – 2 pounds
- Olive oil – 2 tbsps.
- Brown onions – 2, chopped
- Garlic – 2 cloves, minced
- Chicken stock – 14 ounces
- Tomato sauce – 1 cup
- Sweet paprika – 1 tbsp.
- Parsley – 1 tbsp. chopped

Directions:

Heat oil on Sauté. Add onion, garlic, and duck and cook for 5 minutes. Add everything and cover. Cook on High for 25 minutes. Open and serve.

Parmesan Duck Breast

Cook time: 25 minutes| Serves: 4| Per serving: Calories 242; Carbs 7g; Fat 14g; Protein 14g

Ingredients:

- Olive oil – 1 tbsp.
- Duck breasts – 2 pounds, skinless, and boneless
- Salt and pepper to taste
- Chicken stock – 1 cup
- Yellow onion – 1, chopped
- Tomato – 1, cubed
- Parmesan cheese – 1 cup, shredded

Directions:

Heat oil on Sauté. Add onion and duck and cook for 5 minutes. Add everything except for the cheese and cover. Cook on High for 20 minutes. Open and sprinkle with cheese. Serve.

Thyme Duck and Chives

Cook time: 20 minutes| Serves: 4 | Per serving: Calories 293; Carbs 6g; Fat 15g; Protein 14g

Ingredients:

- Duck breasts – 2, boneless, skin scored and halved
- Avocado oil – 1 tbsp.
- Yellow onion – 1, chopped
- Chicken stock – 1 cup
- Salt and pepper to taste

- Thyme – 2 tsps. dried
- Chives – 1 tbsp. chopped

Directions:

Heat oil on Sauté. Add duck breasts, skin side down and cook for 2 minutes. Add the rest of the ingredients except for the chives. Cover and cook on High for 18 minutes. Sprinkle with chives and serve.

Duck and Rice Mix
Cook time: 30 minutes| Serves: 4 | Per serving: Calories 251; Carbs 7g; Fat 17g; Protein 14g

Ingredients:

- Ginger – 1 tbsp. grated
- Garlic – 4 cloves, minced
- Coconut milk – 1 cup
- Wild rice – 1 cup
- Chicken stock – 3 cups
- Duck breasts – 2, skinless, boneless and cubed
- Five spice – 1 tsp.
- Salt and pepper to taste
- Capers – 1 tbsp. drained and chopped

Directions:

Mix the duck with everything in the Pot. Cover and cook on High for 30 minutes. Open and serve.

Duck and Lentils
Cook time: 25 minutes| Serves: 4| Per serving: Calories 273; Carbs 6g; Fat 12g; Protein 13g

Ingredients:

- Duck – 2 breasts, boneless, halved and skin scored
- Red onion – 1, chopped
- Olive oil - 2 tbsps.
- Lentils – 8 ounces
- Parsley – 1 tbsp. chopped
- Chicken stock – 3 cups
- Salt and pepper to taste

Directions:

Heat oil on Sauté. Add onion and duck, skin side down and cook for 5 minutes. Add everything and cover. Cook on High for 20 minutes. Serve.

Chapter 9 Pork Recipes

Chinese Pork Soup

Cook time: 30 minutes| Serves: 5| Per serving: Calories 234; Carbs 2.3g; Fat 7.2g; Protein 29.3g

Ingredients:

- Olive oil – 1 tbsp.
- Ground pork – 1 pound
- Small yellow onion – 1 chopped
- Carrots – 2 cups, chopped
- Chopped cabbage – ½ head
- Homemade chicken broth – 4 cups
- Liquid aminos – ¼ cup
- Ground ginger – 1 tsp.
- Freshly ground black pepper to taste

Directions:

Place the oil in the Instant Pot and press Sauté. Add the pork and cook for 5 minutes. Add the remaining ingredients. Cover and cook on High pressure for 25 minutes. Serve.

Basil-Lime Carnitas

Cook time: 25 minutes |Serves: 4 | Per serving: Calories 344; Carbs 1.1g; Fat 25.3g; Protein 26.7g

Ingredients:

- Avocado oil – 2 tbsps.
- Pork shoulder – 1 pound, chopped
- Finely chopped jalapeno – ½
- Dried oregano – ½ tsp.
- Chili powder – ½ tsp.
- Ground cumin – ½ tsp.
- Dried basil – ½ tsp.
- Salt – ½ tsp.
- Black pepper – ½ tsp.
- Lime juice – ½ tsp.
- Water – 1 cup

Directions:

Press Sauté and heat the oil. Add the pork and brown it. Add salt, black pepper, basil, cumin, chili powder, oregano, jalapeno, and water. Close and cook 25 minutes on High. Do a natural release. Open and stir in lime juice. Serve.

Pork Chops

Cook time: 30 minutes |Serves: 4| Per serving: Calories 232; Carbs 0.8g; Fat 19.9g; Protein 12.2g

Ingredients:

- Coconut oil – 2 tbsps.
- Pork chops – 4, boneless
- Butter – 1 tbsp.
- Crushed red pepper – 1 tsp.
- Dried parsley – ½ tsp.
- Garlic powder – ½ tsp.
- Chili powder – ½ tsp.
- Dried basil – ½ tsp.
- Salt – ½ tsp.
- Ground black pepper – ½ tsp.
- Hot sauce – ¼ cup
- Water – 1 cup

Directions:

Press Sauté and melt the oil in the Instant Pot. Add pork chops and brown on both sides. Add 1-cup water, butter, black pepper, salt, basil, chili powder, garlic powder, parsley, and red pepper. Close and cook 30 minutes on High. Do a natural release. Open the pork chops and rub with hot sauce. Serve.

Pork Parmesan Spinach

Cook time: 8 minutes |Serves: 6 | Per serving: Calories 234; Carbs 6g; Fat 18g; Protein 15g

Ingredients:

- Bell peppers – 1 cup, chopped
- Minced garlic – 2 cloves
- Onion – ½ cup, chopped
- Coconut oil – 1 tbsp.
- Pork – 1 pound, finely ground
- Baby spinach – 4 cups, chopped
- Parmesan cheese – ½ cup, grated

Directions:

Press Sauté and add oil to the Instant Pot. Add the meat stir-fry until browned. Add the spinach, peppers, onions, garlic, and stir-fry for 3 minutes. Close and cook 8 minutes on High. Do a quick release when done. Open the lid and mix in the cheese. Serve.

Cinnamon Pork

Cook time: 15 minutes |Serves: 4| Per serving: Calories 543; Carbs 6g; Fat 36g; Protein 54g

Ingredients:

- Pork – 2 pounds, ground
- Pepper – ¼ tsp.
- Cinnamon – ½ tsp.
- Sweetener – 2 tbsps.
- Grated ginger – ½ tsp.
- Dijon mustard – 2 tbsps.
- Chicken broth – 1 cup
- Olive oil – 1 tbsp.
- Salt – ½ tsp.

Directions:

Season the meat with salt and pepper. Press Sauté and add oil to the Instant Pot. Add the meat and stir-fry until browned. Add the other ingredients and mix well. Close and cook 15 minutes on High. Do a quick release when done. Open and serve.

Creamy Pork Sausage
Cook time: 15 minutes |Serves: 4 | Per serving: Calories 290; Carbs 5g; Fat 30g; Protein 25g

Ingredients:

- Pork sausage – 1 pound
- Arrowroot – ¼ cup
- Garlic cloves – 4, minced
- Milk – 2 cups
- Thyme – 1 tsp.
- Pepper – ¼ tsp.
- Olive oil – ½ tbsp.
- Salt – ½ tsp.

Directions:

Press Sauté and heat the olive oil. Add the thyme and garlic and cook for one minute. Add the sausage and cook it until becomes brown. Pour 1 ½ cups of milk, close the lid and cook on High for 5 minutes. Meanwhile, whisk together the remaining milk, arrowroot, salt, and pepper. Do a quick pressure release and whisk in the arrowroot mixture. Press the Sauté and cook until thickened, about 5 minutes. Serve.

Ginger Pork
Cook time: 42 minutes| Serves: 3 | Per serving: Calories 576; Carbs 2.9g; Fat 24g; Protein 82.7g

Ingredients:

- Pork loin – 2 lbs. chopped into bite-size pieces.
- Eggplant – 1 cup, chopped
- Ghee – 3 tbsps.
- Spring onion – 1, finely chopped

- Garlic cloves – 3
- Beef stock – 3 cups
- Light soy sauce – 2 tbsps.
- Anka sauce – 1 tbsp.
- Balsamic vinegar – 1 tbsp.
- Ginger powder – 2 tsps.
- Anise star – 1
- Cloves – 3
- Sea salt – 2

Directions:

Place the meat at the bottom and add enough water to cover. Press Sauté and bring it to a boil. Cook for 5 minutes and stirring occasionally. Remove from the pot and drain. Set aside. Now grease the inner pot with ghee and heat up. Add cloves, anise, ginger powder and spring onions. Simmer and stir for 1 minute. Add the anka sauce and cook for another minute. Add the meat and mix well. Add the rest of the ingredients. Cover and cook for 35 minutes on high. When done, do a quick pressure release and open the lid. Serve.

Spicy and Smokey Pork
Cook time: 50 minutes |Serves: 4 | Per serving: Calories 660; Carbs 2.2g; Fat 40g; Protein 75g

Ingredients:

- Chili powder – ½ tsp.
- Cumin – 1 tsp.
- Thyme – 1 tsp.
- Oregano – 1 tsp.
- Smoked paprika – 1 tsp.
- Sweetener – 1 tsp.
- Coconut oil – 1 tbsp.
- Ground ginger – 1 tsp.
- Onion powder – ½ tsp.
- Garlic powder – 1 tsp.
- Pork roast – 2 pounds
- Pepper – ½ tsp.
- Beef broth – 1 ½ cups

Directions:

Press Sauté and melt the coconut oil. Combine all the spices and herbs and rub the mixture into the pork. Place the pork in the instant pot and sear on all sides, until browned. Combine the broth and liquid smoke and pour over. Close the lid and cook for 45 minutes on High. Release the pressure naturally. Serve.

Chinese Pulled Pork
Cook time: 1 hour| Serves: 6| Per serving: Calories 459; Carbs 3g; Fat 35g; Protein 30g

Ingredients:

- Pork shoulder – 2 lbs.
- Chicken broth – 1 cup
- Tomato sauce – 4 tbsps.
- Tomato paste – 1 tbsp.
- Garlic paste – 2 tbsps.
- Soy sauce – 4 tbsps.
- Liquid sweetener – 5 drops
- Grated ginger – 2 tsps.
- Smoked paprika – 1 tsp.

Directions:

Except for pork, place all the ingredients in a bowl and mix well. Add pork to the bowl and coat. Transfer the pork to the instant pot and pour over the remaining sauce. Cover and cook on High for 1 hour. Naturally release the pressure. Shred the pork with a fork and mix well to soak up the sauce. Serve.

Easy Pork Ribs
Cook time: 22 minutes |Serves: 5| Per serving: Calories 633; Carbs 7.1g; Fat 40.7g; Protein 54.9g

Ingredients:

- Pork ribs – 2 lbs.
- Cauliflower – 1 cup, chopped into florets
- Celery stalks – 2, chopped
- Red bell peppers – 2, chopped
- Onions – ½ cup, finely chopped
- Portobello mushrooms – 1 cup, chopped
- Tomatoes – 1 cup, diced
- Hot chili sauce – 2 tbsps.
- Garlic – 2 cloves, whole
- Apple cider vinegar – 1 tsp.
- Butter – 3 tbsps.
- Beef broth – 5 cups
- Salt – 2 tsps.
- Black pepper – ½ tsp. freshly ground
- Dried celery – 1 tsp.
- Onion powder – 2 tsps.

Directions:

Place the ribs in the pot and pour in enough water to cover. Add celery stalks and cover. Cook for 15 minutes on High. When done, open the lid. Now stir in the remaining ingredients and sprinkle with onion powder, celery, pepper, and salt. Mix well and seal the lid. Cook for 7 more minutes. When done, do a quick pressure release and open the lid. Serve.

Pork Chops with Peppers

Cook time: 20 minutes| Serves: 5| Per serving: Calories 407; Carbs 5.4g; Fat 30.8g; Protein 25g

Ingredients:

- Pork chops – 1 lb. cut into bite-sized pieces
- Red bell peppers – 2, sliced
- Chili peppers – 2, chopped
- Small onions – 2, finely chopped
- Bacon slices – 2, chopped
- Butter - 2 tbsps. unsalted
- Beef broth – 1 cup
- Italian seasoning – 2 tsps.
- Salt – ¼ tsp.

Directions:

Rinse the meat, pat dry and sprinkle with 1 tsp. of Italian seasoning. Place in the IP and pour in the broth. Cover and cook 10 minutes on High. Open and remove the meat from the pot along with the broth and press Sauté. Grease the inner pot with the butter and add onion. Sauté for 2 minutes and then add peppers. Sprinkle with salt and remaining Italian seasoning and cook for 2 to 3 minutes. Now add the bacon and stir well. If necessary, add some beef broth, about 2 tbsps. at a time. Finally, add the meat and give it a good stir. Cook for 5 minutes. Serve.

Rosemary Pork Shoulder

Cook time: 25 minutes| Serves: 4 | Per serving: Calories 430; Carbs 2g; Fat 19g; Protein 60g

Ingredients:

- Pork shoulder roast – 2 lbs.
- Shallots – 2, sliced
- Garlic – 4 cloves, crushed
- Olive oil – 3 tbsps.
- Dijon mustard – 3 tbsps.
- Salt – 1 tsp.
- Fresh rosemary – 1 tbsp. finely chopped
- White pepper – ½ tsp. freshly ground

Directions:

Rinse the meat well and sprinkle with salt and pepper. Set aside. Coat a bowl with olive oil. Make a layer with shallots and sprinkle with fresh rosemary and garlic. Place the meat on top and brush with Dijon mustard. Loosely cover with aluminum foil and set aside. Set the trivet in the inner pot and pour in one cup of water and place the bowl on the trivet. Cover and cook on High for 25 minutes. Serve.

Green Beans with Pork and Potatoes

Cook time: 22 minutes| Serves: 4| Per serving: Calories 180; Carbs 17g; Fat 6g; Protein 15g

Ingredients:

- Lean pork – 1 pound, cubed
- Tomatoes – 3, chopped
- Carrots – 2, peeled and sliced
- Celery – 2 sticks, sliced
- Green beans – 1 pound
- Medium potatoes – 2, peeled and quartered
- White onion – 1, peeled and chopped
- Salt – ½ tsp.
- Ground black pepper - ½ tsp.
- Olive oil – 2 tbsps.

Directions:

Add oil and Press Sauté on the Instant Pot. Add the meat and cook for 5 minutes or until golden brown. Then add the remaining ingredients and mix. Cover and cook 17 minutes on High. Do a quick release and open. Serve.

Greek Pork
Cook time:50 minutes |Serves: 8|Per serving: Calories 223.9; Carbs 3.3g; Fat 12.2g; Protein 23.7g

Ingredients:

- Pork roast – 4 pounds, cut into 2-inch pieces
- Onion powder – 1 tsp.
- Garlic powder – 1 tsp.
- Salt – 1 tsp.
- Ground black pepper – ½ tsp.
- Dried oregano – 2 tsps.
- Lemon juice – ¼ cup
- Chicken broth – ¼ cup

Directions:

Place the pork in the Instant Pot. In a bowl, whisk remaining ingredients and pour it over the pork and turn to coat. Cover and cook on High for 50 minutes. Do a natural release and open. Shred the pork and serve.

Coffee Flavored Pork Ribs
Cook time: 40 minutes |Serves: 4| Per serving: Calories 345; Carbs 1.3g; Fat 29.3g; Protein 18.1g

Ingredients:

- Baby back ribs – 1 rack
- Olive oil – 2 tsps.
- Oyster sauce – 3 tbsps.

- Salt – ½ tsp.
- Sugar – 1 tsp.
- Water – 1 cup
- Liquid smoke – ½ cup
- Instant coffee powder – 2 tbsps.

Directions:

Add everything in the pot. Cover and cook 40 minutes on High. Do a natural release and serve.

Mushroom and Pork Soup

Cook time: 30 minutes |Serves: 4| Per serving: Calories 283; Carbs 7g; Fat 12g; Protein 10g

Ingredients:

- Pork stew meat – 1 ½, cubed
- Oil – 2 tbsps.
- Salt and pepper to taste
- White mushrooms – ½ pound, sliced
- Yellow onion – 1 cup, chopped
- Garlic – 6 cloves, minced
- Veggie stock – 6 cups
- Parsley -1 tbsp.

Directions:

Heat oil on Sauté. Add meat and brown for 4 minutes. Add mushrooms, onions, garlic, salt, and pepper and cook for 2 minutes more. Add rest of the ingredients, except the parsley and cover. Cook on High for 20 minutes. Serve topped with parsley.

Pork and Fennel Soup

Cook time: 20 minutes| Serves: 4| Per serving: Calories 162; Carbs 8g; Fat 10g; Protein 14g

Ingredients:

- Fennel bulb – 1, shredded
- Chicken stock – 4 cups
- Yellow onion – 1, chopped
- Pork meat – 1 pound, chopped
- Olive oil – 1 tbsp.
- Salt and pepper to taste
- Tomato sauce – 2 tbsps.
- Parsley – 1 tbsp. chopped

Directions:

Heat oil on Sauté. Add onion and meat and cook for 5 minutes. Add the rest of the ingredients, except for the parsley and cover. Cook on High for 15 minutes. Serve topped with parsley.

Chili Pork Soup

Cook time: 25 minutes | Serves: 4 | Per serving: Calories 172; Carbs 9g; Fat 4g; Protein 13g

Ingredients:

- Yellow onion – 1, chopped
- Olive oil – 2 tbsps.
- Jalapeno peppers – 2, minced
- Garlic – 4 cloves, minced
- Oregano – 2 tsps. dried
- Red pepper flakes – ½ tsp. crushed
- Beef stock – 5 cups
- Pork meat – 1 pound, cubed
- Salt and pepper to taste
- Cilantro – 1 tbsp. chopped

Directions:

Heat oil on Sauté. Add onion, garlic, and jalapenos. Cook for 2 minutes and add meat. Cook for 3 minutes more. Add the rest of the ingredients, except for the cilantro. Cover and cook on High for 20 minutes. Serve topped with cilantro.

Cinnamon Pork Stew

Cook time: 10 minutes| Serves: 4 | Per serving: Calories 231; Carbs 7g; Fat 12g; Protein 9g

Ingredients:

- Pork shoulder – 1 ½ pounds, cubed
- Yellow onion – 1, chopped
- Olive oil – 2 tbsps.
- Cinnamon powder – 1 tsp.
- Garlic – 2 cloves, chopped
- Salt and pepper to taste
- Beef stock – ½ cup
- Canned tomatoes – 12 ounces, chopped
- Basil – 1 tbsp. chopped

Directions:

Heat oil on Sauté. Add meat, onion, garlic and cinnamon and cook for 5 minutes. Add the rest of the ingredients, except for the basil. Cover and cook on Low for 25 minutes. Serve topped with basil.

Pesto Pork Stew

Cook time: 30 minutes| Serves: 4| Per serving: Calories 233; Carbs 7g; Fat 12g; Protein 15g

Ingredients:

- Yellow onion – 1, chopped
- Pork stew meat – 1 pound, cubed

- Garlic – 1 clove, minced
- Chicken stock – 1 cup
- Tomato sauce – 12 ounces
- Olive oil – 1 tbsp.
- Juice of ½ lemon
- Parsley – 1 tbsp. chopped
- Basil pesto – 1 tbsp.

Directions:

Heat oil on Sauté. Add meat, onion, and garlic and cook for 5 minutes. Add the rest of the ingredients. Cover and cook on Low for 25 minutes. Serve.

Sweet Potato and Pork Stew
Cook time: 30 minutes| Serves: 4| Per serving: Calories 200; Carbs 7g; Fat 12g; Protein 14g

Ingredients:

- Yellow onion – 1, chopped
- Olive oil – 1 tbsp.
- Garlic – 2 cloves, minced
- Sweet potatoes – 3, chopped
- Pork stew meat – 1 pound, cubed
- Canned tomatoes – 14 ounces, chopped
- Curry powder – 2 tsps.
- Juice of 2 limes
- Cilantro – 1 tbsp. chopped

Directions:

Heat oil on Sauté. Add onion, garlic and meat. Cook for 5 minutes. Add the remaining ingredients, except the cilantro. Cover and cook for 25 minutes on High. Serve topped with cilantro.

Ground Pork Stew
Cook time: 20 minutes| Serves: 4 | Per serving: Calories 177; Carbs 6g; Fat 7g; Protein 14g

Ingredients:

- Yellow onion – 1, chopped
- Olive oil – ½ tbsp.
- Pork meat – 2 ½ pounds, ground
- Tomato paste – 1 cup
- Jalapenos – 2, chopped
- Garlic – 4 tbsps. minced
- Salt and pepper to taste
- Oregano – 1 tsp. dried

Directions:

Heat oil on Sauté. Add pork, onion, and garlic and cook for 4 minutes. Add the rest of the ingredients. Cover and cook on Low for 16 minutes. Serve.

Sage Pork Stew

Cook time: 30 minutes| Serves: 4| Per serving: Calories 220; Carbs 7g; Fat 12g; Protein 16g

Ingredients:

- Yellow onion – 1, chopped
- Pork stew meat – 2 pounds, cubed
- Olive oil – 2 tbsps.
- Carrots – 3, chopped
- Beef stock – 1 cup
- Garlic – 2 cloves, minced
- Salt and pepper to taste
- Sage – 1 tbsp. chopped for garnishing

Directions:

Heat oil on sauté. Add meat, onion, and garlic and cook for 5 minutes. Add rest of the ingredients and cover. Cook on Low for 25 minutes. Serve with sage sprinkled on top.

Orange Pork Stew

Cook time: 30 minutes |Serves: 4 | Per serving: Calories 200; Carbs 7g; Fat 12g; Protein 16g

Ingredients:

- Pork shoulder – 1 ½ pounds, cubed
- Garlic – 3 cloves, minced
- Red onion – 1, chopped
- Juice of 1 orange
- Salt and pepper to taste
- Ginger -1 tbsp. grated
- Rosemary – 1 tsp. dried
- Olive oil – 1 tbsp.

Directions:

Heat oil on sauté. Add onion, meat and the garlic. Cook for 5 minutes. Add the rest of the ingredients and cover. Cook on Low for 25 minutes. Serve.

Pork Bites

Cook time: 30 minutes| Serves: 4| Per serving: Calories 242; Carbs 6g; Fat 12g; Protein 14g

Ingredients:

- Pork roast – 1 pound, cubed and browned
- Italian seasoning – 1 tbsp.
- Beef stock – 1 cup
- Water – 2 tbsps.

- Sweet paprika – 1 tbsp.
- Tomato sauce – 2 tbsps.
- Rosemary – 1 tbsp. chopped

Directions:

Add everything in the pot, except the rosemary. Mix and cover. Cook on High for 30 minutes. Serve sprinkle with rosemary.

Balsamic Pork Chops
Cook time: 25 minutes| Serves: 4| Per serving: Calories 200; Carbs 6g; Fat 11g; Protein 15g

Ingredients:

- Pork chops – 4
- Balsamic vinegar – 2 tbsps.
- Olive oil – 2 tbsps.
- Salt and pepper to taste
- Rosemary – 1 tbsp. chopped
- Beef stock – ½ cup

Directions:

Heat oil on Sauté. Add pork chops and brown 2 minutes per side. Add the rest of the ingredients and cover. Cook on High for 20 minutes. Serve.

Pork Chops with Apples
Cook time: 25 minutes |Serves: 4| Per serving: Calories 210; Carbs 8g; Fat 5g; Protein 12g

Ingredients:

- Pork chops – 4
- Oil – 2 tbsps.
- Garlic – 1 clove, minced
- Lemon juice – 2 tbsps.
- Green apples – 2, cored and cubed
- Yellow onion – 1, chopped
- Beef stock – ½ cup
- Salt and pepper to taste
- Parsley – 1 tbsp. chopped

Directions:

Heat oil on Sauté. Add onion and garlic and sauté for 2 minutes. Add pork chops and cook for 3 minutes. Add the rest of the ingredients, expect for the parsley. Cover and cook for 20 minutes on High. Serve.

Pork and Parsley Sauce
Cook time: 20 minutes| Serves: 4| Per serving: Calories 248; Carbs 6g; Fat 11g; Protein 15g

Ingredients:

- Pork chops – 4
- Olive oil – 2 tbsps.
- Chili powder – 2 tsps.
- Coconut cream - 1 cup
- Garlic cloves – 2, minced
- Salt and pepper to taste
- Parsley – 1 small bunch, chopped

Directions:

Combine the parsley, oil, cream, garlic, chili powder, salt and pepper in a blender and blend well. Put the pork chops in the pot and add the parsley sauce. Cover and cook on High for 20 minutes. Serve.

Tomato Pork Chops
Cook time: 25 minutes| Serves: 4| Per serving: Calories 233; Carbs 7g; Fat 9g ; Protein 14g

Ingredients:

- Pork chops – 4
- Veggie stock – 1 cup
- Tomato puree – ¼ cup
- Sweet paprika – 4 tsps.
- Salt and pepper to taste

Directions:

Combine everything in the pot and cover. Cook on High for 25 minutes. Serve.

Pork and Endives
Cook time: 25 minutes| Serves: 4| Per serving: Calories 227; Carbs 6g; Fat 14g; Protein 16g

Ingredients:

- Pork chops – 4
- Oil – 2 tbsps.
- Salt and pepper to taste
- Garlic – 2 cloves, minced
- Yellow onion – 1, chopped
- Chicken stock – 1 cup
- Endives – 2, sliced
- Tomato sauce – ¼ cup
- Parsley – 1 tbsp. chopped

Directions:

Heat oil on Sauté. Add onion and garlic and sauté for 2 minutes. Add meat and cook for 3 minutes more. Add the rest of the ingredients and cover. Cook on High for 20 minutes. Serve.

Sesame Pork Chops

Cook time: 25 minutes| Serves: 4| Per serving: Calories 236; Carbs 7g; Fat 12g; Protein 15g

Ingredients:

- Pork chops – 4
- Sesame seeds – 2 tsps.
- Oil – 1 tbsp.
- Chili powder – 1 tsp.
- Sweet paprika – 1 tsp.
- Tomato sauce – 1 cup
- Chives – 1 tbsp. chopped

Directions:

Heat oil on Sauté. Add pork chops and brown for 5 minutes. Add the rest of the ingredients, except the sesame seeds. Cover and cook on High for 20 minutes. Serve.

Pork and Fennel

Cook time: 25 minutes| Serves: 4 | Per serving: Calories 273; Carbs 7g; Fat 12g; Protein 17g

Ingredients:

- Pork loin – 1 ½ pounds, cubed
- Stock – 1 cup
- Fennel bulbs – 2, sliced
- Lemon juice – 2 tbsps.
- Oil – 2 tbsps.
- Garlic powder – ¼ cup
- Sweet paprika – 1 tbsp.
- Salt and pepper to taste

Directions:

Heat oil on Saute. Add meat and brown for 5 minutes. Add the rest of the ingredients and cover. Cook on High for 20 minutes. Serve.

Pork Chops and Cauliflower Rice

Cook time: 25 minutes| Serves: 4| Per serving: Calories 244; Carbs 5 g; Fat 12g; Protein 16g

Ingredients:

- Beef stock – 2 cups
- Peppercorns – 1 tbsp. crushed
- Cauliflower rice - 1 cup
- Garlic – 4 cloves, minced
- Pork chops – 4
- Red onion – 1, chopped
- Olive oil – 2 tbsps.
- Salt and pepper to taste

Directions:

Heat oil on Sauté. Add onion and garlic and Sauté for 2 minutes. Add meat and brown for 3 minutes. Add the rest of the ingredients and cover. Cook on High for 20 minutes. Serve.

Rosemary Pork and Green Beans
Cook time: 25 minutes| Serves: 4| Per serving: Calories 254; Carbs 6g; Fat 14g; Protein 17g

Ingredients:

- Pork loin – 1 ½ pounds, sliced
- Green beans – 1 pound, trimmed
- Veggie stock – 1 ½ cup
- Garlic – 3 cloves, minced
- Rosemary – 1 bunch, chopped
- Salt and pepper to taste
- Yellow onion – 1, chopped

Directions:

Combine everything in the pot. Cover and cook on High for 25 minutes. Serve.

Mustard Pork Ribs
Cook time: 30 minutes| Serves: 4| Per serving: Calories 263; Carbs 6g; Fat 14g; Protein 20g

Ingredients:

- Pork ribs – 2 pounds
- Salt and pepper to taste
- Smoked paprika – 1 tbsp.
- Dijon mustard – 2 tbsps.
- Sage – 1 tbsp. chopped
- Olive oil – 1 tbsp.
- Beef stock – 1 ½ cups
- Cilantro – 1 tbsp. chopped

Directions:

Heat oil on Sauté. Add the ribs and the rest of the ingredients, except for the stock and cilantro. Cook for 5 minutes. Add stock and cover. Cook on High for 25 minutes. Serve topped with parsley.

Pesto Pork Chops
Cook time: 25 minutes |Serves: 4| Per serving: Calories 283; Carbs 6g; Fat 13g; Protein 16g

Ingredients:

- Pork chops – 4
- Salt and pepper to taste
- Onion powder – 1 tsp.
- Sweet paprika – ½ tsp.
- Yellow onion – 1, chopped

- Basil pesto – 4 tbsps.
- Beef stock – 1 ½ cups
- Cayenne pepper – 1 pinch

Directions:

Mix everything in a bowl, except the stock and rub well. Add the mixture and stock in the pot. Cover and cook on High for 25 minutes. Serve.

Oregano and Spring Onion Pork
Cook time: 35 minutes | Serves: 4 | Per serving: Calories 253; Carbs 6g; Fat 14g; Protein 17g

Ingredients:

- Green onions – 4, chopped
- Pork chops – 4
- Oil – 2 tsps.
- Garlic – 3 cloves, minced
- Oregano – 1 tbsp. chopped
- Beef stock – 1 ½ cups
- Tomato sauce – 2 tbsps.
- Cilantro – 1 tbsp. chopped

Directions:

Heat oil on Sauté. Add onions and garlic and cook for 2 minutes. Add meat and brown for 3 minutes. Add the rest of the ingredients and cover. Cook on High for 30 minutes. Serve.

Pork and Collard Greens
Cook time: 25 minutes | Serves: 4 | Per serving: Calories 264; Carbs 6g; Fat 14g; Protein 17g

Ingredients:

- Pork loin – 1 ½ pounds, cubed
- Oil – 1 tbsp.
- Yellow onion – 1, chopped
- Salt and pepper to taste
- Tomato paste – ¼ cup
- Collard greens – 1 pound
- Cilantro – 1 tbsp. chopped

Directions:

Heat oil on Sauté. Add onion and cook for 2 minutes. Add meat and brown for 3 minutes more. Add the rest of the ingredients except the cilantro. Cover and cook on High for 20 minutes. Serve.

Pork Chops and Bell Peppers
Cook time: 35 minutes | Serves: 4 | Per serving: Calories 273; Carbs 5g; Fat 13g; Protein 15g

Ingredients:

- Oil – 2 tbsps.
- Pork chops – 4
- Salt and pepper to taste
- Bell peppers – 2, chopped
- Garlic – 3 cloves, chopped
- Red onion – 1, chopped
- Beef stock - 2 cups
- Parsley – 1 tbsp. chopped

Directions:

Heat oil on Sauté. Add pork and brown for 2 minutes. Add onion and garlic and brown for 3 minutes more. Add all the other ingredients, except the parsley. Cover and cook on High for 30 minutes. Sprinkle with parsley and serve.

Orange and Cinnamon Pork
Cook time: 35 minutes| Serves: 4| Per serving: Calories 274; Carbs 6g; Fat 14g; Protein 16g

Ingredients:

- Pork chops – 4
- Garlic – 3 cloves, minced
- Cinnamon powder – 1 tbsp.
- Juice of 1 orange
- Salt and pepper to taste
- Ginger – 1 tbsp. grated
- Beef stock – ½ cup
- Rosemary – 1 tsp. dried

Directions:

Combine everything in the pot and cover. Cook on High for 35 minutes. Open and serve.

Pork, Corn and Green Beans
Cook time: 35 minutes| Serves: 4| Per serving: Calories 264; Carbs 8g; Fat 14g; Protein 12g

Ingredients:

- Pork shoulder – 2 pounds, boneless and cubed
- Garlic – 2 cloves, minced
- Salt and pepper to taste
- Corn – 1 cup
- Green beans – 1 cup trimmed and halved
- Beef stock – 1 cup
- Cumin – 1 tsp. ground

Directions:

Combine everything in the pot. Cover and cook on High for 35 minutes. Open and serve.

Cocoa Pork

Cook time: 30 minutes |Serves: 4| Per serving: Calories 200; Carbs 6g; Fat 9g; Protein 12g

Ingredients:

- Pork chops – 4
- Salt and pepper to taste
- Cocoa powder – 2 tbsps.
- Hot sauce – 2 tbsps.
- Beef stock – 1 cup
- Chili powder – 2 tsps.
- Cumin – ¼ tsp. ground
- Parsley – 1 tbsp. chopped

Directions:

Combine everything in the pot. Cover and cook on High for 30 minutes. Open and serve.

Pork Shoulder and Celery

Cook time: 30 minutes |Serves: 4 | Per serving: Calories 234; Carbs 7g; Fat 11g; Protein 15g

Ingredients:

- Pork shoulder – 2 pounds, boneless and cubed
- Oil – 2 tbsps.
- Salt and pepper to taste
- Chili powder – 2 tbsps.
- Celery – 2 stalks, chopped
- Garlic – 4 cloves, minced
- Beef stock – 1 ½ cups
- Sage – 1 tbsp. chopped

Directions:

Heat oil on Sauté. Add garlic and cook for 2 minutes. Add the meat and cook for 3 minutes more. Add the rest of the ingredients and cover. Cook on High for 25 minutes. Serve.

Pork and Brussels Sprouts

Cook time: 30 minutes |Serves: 4| Per serving: Calories 273; Carbs 6g; Fat 14g; Protein 15g

Ingredients:

- Pork shoulder – 2 pounds, cubed
- Beef stock – 1 ½ cups
- Brussels sprouts – 2 cups, trimmed and halved
- Oil – 2 tbsps.
- Parsley – 1 tbsp. chopped
- Sweet paprika – 1 tbsp.

Directions:

Heat oil on Sauté. Add meat and brown for 5 minutes. Add the rest of the ingredients and cover. Cook on High for 25 minutes. Serve.

Pork, Spinach and Dill
Cook time: 25 minutes| Serves: 4| Per serving: Calories 277; Carbs 7g; Fat 14g; Protein 17g

Ingredients:

- Pork stew meat – 1 ½ pounds, cubed
- Oil – 2 tbsps.
- Yellow onion – ½ cup, chopped
- Baby spinach – 2 cups
- Tomatoes – 2, cubed
- Beef stock – 1 ½ cups
- Dill – 1 tbsp. chopped

Directions:

Heat oil on Sauté. Add onion and meat and cook for 3 minutes. Add the rest of the ingredients and cover. Cook on High for 20 minutes. Serve.

Pork and Tomato Meatloaf
Cook time: 30 minutes| Serves: 4| Per serving: Calories 274; Carbs 7g; Fat 12g; Protein 16g

Ingredients:

- Coconut milk – ½ cup
- Almond meal – ½ cup
- Yellow onion – 1, minced
- Salt and pepper to taste
- Eggs – 2, whisked
- Pork meat – 2 pounds, ground
- Tomato sauce – ½ cup
- Chives – 1 tbsp. chopped
- Water – 1 cup

Directions:

Mix everything in a bowl, except the water. Shape a meatloaf and put it in a loaf pan. Add water to the IP and add the steamer basket. Place the pan on top of the steamer basket and cover. Cook on High for 30 minutes. Open, slice and serve.

Pork and Ginger Broccoli
Cook time: 30 minutes |Serves: 4 | Per serving: Calories 269; Carbs 5g; Fat 12g; Protein 16g

Ingredients:

- Pork stew meat – 1 ½ pounds, cubed
- Oil – 1 tbsp.
- Broccoli florets – 2 cups

- Ginger – 1 tbsp. grated
- Parmesan – ¾ cup, grated
- Salt and pepper to taste
- Tomato puree – ¼ cup
- Beef stock – 1 ½ cups
- Basil – 1 tbsp. chopped

Directions:

Heat oil on Sauté. Add meat and cook for 5 minutes. Add the rest of the ingredients, except the basil and parmesan. Cover and cook on High for 25 minutes. Open and sprinkle with parmesan and basil. Cover and leave aside for 5 minutes. Serve.

Nutmeg Pork
Cook time: 30 minutes| Serves: 4| Per serving: Calories 293; Carbs 6g; Fat 14g; Protein 18g

Ingredients:

- Pork meat – 1 ½ pounds, cubed
- Parsley – 2 tbsps. chopped
- Garlic – 2 cloves, minced
- Salt and pepper to taste
- Beef stock – 1 cup
- Nutmeg – 2 tsps. ground
- Sweet paprika – ½ tsp.
- Olive oil – 2 tbsps.

Directions:

Heat oil on Sauté. Add meat and garlic and cook for 5 minutes. Add the rest of the ingredients and cover. Cook on High for 25 minutes. Open and serve.

Tarragon Pork Mix
Cook time: 30 minutes |Serves: 4 | Per serving: Calories 263; Carbs 6g; Fat 12g; Protein 13g

Ingredients:

- Red onion – 1, chopped
- Tarragon – 1 tbsp. chopped
- Oregano – ½ tsp. dried
- Salt and pepper to taste
- Pork stew meat - 1 ½ pounds, cubed
- Olive oil – 1 tbsp.
- Tomato puree – 1 cup

Directions:

Heat oil on Sauté. Add meat and onion and cook for 5 minutes. Add the rest of the ingredients and cover. Cook on High for 25 minutes. Open and serve.

Pork Roast and Creamy Potatoes

Cook time: 40 minutes| Serves: 4| Per serving: Calories 263; Carbs 7g; Fat 14g ; Protein 19g

Ingredients:

- Pork shoulders – 2 pounds, sliced
- Sweet potatoes – 2, peeled and cubed
- Red onions – 2, chopped
- Coconut cream – 1 cup
- Chili powder - 1 cup
- Rosemary – ½ tsp. chopped
- Oil – 1 tbsp.
- Beef stock – 1 cup
- Parsley – 1 tbsp. chopped
- Salt and pepper to taste

Directions:

Heat oil on Sauté. Add the meat and onions and cook for 5 minutes. Add the rest of the ingredients, except for the coconut cream and parsley. Cover and cook on High for 25 minutes. Open and press Sauté. Add cream and cook 10 minutes more. Serve topped with parsley.

Chapter 10 Beef and Lamb Recipes

Spicy Lamb
Cook time: 30 minutes| Serves: 6| Per serving: Calories 350; Carbs 1.9 g; Fat 17.4g; Protein 43.3g

Ingredients:

- Boneless leg of lamb – 2 lbs. cut into bite-sized pieces
- Heavy cream – ¼ cup
- Ghee – 2 tbsps.
- Cherry tomatoes – 2 cups, chopped
- Vegetable stock – 3 cups
- Salt – 1 tsp.
- Coriander powder – 1 tbsp.
- Ginger powder – 1 tsp.
- Cumin powder – 1 tsp.
- Chili powder – 2 tbsps.
- Garam masala – 1 tsp.
- Garlic powder – ½ tsp.
- Fennel seeds – 2 tsps.
- Cumin seeds – 1 ½ tsp.
- Whole cloves – 3
- Cinnamon stick – 1
- Bay leaves – 3

Directions:

Place the chopped lamb pieces in a deep bowl and add heavy cream and garam masala. Mix and tightly wrap with aluminum foil. Refrigerate overnight. Grease the inner pot with ghee and press Sauté. Add fennel seeds, cumin seeds, cloves, cinnamon, cardamom, and bay leaves. Cook and stir for 1 to 2 minutes. Now add the remaining spices and stir well. Cook for another minute. Add the marinated meat. Pour in the stock and add cherry tomatoes. Stir well and close. Cook 25 minutes on High. Serve.

Herb Lamb
Cook time: 70 minutes |Serves: 4| Per serving: Calories 620; Carbs 3g; Fat 26g; Protein 58g

Ingredients:

- Sage – 1 ½ tsps.
- Marjoram – 1 ½ tsps.
- Thyme – ¼ tsp.
- Bay leaf -1
- Minced garlic – 2 tsps.
- Arrowroot – 2 tbsps.
- Chicken broth – 1 ½ cups
- Leg of lamb – 6 pounds

- Salt and pepper to taste

Directions:

Press Sauté and heat the oil in the instant pot. Combine the herbs with garlic and salt and pepper. Rub into meat. Place the lamb in the instant pot and sear on all sides, until browned. Pour the broth over and add the bay leaf. Close and cook for 60 minutes on Meat/Stew. Release the pressure quickly and transfer the lamb to a plate. Press Sauté and whisk in the arrowroot. Cook until the sauce is thickened. Drizzle over the lamb. Serve.

Lamb Curry with Zucchini
Cook time: 27 minutes |Serves: 4| Per serving: Calories 338; Carbs 7.5g; Fat 21g; Protein 23g

Ingredients:

- Ghee – 1 tbsp.
- Minced garlic – 2 tsps.
- Lamb – 1 pound, cut into cubes
- Grated ginger – 1 tsp.
- Diced tomatoes – 1 cup
- Coconut milk – ½ cup
- Zucchini – 1, diced
- Onion – 1, diced
- Carrot – 1, thinly sliced
- Curry powder – 1 ½ tbsps.

Directions:

In a bowl, place the coconut milk, lamb, ginger, and garlic. Cover and place in the fridge for 3 hours. Now add the lamb and the juices to the pot. Add the ghee, tomatoes, onion, and carrot. Close and cook for 20 minutes on High. Do a natural pressure release. Stir in the zucchini and cook on Sauté for 5 to 6 minutes. Serve.

Herb, Butter Lamb
Cook time: 45 minutes |Serves: 6 | Per serving: Calories 360; Carbs 0.7g; Fat 17.g; Protein 45.8g

Ingredients:

- Lamb shoulder – 2 lbs. cut into 3 pieces
- Beef broth – 4 cups
- Butter – 3 tbsps. softened
- Balsamic vinegar – ¼ cup
- Salt - 2 tsps.
- Black pepper – 1 tsp. freshly ground
- Rosemary springs – 2

Directions:

Rinse and pat dry the meat. Rub each piece with salt and pepper. Place at the bottom of the pot and add rosemary springs. Pour in the vinegar and broth. Cover and cook for 25 minutes on High.

When done, do a Quick release and open the lid. Meanwhile, preheat the oven to 450F. Take the meat out of the pot and brush with butter. Sprinkle with more salt and pepper and place on a baking sheet lined with some parchment paper. Roast for 15 to 20 minutes, turning once. Serve.

Cheesy Cajun Beef
Cook time: 17 minutes |Serves: 4| Per serving: Calories 400; Carbs 4g; Fat 16g; Protein 33g

Ingredients:

- Cajun seasoning – 1 tbsp.
- Mexican cheese blend – 12 ounces
- Beef broth – 1 cup
- Ground beef – 1 pound
- Tomato paste – 2 tbsps.
- Olive oil – 1 tbsp.

Directions:

Press Sauté and heat the oil. Add beef and cook until browned. Stir in the tomato paste and seasoning. Pour the broth over and close the lid. Cook on High for 7 minutes. Stir in the cheese and cook on High for 5 more minutes. Do a quick pressure release. Serve.

Pepper Short Ribs
Cook time: 30 minutes |Serves: 8| Per serving: Calories 416; Carbs 2.3g; Fat 21.2g; Protein 20.4g

Ingredients:

- Beef short ribs – 3 lbs.
- Medium red onion – 1, diced
- Garlic cloves – 4, crushed
- Heavy cream – 1 cup
- Beef stock – 2 cups
- Italian seasoning – 1 tsp.
- Black pepper – 2 tsps. ground
- Fresh thyme – 1 tsp. chopped
- Fresh sage – 1 tsp. chopped

Directions:

Add the onions and garlic in the pot and cook until onions are translucent. Add the ribs and pour in the broth. Sprinkle with sage, thyme, and Italian seasoning. Close the lid cook for 20 minutes on High. When done, do a quick pressure release and open the pot. Stir in heavy cream and press the Sauté. Simmer for 10 minutes. Transfer the meat to a serving plate and drizzle over the cream sauce.

Balsamic Fried Beef Roast
Cook time: 27 minutes| Serves: 8| Per serving: Calories 464; Carbs 2.5g; Fat 36.1g; Protein 30.2g

Ingredients:

- Beef chuck roast – 2 lbs. cut into bite-sized pieces
- Shallots – ½ cup, chopped
- Garlic – 3 cloves, crushed
- Balsamic vinegar – ¼ cup
- Heavy cream – ½ cup
- Olive oil – 1 tbsp.
- Salt – 1 tsp.
- Dried oregano – 1 tsp. ground
- Black pepper – 1 tsp. ground
- Dried parsley – 1 tbsp. finely chopped
- Dried marjoram – ¼ tsp. ground

Directions:

Rub the beef pieces with salt and pepper and set aside. Grease the instant pot with oil. Add shallots and garlic. Stir-fry for 2 to 3 minutes, stirring constantly. Add the meat and cook for 10 minutes. Pour in the balsamic vinegar and heavy cream. Sprinkle with the remaining spices and mix. Bring to a boil and cook until sauce thickens, about 10 to 15 minutes. Transfer to a serving dish. Drizzle with lemon juice and serve.

Creamy Beef Chili
Cook time: 20 minutes |Serves: 4| Per serving: Calories 390; Carbs 7.7g; Fat 22.3g; Protein 37.3g

Ingredients:

- Ground beef – 1 lb.
- Tomatoes – 2 cups, diced
- Medium red bell pepper – 1, chopped
- Small red onion – 1, chopped
- Garlic cloves – 3, minced
- Olive oil – 1 tbsp.
- Heavy cream – 1 cup
- Beef broth – ½ cup
- Chili powder – ½ tsp.
- Kosher salt – 1 tsp.
- Garlic powder – 1 tsp.
- Smoked paprika – ½ tsp.
- Dried rosemary – ½ tsp. ground

Directions:

Grease the instant pot with olive oil and press Sauté. Add ground beef, onion and bell pepper. Sprinkle with garlic powder and salt. Stir and cook for 5 minutes. Add broth and tomatoes. Cover and cook for 5 minutes on High. When done, do a quick pressure release and open the pot. Stir in the heavy cream and sprinkle with rosemary, paprika, salt and chili powder. Press Sauté and cook for 10 minutes. Transfer to a serving dish and enjoy.

Beef Stroganoff

Cook time: 20 minutes |Serves: 4| Per serving: Calories 260; Carbs 4.8g; Fat 14g; Protein 26.5g

Ingredients:

- Small onion – 1, diced
- Garlic – 2 cloves, crushed
- Bacon – 2 rashers, diced
- Beef Sirloin Steak – 1 lbs. (cut into ½ inch strips)
- Smoked paprika – 1 tsp.
- Tomato paste – 3 tbsps.
- Beef broth – 1 cup
- Mushrooms – ½ lbs. quartered
- Sour cream – ½ cup

Directions:

Except for the sour cream, place all ingredients in the pot and stir to combine. Cover and cook for 20 minutes on high. Naturally release the pressure, then stir in the sour cream. Serve warm.

High Protein Chili

Cook time: 20 minutes| Serves: 5| Per serving: Calories 233; Carbs 2.7g; Fat 10.2g; Protein 30.6g

Ingredients:

- Avocado oil – 2 tbsps.
- Garlic – 2 cloves, minced
- Beef – 1 pound, ground
- Crushed red pepper – ½ tsp.
- Chili powder – ½ tsp.
- Full-fat cheddar cheese – ½ cup, shredded
- Dried basil – ½ tsp.
- Salt – ½ tsp.
- Black pepper – ½ tsp.
- Crushed tomatoes – 1 (14-ounce) can
- Water – ½ cup

Directions:

Press Sauté and heat the oil in the Instant Pot. Add the garlic and sauté for 2 minutes. Add beef, water, tomatoes, black pepper, salt, basil, cheese, chili powder, and red pepper. Close and cook on High for 18 minutes. Do a natural release. Open and serve.

Classic Beef Stew

Cook time: 15 minutes |Serves: 5| Per serving: Calories 208; Carbs 4.7g; Fat 6.4g; Protein 31.2g

Ingredients:

- Avocado oil - 2 tbsps.
- Beef stew meat – 1 pound, cubed
- Garlic – 1 clove, minced
- Bone broth – 3 cups
- Wild mushrooms – 2 ounces
- Carrots – 2
- Bay leaf – 1
- Dried parsley – ½ tsp.
- Salt – ½ tsp.
- Ground black pepper – ½ tsp.

Directions:

Press Sauté, add oil and heat. Add beef and cook until browned. Stirring occasionally. Add garlic and cook for 1 minute more. Add the salt, black pepper, parsley, bay leaf, carrots, mushrooms, and bone broth. Close and cook 15 minutes on High. Do a natural release. Open, remove bay leaf and serve.

Sloppy Joes
Cook time: 15 minutes | Serves: 4| Per serving: Calories 249; Carbs 7.1g; Fat 8.2g; Protein 35.2g

Ingredients:

- Avocado oil – 2 tbsps.
- Garlic – 2 cloves, minced
- Small onion – ¼, sliced
- Beef – 1 pound, ground
- Celery – 1 stalk, chopped
- Tomato paste – 1 tsp.
- Worcestershire sauce – 1 tbsp.
- Chili powder – 1 tsp.
- Hot sauce – 1 tsp.
- Cayenne pepper – ½ tsp. ground
- Coriander – ½ tsp.
- Salt – ½ tsp.
- Ground black pepper - ½ tsp.
- Ketchup – ¼ cup
- Water – 1 cup

Directions:

Press Sauté and heat the oil in the Instant Pot. Then sauté the onion and garlic for 2 minutes. Add beef, ketchup, black pepper, salt, coriander, cayenne pepper, hot sauce, chili powder,

Worcestershire sauce, tomato paste, celery, and water. Close and cook 15 minutes on High. Do a natural release when done. Open and drain any excess liquid. Serve with buns.

Traditional Goulash
Cook time: 18 minutes| Serves: 5| Per serving: Calories 255; Carbs 7.5g; Fat 12.3g; Protein 29g

Ingredients:

- Coconut oil – 2 tbsps.
- Beef stew meat – 1 pound, cubed
- Avocado oil – 2 tbsps.
- Paprika – 2 tbsps.
- Minced garlic – 1 tsp.
- Ground cumin – ½ tsp.
- Coriander – ½ tsp.
- Onion – ½, chopped
- Ground cayenne pepper – ½ tsp.
- Salt – ½ tsp.
- Ground black pepper – ½ tsp.
- Diced tomatoes – 1 (14-ounce) can
- Water – 4 cups

Directions:

Melt the coconut oil on Sauté in the Instant Pot. Brown the beef and set aside. Clean the inner pot and add avocado oil. Sauté tomatoes, black pepper, salt, cayenne pepper, onion, coriander, cumin, garlic, and paprika for 3 minutes. Add water and stir. Close and cook 18 minutes on High. Do a natural release. Open and serve.

Bacon Cheeseburger
Cook time: 15 minutes| Serves: 2| Per serving: Calories 591; Carbs 4.1g; Fat 48.7g; Protein 33.4g

Ingredients:

- Bacon – 6 slices
- Butter – 2 tbsps. softened
- Beef – 1 pound, ground
- Cayenne pepper – ½ tsp. ground
- Crushed red pepper – ½ tsp.
- Fresh paprika – ½ tsp.
- Ground black pepper – ½ tsp.
- Salt – ½ tsp.
- Full-fat cheddar cheese – ½ cup, shredded
- Full-fat Monterey Jack cheese – ½ cup, shredded
- Water – ½ cup

- Burger buns for serving

Directions:

Place the bacon slices on aluminum foil. Fold the edges. Press Sauté and melt the butter in the Instant Pot. In a bowl, mix the beef, salt, black pepper, paprika, red pepper, and cayenne pepper. Make 2 thin patties. Add ½ water to the Instant Pot and add the patties. Add the trivet. Pace the bacon with the foil on top. Close and cook 15 minutes on High. Do a natural release. Open the lid and remove the food. Top the burgers with the bacon, Monterey jack, and cheddar. Serve.

Mushroom Burgers
Cook time: 20 minutes| Serves: 2| Per serving: Calories 510; Carbs 7.6g; Fat 33.5g; Protein 40.5g

Ingredients:

- Beef – 1 pound, ground
- Cayenne pepper – ½ tsp. ground
- Oregano – ½ tsp. dried
- Ground black pepper – ½ tsp.
- Salt – ½ tsp.
- Portobello mushroom caps – 4
- Lettuce – 1 cup, shredded
- Tomatoes – 1 cup, diced
- Dijon mustard – 1 tsp.
- Small onion – ¼, thinly sliced
- Full-fat cheddar cheese – ½ cup shredded

Directions:

Preheat the oven to 350F. Lightly grease a baking sheet and place the mushroom caps on it. Add ½ cup water to the Instant Pot. Insert the trivet. Mix beef, salt, black pepper, oregano, and cayenne pepper in a bowl. Make 2 patties and place the patties on top of the trivet. Close and cook 20 minutes on High. Meanwhile, Bake the mushroom caps in the oven, 5 minutes per side. Do a natural pressure release. Open the lid and remove the meat. Arrange the burgers with mushroom caps, patties, and remaining ingredients. Serve.

Classic Meatballs
Cook time: 16 minutes| Serves: 4| Per serving: Calories 343; Carbs 6.2g; Fat 22.7g; Protein 26.4g

Ingredients:

- Avocado oil – 2 tbsps.
- Coconut oil – 2 tbsps.
- Beef – 1 pound, ground
- Cayenne pepper – ½ tsp. ground
- Crushed red pepper – ½ tsp.

- Dried basil – ½ tsp.
- Salt – ½ tsp.
- Ground black pepper – ½ tsp.
- Roasted tomatoes – 2 (14-ounce cans)

Directions:

Heat the avocado oil in the Instant Pot on Sauté. In a bowl, mix together black pepper, salt, basil, red pepper, cayenne pepper, beef, and coconut oil. Make 1 ½-inch meatball with the mixture and place into the Instant Pot. Pour the tomato over the meatballs. Close cook 16 minutes on High. Do a natural release when done. Open and serve.

Steak and Cauliflower Rice
Cook time: 20 minutes| Serves: 4|Per serving: Calories 418; Carbs 8.5 g; Fat 22.1g; Protein 54.4g

Ingredients:

- Ribeye steak – 1
- Fresh paprika – ½ tsp.
- Ground turmeric – ½ tsp.
- Dried parsley – ½ tsp.
- Ground cumin – ½ tsp.
- Ground black pepper – ½ tsp.
- Salt – ½ tsp.
- Cauliflower head – 1, chopped
- Butter – 2 tbsps. softened
- Avocado – 1, mashed

Directions:

Add 1-cup of water into the Instant Pot and place in the trivet. In a bowl, mix salt, black pepper, cumin, parsley, turmeric, and paprika. Coat the steak with this mixture. Place the coated steak onto a greased dish. Place the cauliflower beside the steak. Place the dish on top of the trivet and cover loosely with foil. Close and cook for 20 minutes on High. Do a natural release. Remove the dish and add butter to the steak. Serve with avocado.

Steak Nachos
Cook time: 20 minutes| Serves: 6| Per serving: Calories 449; Carbs 10g; Fat 32.5g; Protein 30.5g

Ingredients:

- Butter – 2 tbsps. softened
- Fire roasted tomatoes – 1 (14-ounce) can, drained
- Beefsteak – 1 pound, sliced into thin strips
- Cauliflower – ½ pound, chopped
- Full-fat cheddar cheese – ½ cup, shredded

- Full-fat Monterey Jack cheese – ½ cup, shredded
- Chili powder – ½ tsp.
- Seeded jalapeno – ½, chopped
- Ground turmeric – ½ tsp.
- Ground cumin - ½ tsp.
- Curry powder – ½ tsp.
- Coconut oil – ¼ cup
- Avocado – 1, mashed
- Sour cream – ¼ cup, at room temperature

Directions:

Add 1 cup of water into the Instant Pot and place in the trivet. In a bowl, combine coconut oil, curry powder, cumin, turmeric, jalapeno, chili powder, Monterey Jack, cheddar, cauliflower, steak, tomatoes, and butter. Mix well. Place the mixture into a greased dish. Place the dish onto the trivet and cover with aluminum foil. Close and cook for 20 minutes on high. Do a natural release when done. Open the Instant Pot and cool. Add the sour cream and avocado on top. Serve.

Balsamic Beef
Cook time: 22 minutes| Serves: 4| Per serving: Calories 323; Carbs 3.1g; Fat 15.6g; Protein 39.5g

Ingredients:

- Chunk roast – 1 pound
- Garlic – 2 cloves, minced
- Bone broth – 1 cup
- Ground rosemary – ½ tsp.
- Ground black pepper – ½ tsp.
- Salt – ½ tsp.
- Ground thyme – ½ tsp.
- Crushed red pepper – ½ tsp.
- Balsamic vinegar – ¼ cup
- Butter – 4 tbsps. softened
- Broccoli – 1 cup, chopped
- Water – ½ cup

Directions:

Add the water and chuck roast to the pot. Close and cook for 20 minutes on High. Combine 2 tbsps. butter, vinegar, red pepper, thyme, salt, black pepper, rosemary, bone broth, and garlic in a bowl. Mix well. Do a natural release when cooked. Open the pot and remove the dish. Press Sauté and add 2 tbsps. butter and broccoli. Cook broccoli until cooked. Remove broccoli. Serve the beef with broccoli, and sauce.

Feta Lamb Meatballs in Tomato Sauce

Cook time: 12 minutes| Serves: 6 | Per serving: Calories 345; Carbs 8g; Fat 17g; Protein 35g

Ingredients:

- Egg - 1
- Olive oil – 2 tbsps.
- Minced garlic – 2 tsps.
- Bell pepper – 1, diced
- Onion – 1, chopped
- Crumbled feta cheese – ½ cup
- Chopped mint – 1 tbsp.
- Water – 1 tbsp.
- Oregano – 1 tsp.
- Ground lamb – 1 ½ pounds
- Almond flour – ½ cup
- Canned diced tomatoes – 24 ounces
- Chopped parsley – 2 tbsps.

Directions:

In a bowl, combine feta, parsley, mint, water, almond flour, half of the garlic, lamb and egg. Make meatballs from the mixture. Heat oil in the Instant Pot on Sauté. Add the pepper and onion and cook for 3 minutes. Add the remaining ingredients and stir to combine. Place the meatballs inside. Close and cook on High for 8 minutes. Serve.

Lamb with Tomatoes

Cook time: 26 minutes| Serves: 4| Per serving: Calories 338; Carbs 7.5g; Fat 21g; Protein 23g

Ingredients:

- Ghee – 1 tbsp.
- Minced garlic – 2 tsps.
- Lamb – 1 pound, cut into cubes
- Grated ginger – 1 tsp.
- Diced tomatoes – 1 cup
- Coconut milk – ½ cup
- Zucchini – 1, diced
- Onion – 1, diced
- Carrot – 1, thinly sliced
- Curry powder – 1 ½ tbsp.

Directions:

In a bowl, place the coconut milk, lamb, ginger, and garlic. Cover and place in the fridge for 3 hours. Now add the lamb and the juices to the Instant Pot. Add the ghee, tomatoes, onion, and carrot. Close and cook for 20 minutes on High. Do a natural pressure release. Stir in the zucchini and cook on Sauté for 5 to 6 minutes. Serve.

Beef Kale Patties
Cook time: 17 minutes| Serves: 4| Per serving: Calories 279; Carbs 1.9g; Fat 12.7g; Protein 36.9g

Ingredients:

- Ground beef – 1 lb.
- Fresh kale – 1 cup, finely chopped
- Egg – 1, beaten
- Almond flour – 1 tbsp.
- Olive oil – 1 tbsp.
- Dried rosemary – ½ tsp. ground
- Dried oregano – ½ tsp. ground
- Sea salt – 1 tsp.
- Black pepper – ½ tsp. ground
- Water – 1 cup

Directions:

In a bowl, combine flour, egg, kale, and beef. Mix with your hand until mixed thoroughly. Add flour and all spices. Mix and shape about 8 patties, about 2-inch in diameter. Grease a fitting springform pan with olive oil. Add the patties and set aside. Pour 1-cup water in the inner pot of the IP. Position a trivet on the bottom and place the pan on top. Cover and cook on High for 15 minutes. Do a quick release and open the pot. Cool and serve. Optionally, brown the patties on Sauté mode for 1 minute on both sides.

Picadillo
Cook time: 20 minutes| Serves: 6| Per serving: Calories 207; Carbs 4g; Fat 8.5g; Protein 25g

Ingredients:

- Olive oil – 1 tbsp.
- Lean ground beef – 1 ½ lbs.
- Salt – 1 tsp.
- Ground black pepper – 1 tsp.
- Onion – 3 ½ oz. diced
- Garlic – 2 cloves, minced
- Tomato – 6 oz. diced
- Coriander leaves – 2 tbsps. chopped
- Olives – 6, stuffed with pepper
- Capers – 6
- Cumin – 1 tsp.
- Red bell pepper – ½ diced

- Tomato sauce – 4 oz.
- Bay leaf – 1
- Water – 5 tbsps.

Directions:

Press Sauté and add 1 tbsp. oil in the Instant Pot. Add the beef and stir-fry until brown, about 3 to 4 minutes. Add coriander leaves, salt, pepper, chopped tomato, garlic, and onion. Stir-fry for 1 minute. Add the water, bay leaf, tomato sauce, bell pepper, cumin, capers, and olives. Stir to combine. Cover and cook on High for 15 minutes. Do a natural release and serve.

Beef Meatballs

Cook time: 15 minutes| Serves: 6| Per serving: Calories 383; Carbs 4.3g; Fat 16.1g; Protein 51.7g

Ingredients:

- Ground beef – 2 lbs.
- Fresh parsley – 1 cup, finely chopped
- Feta cheese – ¼ cup
- Medium-sized yellow bell pepper – 1, chopped
- Large eggs – 3
- Tomatoes – 1 cup, diced
- Small red onion – 1, chopped
- Garlic – 3 cloves
- Beef broth – 1 cup
- Olive oil – 1 tbsp.
- Sea salt – 1 tsp.
- Red pepper flakes – ½ tsp.
- Dried oregano – ½ tsp. ground
- Dried thyme – ¼ tsp. ground

Directions:

In a bowl, combine cheese, parsley, eggs, and beef. Add 2 tbsps. warm water and mix with your hands. Add all the spices and mix well. Shape balls with the mixture. Set aside. Grease the pot with olive oil. Press sauté and add garlic and onions. Stir-fry for 3 to 4 minutes or until the onions are translucent. Pour in the broth and stir in the tomatoes. Gently place the meatballs in the pot and close the lid. Press Manual and cook on High for 10 minutes. When cooked, do a quick release and open the pot. Transfer the meatballs to a serving bowl and drizzle with the remaining sauce from the pot.

Grilled Beef Tenderloin

Cook time: 25 minutes| Serves: 6| Per serving: Calories 562; Carbs 2.4g; Fat 28.3g; Protein 69.7g

Ingredients:

- Beef tenderloin – 2 lbs. cut into bite-sized pieces
- Garlic – 4 cloves, finely chopped

- Beef broth – 3 cups
- Olive oil – 1 tbsp.
- Butter – 1 tbsp.
- Onion powder – 1 tsp.
- Dried oregano – 1 tsp. ground
- Dried rosemary – 1 tsp. ground
- Sea salt – 1 tsp.
- Black pepper – 1 tsp. ground
- Chives and thyme for garnish

Directions:

Place the chopped meat in a bowl. Add all the spices. Rub well and set aside. Grease the insert with olive oil and press Sauté. Add garlic and chopped tenderloin, cook for 5 minutes. Add beef broth and cover the lid. Cook on High for 20 minutes. Do a quick release and open. Garnish with chives and thyme and serve.

Balsamic Beef Dish
Cook time: 50 minutes| Serves: 8| Per serving: Calories 393; Carbs 5g; Fat 15g; Protein 37g

Ingredients:

- Chuck roast – 3 pounds
- Garlic – 3 cloves, sliced
- Olive oil - 2 tbsps.
- Flavored vinegar – 1 tsp.
- Pepper – ½ tsp.
- Rosemary – ½ tsp.
- Thyme – ½ tsp.
- Balsamic vinegar – ¼ cup
- Beef broth – 1 cup

Directions:

Cut slits in the roast and stuff garlic slices. In a bowl, mix flavored vinegar, rosemary, pepper, thyme, and rub the mixture over the roast. Add oil and heat on Sauté. Add beef and brown both sides for 5 minutes each. Remove and set aside. Add broth, balsamic vinegar and deglaze the pot. Transfer the roast back and cover. Cook on High for 40 minutes. Do a quick release, shred the meat, and serve.

Beef Stew
Cook time: 25 minutes | Serves: 8| Per serving: Calories 268; Carbs 21g; Fat 8.1g; Protein 29g

Ingredients:

- Stew beef – 1 ½ pound, cut into bite-sized pieces
- Red pepper – 1, chopped

- Small potatoes – 4, cubed
- Zucchini – 2, sliced
- Mushrooms – 10 ounces, chopped
- Salt – ½ tsp.
- Ground black pepper – 1 tsp.
- Dried sage – ½ tsp.
- Dried thyme – 1 tsp.
- Olive oil – 1 tbsp.
- Red wine – 1 ½ cup
- Water – 1 ½ cup

Directions:

Press Sauté and add oil to the Instant Pot. Add beef and cook for 5 minutes. Add remaining ingredients and mix. Cover. Cook on High for 20 minutes. Open and serve.

Lamb Chops
Cook time: 8 minutes| Serves: 8| Per serving: Calories 160; Carbs 0g; Fat 7g; Protein 25g

Ingredients:

- Lamb chops – 3 pounds
- Shallot – 1, peeled and halved
- Salt – 1 tsp.
- Rosemary – 4 sprigs, leaves removed
- Tomato paste – 1 tbsp.
- Olive oil – 3 tbsps.
- Beef stock – 1 cup

Directions:

Season the lamb chops with rosemary and salt and marinate for 30 minutes. Press Sauté on the Instant Pot and add oil and lamb chops. Cook 1 minute per side and transfer to a plate. Add shallots and tomato paste into the pot and cook for 2 minutes. Add beef stock to deglaze the pot. Return lamb chops into the pot and cover. Cook 2 minutes on High. Do a natural release and serve.

Rosemary Lamb
Cook time: 50 minutes| Serves: 8| Per serving: Calories 318; Carbs 3g; Fat 17g; Protein 37g

Ingredients:

- Onions – 2, chopped
- Rosemary – 2 sprigs
- Beef broth – 3 cups, low-sodium
- Lamb shanks – 2, about 1 pound each
- Bay leaves – 2

211

- Olive oil – 3 tbsps.
- Salt to taste

Directions:

Add oil in the Instant Pot and press Sauté. Add meat and cook for 5 minutes or until browned. Set aside. Add onions. Cook for 3 to 4 minutes or until translucent. Add meat and pour in the broth. Add remaining ingredients and cover. Cook on High for 40 minutes. Then do a quick release. Open and remove the rosemary and bay leaves. Serve.

Smoked Beef Chili
Cook time: 22 minutes| Serves: 4| Per serving: Calories 368; Carbs 7.8g; Fat 17.4g; Protein 41.3g

Ingredients:

- Ground beef – 1 pound
- Cherry tomatoes – 2 cups, chopped
- Chili pepper -2, chopped
- Onions – 2, chopped
- Olive oil – 3 tbsps.
- Beef broth – 4 cups
- Button mushrooms – 1 cup, sliced
- Smoked paprika – 1 tsp.
- Dried basil – ¼ tsp.
- Chili powder – ¼ tsp.
- Salt – to taste

Directions:

Add oil in the Instant Pot and press Sauté. Add onion and cook for 2 minutes. Add chili pepper and cook for 2 minutes more. Add ground beef, sprinkle with salt, chili powder, smoked paprika, and dried basil. Cook for 5 minutes. Pour in the beef broth, add cherry tomatoes, and mushrooms. Cover and cook on High for 12 minutes. Do a quick release and open. Serve.

Lamb Stew with Bacon
Cook time: 28 minutes |Serves: 6| Per serving: Calories 453; Carbs 3.8g; Fat 23.6g; Protein 52.5g

Ingredients:

- Lamb leg – 2 pounds, chopped
- Olive oil – 2 tbsps.
- Garlic – 8 cloves
- Bacon – 6 slices
- Beef broth – 3 cups
- Onion – 1, chopped
- Black pepper – ¼ tsp.

- Dried rosemary – 1 tsp.
- Salt – ½ tsp.

Directions:

Press Sauté on the Instant Pot and add oil. Add onions and bacon and stir-fry for 3 minutes. Meanwhile, make 8 incisions into the meat and place a garlic clove in each. Rub with spices and transfer to the pot. Pour in broth and the remaining ingredients, cover. Cook 25 minutes on High. Open and serve.

Beef Ragout
Cook time: 20 minutes| Serves: 6 | Per serving: Calories 400; Carbs 4g; Fat 20.4g; Protein 46.9g

Ingredients:

- Beef stew meat – 2 pounds, cut into 1-inch pieces
- Cauliflower – 1 cup, chopped
- Olive oil – 5 Tbsps.
- Onions – 3, chopped
- Cherry tomatoes – 1 cup, chopped
- Celery rib – 1, sliced
- Balsamic vinegar – 2 Tbsps.
- Black pepper – ½ tsp.
- Smoked paprika – 1 Tbsp.
- Salt – 1 tsp.

Directions:

Add oil in the Instant Pot. Rub the meat with salt and arrange on the bottom of the Instant Pot. Add cherry tomatoes, cauliflower and season with salt, smoked paprika, and black pepper. Sprinkle with onions and pour in vinegar and beef broth. Top with celery rib and cover. Cook on High for 20 minutes. Do a natural release and open. Serve.

Greek Lamb Stew
Cook time: 30 minutes | Serves: 4| Per serving: Calories 242; Carbs 9g; Fat 12g; Protein 15g

Ingredients:

- Lamb shoulder – 2 pounds, cubed
- Garlic – 1 tbsp. minced
- Canned tomatoes – 14 ounces, chopped
- Yellow onion – 2, chopped
- Olive oil – 1 tbsp.
- Oregano – 1 tsp. dried
- Basil – 1 tsp. dried
- Salt and pepper to taste
- Parsley – ½ cup, chopped

Directions:

Heat oil on Sauté. Add onion, garlic and meat and cook for 5 minutes. Add the rest of the ingredients except the parsley. Cover and cook on High for 25 minutes. Serve garnished with parsley.

Lamb and Tomato Stew
Cook time: 40 minutes| Serves: 4| Per serving: Calories 230; Carbs 7g; Fat 14g; Protein 11g

Ingredients:

- Lamb shanks – 4
- Oil – 2 tbsps.
- Yellow onion – 1, minced
- Garlic – 2 cloves, minced
- Tomatoes – 1 ½ cups, cubed
- Oregano – 1 tbsp. chopped
- Salt and pepper to taste
- Beef stock – 2 cups

Directions:

Heat oil on Sauté. Add lamb and brown for 4 minutes. Add the rest of the ingredients and cover. Cook on Low for 35 minutes. Serve.

Lamb Ribs
Cook time: 25 minutes| Serves: 4| Per serving: Calories 263; Carbs 7g; Fat 12g; Protein 12g

Ingredients:

- Lamb ribs – 4
- Garlic – 4 cloves, minced
- Sage – 1 tbsp. chopped
- Veggie stock – 1 ½ cups
- Olive oil – 2 tbsps.
- Salt and pepper to taste
- Tomatoes – 2, cubed

Directions:

Heat oil on Sauté. Add lamb, garlic, sage, salt, and pepper and brown for 5 minutes. Add the stock and tomatoes and cover. Cook on High for 20 minutes. Serve.

Herbed Lamb Shanks
Cook time: 40 minutes |Serves: 4| Per serving: Calories 263; Carbs 7g; Fat 12g; Protein 10g

Ingredients:

- Lamb shanks – 4
- Oil – 2 tbsps.
- Salt and pepper to taste

- Marjoram – 1 tsp. dried
- Rosemary – 1 tbsp. dried
- Sage – 1 tsp. dried
- Thyme – 1 tsp. dried
- Garlic – 3 cloves, minced
- Veggie stock – 2 cups

Directions:

Heat oil on Sauté. Add meat and brown for 4 minutes. Add the rest of the ingredients and cover. Cook on High for 35 minutes. Serve.

Lamb Chops
Cook time: 40 minutes| Serves: 4| Per serving: Calories 238; Carbs 5g; Fat 10g; Protein 15g

Ingredients:

- Lamb chops – 4
- Veggie stock – 1 cup
- Dill – 1 tsp. dried
- Garlic powder – 1 tsp.
- Chili flakes – 1 tsp. crushed
- Chives – 1 tbsp. chopped
- Oil – 1 tbsp.
- Salt and pepper to taste

Directions:

Heat oil on Sauté. Add lamb chops and brown for 2 minutes on each side. Add the rest of the ingredient and cover. Cook on Low for 35 minutes. Serve.

Lamb Couscous
Cook time: 40 minutes |Serves: 4| Per serving: Calories 247; Carbs 6g; Fat 15g; Protein 15g

Ingredients:

- Lamb chops – 4
- Couscous – 1 ½ cups
- Veggie stock – 3 cups
- Almonds – 1 tbsp. toasted and chopped
- Salt and pepper to taste
- Oregano – 1 tbsp. chopped
- Basil – 1 tbsp. chopped
- Olive oil – 1 tbsp.
- Celery – 2 stalks, chopped

Directions:

Heat oil on Sauté. Add the meat and brown for 3 minutes on each side. Add the rest of the ingredients except the almonds. Cover and cook on Low for 40 minutes. Top with almonds and serve.

Beef and Lamb Mix

Cook time: 35 minutes| Serves: 4| Per serving: Calories 272; Carbs 7g; Fat 14g; Protein 17g

Ingredients:

- Beef stew meat – 1 pound, cubed
- Lamb shoulder – 1 pound, cubed
- Garlic – 4 cloves, minced
- Red bell peppers – 2, cut into strips
- Oil – 1 tbsp.
- Celery stalks – 2, chopped
- Carrots – 2, chopped
- Thyme – ¼ tsp. dried
- Salt and pepper to taste
- Oregano – 1 tbsp. chopped
- Beef stock – 1 ½ cups

Directions:

Heat oil on Sauté. Add the garlic and the meat and brown for 5 minutes. Add the rest of the ingredients and cover. Cook on High for 30 minutes. Open and serve.

Turmeric Lamb Shanks

Cook time: 30 minutes| Serves: 4| Per serving: Calories 232; Carbs 6g; Fat 9g; Protein 10g

Ingredients:

- Lamb shanks – 4
- Salt and pepper to taste
- Turmeric powder – 3 tsps.
- Cinnamon powder – 1 tsp.
- Ginger – 1 tbsp. grated
- Tomatoes – 2, chopped
- Garlic – 2 cloves, minced
- Veggie stock – 2 ½ cups
- Coriander – 1 tsp. chopped

Directions:

Heat oil on Sauté. Add lamb and garlic and brown for 5 minutes. Add the rest of the ingredients and cover. Cook on High for 25 minutes. Serve.

Chapter 11 Fish and Seafood Recipes

Lobster Bisque

Cook time: 7 minutes| Serves: 5 | Per serving: Calories 366; Carbs 8g; Fat 18g; Protein 30.1g

Ingredients:

- Lobster tails – 3 (meat removed, chopped and refrigerate, covered)
- Bone broth – 3 cups
- Canned diced tomatoes – 3 cups
- Old Bay seasoning – 2 tbsps.
- Garlic – 1 clove, crushed
- Thyme – 1 tsp. ground
- Hot sauce – 1 tsp.
- Fresh paprika – ½ tsp.
- Salt – ½ tsp.
- Freshly ground black pepper – ½ tsp.
- Heavy whipping cream – 2 cups

Directions:

Place the lobster shells in the Instant Pot. Then add the salt, pepper, paprika, hot sauce, thyme, garlic, Old Bay, tomatoes, and bone broth. Close the lid and press Manual. Cook 4 minutes on High. Do a quick release. Open, remove and discard the shells. Press Keep Warm and mix in whipping cream. Blend with a hand mixer until the mixture becomes smooth. Stir in lobster tails and cover. Press Manual and cook 3 minutes. Do a quick release and open. Serve.

Salmon with Vegetables

Cook time: 5 minutes| Serves: 4| Per serving: Calories 188; Carbs 7g; Fat 8.9g; Protein 17.7g

Ingredients:

- Fresh parsley – a ½ bunch, plus more for garnish
- Fresh tarragon – 2 to 3 sprigs
- Wild salmon fillets – 1 ½ pounds
- Olive oil – 1 tbsp.
- Sea salt and black pepper to taste
- Lemon – 1, sliced
- Medium zucchinis – 2, julienned
- Medium bell pepper – 2, seeded and julienned
- Medium carrots – 2, julienned

Directions:

Add tarragon, parsley and ¾ cup water into the Instant Pot. Place the steamer rack in the IP. Drizzle the salmon with olive oil and season with salt and pepper. Place the salmon on the rack (skin-side down). Top with lemon slices. Close the lid and press Steam. Steam for 3 minutes. Do a quick release and remove the rack with the salmon. Keep the salmon warm. Keep the liquid and discard the herbs. Add the carrots, peppers, and zucchinis to the IP and close the lid. Press Sauté and cook for 2 to 3 minutes. When the vegetables are tender, remove and season with salt and pepper. Serve.

Poached Salmon
Cook time: 3 minutes |Serves: 4| Per serving: Calories 472; Carbs 4.6g; Fat 25g; Protein 35.2g

Ingredients:

- Lemons- 2, sliced
- Salmon fillets – 4
- Butter- 8 tbsps. softened
- Dijon mustard – 2 tsps.
- Garlic – 1 clove, chopped
- Thyme – 1 tsp. ground
- Dried parsley – ½ tsp.
- Salt – ½ tsp.
- Freshly ground black pepper - ½ tsp.
- Water as needed

Directions:

Add 1-inch water into the Instant Pot. Place in the trivet. Place the salmon in an aluminum foil and top with lemon slices. Fold to make a pocket and place on the trivet. Close and cook on Steam for 3 minutes. Meanwhile, melt the butter in the microwave then add salt, pepper, parsley, thyme, garlic, and mustard. Mix well. Do a quick release when done, open and discard the lemon slices. Serve salmon with sauce.

Simple Crab Legs
Cook time: 3 minutes| Serves: 5| Per serving: Calories 152; Carbs 0g; Fat 23g; Protein 16g

Ingredients:

- Crab legs – 2 pounds, thawed
- Water – 1 cup for the pot

Directions:

Add 1-cup water into the IP and insert trivet. Place the crab legs on top of the trivet. Press Manual and cook on High for 3 minutes. Do a quick release. Serve crab legs with your favorite sauce.

Clambake
Cook time: 6 minutes| Serves: 4| Per serving: Calories 137; Carbs 3g; Fat 2g; Protein 26.1g

Ingredients:

- Avocado oil – 2 tbsps.
- Bone broth – 1 cup
- Clams – 20, scrubbed
- Lobster tails – 2, thawed if frozen
- Salt – ½ tsp.
- Freshly ground black pepper to taste

Directions:

Press Sauté and heat the oil. Add the bone broth in the Instant Pot. Add the lobster tails, clams, salt, and pepper to the Instant Pot. Working in batches if necessary. Close and cook for 6 minutes on High. Do a natural release and remove lobster tails and clams. Serve.

Crab Bisque
Cook time: 3 minutes| Serves: 4| Per serving: Calories 415; Carbs 8g; Fat 35.1g ; Protein 13g

Ingredients:

- Butter – 4 tbsps.
- Bone broth – 3 cups
- Full-fat cream cheese – 8 ounces, softened
- Celery – 2 stalks, chopped
- Crab meat – 1 pound, thawed
- Old Bay Seasoning – 1 tsp.
- Cayenne pepper – ½ tsp. ground
- Ground black pepper – ½ tsp.
- Salt – ½ tsp.
- Bell peppers – ¼ cup, chopped
- Heavy whipping cream – ¼ cup
- Small onion – ¼, sliced
- Crushed tomatoes – 1 (14-ounce) can

Directions:

Melt the butter on Sauté in the Instant Pot. Pour in the bone broth and add tomatoes, onion, whipping cream, bell pepper, salt, pepper, cayenne pepper, Old Bay, crab, celery, and cream cheese. Mix. Close the lid and cook on Manual for 3 minutes on Low. Do a quick release and open. Blend with a hand mixer. Serve.

Mahi Mahi
Cook time: 4 minutes |Serves: 4| Per serving: Calories 310; Carbs 1.3g; Fat 11.4g; Protein 47.4g

Ingredients:

- Butter – 3 tbsps. softened

- Grated ginger – 1 piece
- Lime – ½, juiced
- Lemon – ½, juiced
- Dried basil – ½ tsp.
- Black pepper – ½ tsp.
- Salt – ½ tsp.
- Minced garlic – ½ tsp.
- Mahi Mahi fillets – 4
- Water – ½ for the pot

Directions:

Add ½ cup water into the Instant Pot. Insert the trivet. Combine garlic, salt, black pepper, basil, lemon juice, lime juice, ginger, and butter in a bowl. Mix well. Coat the fish with this mixture. Grease a dish and place fillets on it. Place the dish on the trivet and cover loosely with aluminum foil. Close the lid. Press Manual and cook 4 minutes on Low. Once cooked do a natural pressure release. Open and serve.

Salmon with Broccoli
Cook time: 4 minutes |Serves: 4 | Per serving: Calories 119; Carbs 4g; Fat 5g; Protein 16g

Ingredients:

- Salmon fillets – 4
- Water – 1 ½ cups
- Broccoli fillets – 10 ounces
- Garlic powder – 1 tsp.
- Salt and pepper to taste

Directions:

Season the salmon with garlic powder, salt, and pepper. Pour the water into the Instant Pot. Place the salmon in the steaming basket and add the broccoli around the fish. Close the lid and cook on High for 4 minutes. Quick release and serve.

Creamy Haddock
Cook time: 10 minutes |Serves: 4| Per serving: Calories 195; Carbs 5.5g; Fat 18g; Protein 18g

Ingredients:

- Haddock fillets – 12 ounces
- Butter – 1 tbsp.
- Heavy cream – ½ cup
- Cheddar cheese – 5 ounces, grated
- Diced onions – 3 tbsps.
- Garlic salt – ¼ tsp.

- Pepper – ¼ tsp.

Directions:

On Sauté setting, melt the butter in the Instant Pot. Sauté the onions for 2 minutes. Season the fish with salt and pepper. Place in the Instant Pot and cook for 2 minutes per side. Pour the cream over and top with the cheese. Cook on Manual for 5 minutes. Do natural pressure release. Serve.

Cajun Shrimp with Asparagus
Cook time: 2 minutes| Serves: 4 | Per serving: Calories 330; Carbs 7g; Fat 7g; Protein 45g

Ingredients:

- Cajun seasoning – 1 tbsp.
- Shrimp – 1 pound, peeled and deveined
- Asparagus – 1 bunch, trimmed
- Olive oil – 1 tsp.
- Salt and pepper to taste

Directions:

Pour the water into the IP. Arrange the asparagus in a single layer on the IP's rack. Top with the shrimp. Drizzle with oil and season with Cajun, salt and pepper. Close the lid and cook on Steam for 2 minutes. Do a quick pressure release. Serve.

Almond Tuna
Cook time: 3 minutes |Serves: 4| Per serving: Calories 150; Carbs 4g; Fat 5g; Protein 10g

Ingredients:

- Tuna – 2 cans, drained
- Shaved almond – 1 cup
- Butter – 2 tbsps.
- Garlic powder – 1 tsp.
- Grated Cheddar Cheese – 1 cup

Directions:

Melt the butter in the IP on Sauté. Add cheddar, almonds, and tuna. Cook on Sauté for 3 minutes. Serve with cauliflower rice.

Dijon Halibut
Cook time: 3 minutes| Serves: 4| Per serving: Calories 190; Carbs 0.1g; Fat 2g; Protein 40g

Ingredients:

- Dijon mustard – 1 ½ tbsps.
- Halibut fillets – 4
- Water – 1 ½ cups

Directions:

Pour the water into the IP. Brush the halibut with Dijon and place in the steaming basket. Lower the basket and close the lid. Set the IP to Manual. Cook on High for 3 minutes. Do a quick pressure release. Serve.

Trout Casserole

Cook time: 20 minutes |Serves: 4| Per serving: Calories 361; Carbs 3.7g; Fat 23.8g; Protein 31.6g

Ingredients:

- Trout fillets – 1 lb. without skin
- Cherry tomatoes – 1 cup, halved
- Zucchini – ½, sliced
- Cauliflower – 1 cup, chopped into florets
- Small onion – 1, sliced
- Olive oil – 4 tbsps.
- Sea salt – 2 tsps.
- Dried rosemary -1 tsp.
- Dried thyme – 1 tsp.
- Garlic powder – ½ tsp.

Directions:

Line a small square pan with some parchment paper and sprinkle with 2 tbsps. of olive oil. Arrange onions at the bottom of the pan and make a layer with zucchini. Top with onions and cherry tomatoes. Drizzle with oil and sprinkle with salt. Top with trout fillets and season with garlic powder, thyme, rosemary, and more salt. Tightly wrap with aluminum foil and set aside. Pour in 2 cups of water in the IP. Set the trivet at the bottom of the inner pot and place the pan on top. Cover and cook for 20 minutes on High. When cooked, do a quick pressure release and open the lid. Carefully open the pan and chill for a while. Remove the aluminum foil and serve.

Sockeye Salmon

Cook time: 4 minutes |Serves: 4| Per serving: Calories 195; Carbs 1g; Fat 10g; Protein 24g

Ingredients:

- Dijon mustard – 1 tsp.
- Garlic powder – 1 tsp.
- Onion powder – ¼ tsp.
- Garlic – 1 clove, minced
- Salmon fillets – 4 (2 to 3 ounce each)
- Lemon juice – 1 tbsp.
- Salt and pepper to taste
- Water – 1 ½ cups

Directions:

Combine the lemon juice, minced garlic, garlic powder, onion powder, and mustard in a small bowl. Brush the mixture over the salmon. Pour the water into the IP and lower the rack. Arrange the salmon on the rack and close the lid. Cook on High for 4 minutes. Do a quick pressure release. Serve.

Lemon-Garlic Prawns
Cook time: 3 minutes| Serves: 4| Per serving: Calories 160; Carbs 2g; Fat 2g; Protein 18g

Ingredients:

- Minced garlic – 2 tbsps.
- Olive oil – 2 tbsps.
- Lemon zest – 2 tbsps.
- Lemon juice – 2 tbsps.
- Ghee – 1 tbsp.
- Prawns – 1 pound
- Fish stock – 2/3 cup
- Salt and pepper to taste

Directions:

Melt the ghee along with oil in the Instant Pot on Sauté. Add the remaining ingredients and stir to combine. Close the lid and cook on High for 3 minutes. Drain the prawns. Serve.

Shrimp Zoodles
Cook time: 5 minutes| Serves: 4 | Per serving: Calories 300; Carbs 3g; Fat 20g; Protein 30g

Ingredients:

- Zoodles – 4 cups
- Ghee – 2 tbsp.
- Veggie stock – 1 cup
- Olive oil – 2 tbsps.
- Minced garlic – 3 tsps.
- Shrimp – 1 pound, peeled and deveined
- Juice of ½ lemon
- Chopped basil – 1 tbsp.
- Paprika – ½ tsp.

Directions:

Melt the ghee along with olive oil in the Instant Pot on Sauté. Add garlic and cook for 1 minute. Add shrimp and lemon juice. Cook for 1 minute. Add stock, paprika, and zoodles. Cook on High for 3 minutes. Serve topped with basil. Enjoy.

Caramelized Tilapia
Cook time: 10 minutes| Serves: 4| Per serving: Calories 150; Carbs 3g ; Fat 4g ; Protein 21g

Ingredients:

- Tilapia fillets – 1 pound
- Red chili – 1, minced
- Minced garlic – 3 tsps.
- Granulated sweetener – ¼ tsp.
- Spring onion – 1, minced
- Coconut water – ¾ cup
- Water – 1/3 cup
- Fish sauce – 3 tbsps.
- Salt and pepper to taste

Directions:

Combine the garlic, fish sauce, salt and pepper in a bowl. Place the tilapia inside and mix to coat. Cover and let sit in the fridge for 30 minutes. Meanwhile, combine the water and sweetener in the Instant Pot. Cook on Sauté until caramelized. Add fish and pour the coconut water over. Close and cook on High for 10 minutes. Do a quick pressure release. Top the fish with spring onion and chili. Serve.

Steamed Tuna Steaks
Cook time: 4 minutes| Serves: 4| Per serving: Calories 190; Carbs 1g ; Fat 3g; Protein 39.5g

Ingredients:

- Tuna steaks – 4 (4-ounce each)
- Capers – 2 tbsps.
- Lemon pepper seasoning – 1 tbsp.
- Lemon juice – 2 tbsps.
- Water – 1 cup

Directions:

Pour water in the Instant Pot. Then insert a steamer basket. Season tuna with lemon pepper seasoning and sprinkle with capers. Place into the steamer basket and drizzle with lemon juice. Cover the pot and cook on Steam for 4 minutes on High. Do a natural release and open. Serve.

Cod with Tomatoes
Cook time: 15 minutes | Serves: 6| Per serving: Calories 333; Carbs 18.9g; Fat 9.3g; Protein 43.9g

Ingredients:

- Cod – 6 pieces
- Diced tomatoes – 14 ounces
- Salt – ½ tsp.
- Ground black pepper to taste
- Oregano – 1 tsp.

- Lemon juice – 1 tbsp.
- Olive oil – 3 tbsps.

Directions:

Add everything in the Instant Pot, except the fish. Cook on Sauté for 8 to 10 minutes. Press Cancel and add cod. Coat the fish well. Cover the pot. Cook on High for 5 minutes. Do a natural release and open. Serve.

Shrimp with Tomatoes and Feta
Cook time: 2 minutes | Serves: 6 | Per serving: Calories 211; Carbs 6g; Fat 11g; Protein 19g

Ingredients:

- Frozen shrimp - 1 pound, shelled
- Sliced black olives – ½ cup
- Chopped white onion – 1 ½ cups
- Tomatoes – 14.5 ounces
- Minced garlic – 1 tbsp.
- Salt – 1 tsp.
- Red pepper flakes – ½ tsp.
- Dried oregano – 1 tsp.
- Olive oil – 2 tbsps.
- Feta cheese – 1 cup, crumbled
- Chopped parsley – ¼ cup

Directions:

Heat the oil on Sauté in the Instant Pot. Add garlic and red pepper. Cook for 1 minute. Add onion and tomatoes and season with salt and oregano. Add shrimps, mix, and cover. Cook on Low for 1 minute. Do a natural release and open. Stir shrimps. Sprinkle with olives, cheese, and parsley. Serve.

Mussels
Cook time: 11 minutes| Serves: 4| Per serving: Calories 189; Carbs 8g; Fat 8g; Protein 14g

Ingredients:

- Mussels – 2 pounds, picked, cleaned and rinsed
- Shallots – 2 medium, peeled and chopped
- Minced garlic – 2 tsps.
- Olive oil – 2 tbsps.
- White wine – ½ cup
- Chicken broth – ½ cup
- Chopped parsley – 2 tbsps. for serving

Directions:

Press Sauté and add oil in the Instant Pot. Add onion and stir-fry for 5 minutes. Then add garlic and cook for one minute more. Stir in wine and broth. Add mussels and cover the pot. Cook 5 minutes on High. Do a natural release and open. Garnish with parsley and serve.

Clam Chowder II
Cook time: 12 minutes| Serves: 6| Per serving: Calories 252; Carbs 25g; Fat 11g; Protein 12g

Ingredients:

- Bacon – 4 strips, chopped
- Chopped clams – 6.5 ounces
- Large carrots – 3, chopped
- Diced turnip – ¾ cup
- Radishes – 10 medium, trimmed, peeled and quartered
- Red bell pepper – 1, chopped
- Fresh leeks – ¾ cup, diced
- Celery – 3 stalks, diced
- Diced tomatoes – 28 ounces
- Minced garlic – 2 tsps.
- Sea salt – 1 tsp.
- Dried oregano – 1 tbsp.
- Ground thyme – 1 ½ tsps.
- Sambal oiled paste – 1 tsp. (or any chili paste)
- Clam juice – 16 ounces
- Tomato paste – 1 ½ tbsps.
- Bay leaves – 2
- Chopped parsley – 3 tbsps.

Directions:

Cook the bacon on Sauté in the Instant Pot for 2 minutes or until beginning to brown. Remove the bacon and leave 2 tbsps. bacon grease in the pot. Add carrots, bell pepper, and leeks and cook on sauté for 5 minutes. Add the remaining ingredients except for clams and parsley and stir to mix. Cover and cook for 5 minutes on High. Then do a natural release. Add clams and parsley. Stir and serve with crumbled bacon.

Tilapia with Veggies and Olives
Cook time: 20 minutes |Serves: 4| Per serving: Calories 189; Carbs 9.3g; Fat 5.3g; Protein 28.1g

Ingredients:

- Zucchini -1 ½ cups, diced
- Grape tomatoes – 1 ½ cups, sliced
- Onion – 1 cup, sliced
- Kalamata olives – ½ cup, chopped

- Olive oil – ½ tbsp.
- Lemon juice – 2 tbsps.
- Fresh thyme – 1 tbsp. chopped
- Fresh oregano – 1 tbsp. chopped
- Salt – ½ tbsp. divided
- Pepper – ½ tsp. divided
- Tilapia fillets – 4
- Water – 2 cups

Directions:

In a bowl, combine tomatoes, zucchini, onions, olives, olive oil, lemon juice, thyme, oregano, 1 tsp. salt and ¼ tsp. pepper. Mix well. Spread oil over the work area and put the fish fillets on top of the foil. Season with remaining salt and pepper. Top the fillets with the vegetable mixture. Wrap the foil. Pour water into the Instant Pot, then add the steamer basket. Place the tilapia and veggie packet on top of the steamer. Seal the pot and cook on Low for 20 minutes. Serve.

Salmon with Green Beans
Cook time: 5 minutes| Serves: 4| Per serving: Calories 303; Carbs 9.3g Fat 14.2g; Protein 36.9g

Ingredients:

- Lemon juice – ¼ cup
- Water – ¾ cup
- Salmon fillets – 4
- Fresh dill – 1 tbsp.
- Salt and pepper to taste
- Lemon slices – 4
- Green beans – 4 cups
- Olive oil – 1 tbsp.

Directions:

Pour the lemon juice and water into the Instant Pot. Add a steamer basket. Place the salmon fillets and green beans on top of the steamer. Sprinkle the dill on top of the salmon and season the salmon and green beans with salt and pepper. Top the fish and green beans with lemon slices. Cover the pot. Then cook on High for 5 minutes. Do a quick release and serve.

Seafood Stew
Cook time: 25 minutes |Serves: 4| Per serving: Calories 221; Carbs 7g ; Fat 8g; Protein 28g

Ingredients:

- Olive oil – 1 tbsp.
- Onion – 1, chopped
- Garlic – ½ tsp. minced
- Red pepper flakes – 1/8 tsp. crushed

- Lemon zest – ½ tsp. grated
- Tomatoes – ¼ lb. diced
- White wine – 1/3 cup
- Clam juice – ½ cup
- Salt – ½ tsp.
- Tomato paste – 1 tbsp.
- Scallops – ½ lb.
- Red snapper fillets – ½ lb. cubed
- Shrimp – ½ lb. peeled and deveined
- Parsley – ¼ cup

Directions:

Press Sauté and add the oil in the Instant Pot. Add onion and sauté for 5 minutes. Add garlic and cook for 1 minute. Add pepper flakes, lemon zest, and tomatoes. Cook for 2 minutes. Add the clam juice, wine, salt, and tomato paste. Simmer for 10 minutes. Add the seafood. Cover the pot. Then cook on High for 8 minutes. Open and stir in parsley. Serve.

Sea Bass with Vegetables
Cook time: 17 minutes| Serves: 4 | Per serving: Calories 235; Carbs 7.5g; Fat 9.3g; Protein 25.3g

Ingredients:

- Olive oil – 4 tsps. divided
- Sea bass fillets – 4
- Onion – 1, diced
- White wine – ½ cup
- Black olives – ½ cup, pitted and chopped
- Capers – 2 tbsps.
- Canned diced tomatoes with juice – 1 cup
- Red pepper – ¼ tsp. crushed
- Baby spinach – 2 cups
- Salt and pepper to taste

Directions:

Press Sauté and add half the oil in the Instant Pot. Add the fish and cook for 5 minutes and remove to a platter. Add the remaining oil and add onion in the Instant Pot. Sauté for 2 minutes. Add the wine and simmer for 2 minutes. Add the capers, olives, tomatoes, and crushed red pepper. Cook for 3 minutes. Stir in the spinach and cook for 5 minutes. Pour the sauce over the fish and serve.

Salmon and Citrus Sauce
Cook time: 12 minutes| Serves: 4 | Per serving: Calories 200; Carbs 6g Fat 12g; Protein 11g

Ingredients:

- Salmon fillets – 4, boneless
- Spring onions – 4, chopped
- Oil – 1 tbsp.
- Ginger -1 tbsp. grated
- Salt and pepper to taste
- Juice of 1 orange
- Cilantro – 1 tbsp. chopped

Directions:

Heat oil on Sauté. Add ginger and spring onions and cook for 2 minutes. Add the salmon fillets and rest of the ingredients. Cover and cook on High for 10 minutes. Serve.

Fish Bowls

Cook time: 10 minutes| Serves: 4| Per serving: Calories 132; Carbs 5 g; Fat 9g; Protein 11g

Ingredients:

- White fish fillets – 1 pound, boneless, skinless and cubed
- Black olives – 1 cup, pitted and chopped
- Cherry tomatoes – 1 pound, halved
- Garlic – 2 cloves, minced
- Oil - 1 tbsp.
- Salt and pepper to taste
- Oregano – 1 tbsp. chopped
- Parsley - 1 tbsp. chopped

Directions:

Heat oil on Sauté. Add fish and sear for 1 minute on each side. Add the rest of the ingredients and cover. Cook on High for 8 minutes. Open and serve.

Trout Curry

Cook time: 12 minutes| Serves: 4| Per serving: Calories 200; Carbs 6g; Fat 12g; Protein 11g

Ingredients:

- Trout fillets – 1 pound, boneless, skinless and cubed
- Tomato – 1, chopped
- Coconut milk – 1 ½ cup
- Red onions – 2, chopped
- Garlic – 2 cloves, sliced
- Coriander -1 tbsp. ground
- Turmeric powder – ½ tsp.
- Ginger – 1 tbsp. grated
- Salt and black pepper to taste
- Lemon juice – 2 tbsps.

Directions:

Heat oil on Sauté. Add onions, garlic, and ginger and cook for 2 minutes. Add the fish and rest of the ingredients. Cover and cook on High for 10 minutes. Serve.

Trout and Capers Sauce

Cook time: 12 minutes| Serves: 4| Per serving: Calories 200; Carbs 6g; Fat 12g; Protein 9g

Ingredients:

- Trout fillets – 4, boneless
- Cherry tomatoes – 1 cup, halved
- Garlic – 2 cloves, minced
- Capers – 2 tbsps. drained and chopped
- Salt and pepper to taste
- Parsley – 1 tbsp. chopped
- Oil – 1 tbsp.
- Veggie stock - ½ cup

Directions:

Heat oil on Sauté. Add garlic, capers, salt and pepper and cook for 2 minutes. Add the rest of the ingredients and cover. Cook on High for 10 minutes. Serve.

Paprika Salmon

Cook time: 10 minutes| Serves: 4| Per serving: Calories 211; Carbs 7g ; Fat 13g ; Protein 11g

Ingredients:

- Salmon fillets – 4, boneless
- Parsley – 1 tbsp. chopped
- Fish stock – ½ cup
- Oregano – ½ tsp. dried
- Sweet paprika – 2 tsps.
- Garlic – 2 cloves, chopped
- Salt and pepper to taste

Directions:

Add everything in the pot and cover. Cook on High for 10 minutes. Serve.

Lemon Cod and Scallions

Cook time: 12 minutes| Serves: 4 | Per serving: Calories 200; Carbs 6g ; Fat 12g; Protein 8g

Ingredients:

- Cod fillets – 4, boneless
- Zest of 1 lemon, grated
- Juice of ½ lemon
- Scallions – 4, chopped
- White wine vinegar – 1 tsp.
- Chicken stock – 1 cup

- Parsley – ¼ cup, chopped
- Salt and pepper to taste

Directions:

Combine everything in the Pot. Cover and cook on High for 12 minutes. Serve.

Shrimp and Parsley Mix
Cook time: 4 minutes |Serves: 4| Per serving: Calories 232; Carbs 7g; Fat 7g; Protein 9g

Ingredients:

- Shrimp – 1 ½ pounds, peeled and deveined
- Salt and pepper to taste
- Parsley – 1 tbsp. chopped
- Tomato sauce – 2 tbsps.
- Sweet paprika – ½ tbsp. chopped
- Garlic – 2 cloves, minced

Directions:

Add everything in the pot and cover. Cook on High for 4 minutes. Serve.

Cod and Cauliflower Rice
Cook time: 12 minutes| Serves: 4| Per serving: Calories 232; Carbs 6g; Fat 9g; Protein 8g

Ingredients:

- Cod filets – 4, boneless
- Salt and pepper to taste
- Cauliflower – 1 cup, riced
- Chicken stock – 1 cup
- Tomato puree – 2 tbsps.
- Cilantro - 1 tbsp. chopped

Directions:

Combine everything in the pot and cover. Cook on High for 12 minutes. Serve.

Salmon and Baby Carrots
Cook time: 12 minutes| Serves: 4 | Per serving: Calories 200; Carbs 6g; Fat 13g; Protein 11g

Ingredients:

- Salmon fillets – 4, boneless
- Veggie stock – ½ cup
- Garlic – 2 cloves, minced
- Red onion – 1, minced
- Oil – 1 tbsp.
- Baby carrots – 2 cups, trimmed
- Salt and pepper to taste

- Rosemary – 1 tbsp. chopped

Directions:

Heat oil on Sauté. Add onion and garlic and cook for 2 minutes. Add the rest of the ingredients and cover. Cook on High for 10 minutes. Serve.

Spicy Trout
Cook time: 12 minutes | Serves: 4| Per serving: Calories 200; Carbs 6g; Fat 12g; Protein 9g

Ingredients:

- Trout fillets – 4 boneless
- Chili pepper – 2 tbsps. minced
- Juice of 1 lime
- Veggie stock – ½ cup
- Salt and pepper to taste
- Cayenne pepper to taste
- Chives – 1 tbsp. chopped, for garnish

Directions:

Add everything in the pot, except the chives. Cover and cook on High for 10 minutes. Sprinkle with chives and serve.

Thyme Cod and Tomatoes
Cook time: 15 minutes| Serves: 4| Per serving: Calories 200; Carbs 5g; Fat 12g Protein 6g

Ingredients:

- Cod fillets – 4, boneless
- Red onion – 1, chopped
- Tomatoes – 3, chopped
- Thyme – 2 tbsps. chopped
- Oil – 3 tbsps.
- Salt and pepper to taste
- Tomato puree – 2 tbsps.

Directions:

Heat oil on Sauté. Add onion, salt and pepper and cook for 2 minutes. Add cod and rest of the ingredients and cover. Cook on High for 10 minutes. Serve.

Salmon Cakes and Sauce
Cook time: 15 minutes | Serves: 4| Per serving: Calories 192; Carbs 8g; Fat 9g; Protein 7g

Ingredients:

- Oil – 1 tsp.
- Egg – 1, whisked
- Salmon meat – 1 pound, minced

- Lemon zest – 2 tbsps. grated
- Lemon juice – 1 tsp.
- Salt and pepper to taste
- Tomato sauce – 1 cup

Directions:

In a bowl, combine everything except the tomato sauce and oil. Mix and make cakes out of this mix. Heat oil on Sauté and cook the cakes 2 minutes per side. Add tomato sauce and cover. Cook on High for 8 minutes. Serve.

Sea Bass and Artichokes
Cook time: 15 minutes |Serves: 4| Per serving: Calories 210; Carbs 6g; Fat 9g; Protein 7g

Ingredients:

- Sea bass – 1 pound, skinless, boneless, and cubed
- Yellow onion – 1, chopped
- Canned artichokes – 12 ounces, chopped
- Coconut cream – 1 ½ cups
- Salt and pepper to taste
- Cilantro – 1 tbsp. chopped

Directions:

Combine everything in the pot except the cilantro. Cover and cook on High for 15 minutes. Sprinkle with cilantro and serve.

Cod and Strawberries Sauce
Cook time: 15 minutes| Serves: 4| Per serving: Calories 200; Carbs 5g; Fat 10g; Protein 9g

Ingredients:

- Cod fillets – 6, boneless
- Olive oil – 2 tbsps.
- Shallots – 2, minced
- Garlic – 2 cloves, minced
- Parsley – 2 tbsps. chopped
- Strawberries – 1 cup, chopped
- Lemon juice – 2 tbsps.
- Salt and pepper to taste
- Balsamic vinegar – 2 tbsps.

Directions:

Heat oil on Sauté. Add the shallots and garlic and cook for 2 minutes. Add the vinegar, berries, salt and pepper and cook for 2 minutes more. Add the fish and cover and cook on High for 10 minutes. Open, sprinkle with parsley and drizzle with lemon juice. Serve.

Chapter 12 Desserts

Cheesecake
Cook time: 25 minutes |Serves: 6| Per serving: Calories 337; Carbs 5.6 g; Fat 31.8g; Protein 8.2g

Ingredients:

- Full-fat cream cheese – 16 ounces, softened
- Swerve, confectioners – ½ cup or to taste
- Vanilla extract – 4 tsps.
- Eggs – 2
- Water – 2 cups for the pot

Toppings

- Swerve, confectioners – ½ cup or to taste
- Heavy whipping cream – 2 tbsps.
- Coconut - 1 tbsp. shredded and lightly toasted
- Slivered almonds – 1 tbsp. lightly toasted
- Sugar free chocolate chips – 2 tbsps.

Directions:

In a bowl, combine eggs, vanilla, swerve, and cream cheese. Mix thoroughly. Place mixture in a greased springform pan. Add 2 cups water to the Instant Pot and place the trivet. Place the springform pan on top and cover with foil. Close the lid and cook 25 minutes on High. Do a natural release. Remove the pan, leave the foil on. Cool for 30 minutes and chill in the refrigerator for 45 minutes. Remove from the refrigerator and discard the foil. Whip the whipping cream and swerve with a hand mixer until thickened. Spread evenly on top of the cake. Sprinkle with chocolate chips, slivered almonds, and toasted coconut. Serve.

Mint Chocolate Chip Ice Cream
Cook time: 5 minutes |Serves: 6| Per serving: Calories 351; Carbs 6.8 g; Fat 31.4g; Protein 8.8g

Ingredients:

- Egg whites – 6
- Vanilla extract – 4 tsps.
- Mint extract – 1 tsp.
- Swerve, confectioners – ½ cup
- Slivered almonds – ¼ cup
- Shredded coconut – ¼ cup
- Heavy whipping cream – 2 and 2/3 cups
- Sugar-free chocolate chips – ½ cup

Directions:

Beat egg whites until stiff peaks form. Gently fold in whipping cream, coconut, almond, swerve, mint, and vanilla. Mix thoroughly. Cover and freeze for 2 to 4 hours. Before serving, press Sauté on the Instant Pot. Add the chocolate chips and continue to stir until melts. Do not burn. Press Cancel and remove melted chocolate. Scoop ice cream on serving bowls. Drizzle with melted chocolate and serve.

Coconut Crusted Chocolate Bark
Cook time: 20 minutes| Serves: 20| Per serving: Calories 258; Carbs 7g; Fat 22g; Protein 2g

Ingredients:

- Raw dark chocolate – 16 ounces
- Raw coconut butter – 3 tbsps.
- Coconut oil - 2 tbsps.
- Macadamia nuts – 2 cups, chopped
- Almond butter – 1 tbsp. smooth
- Salt – ½ tsp.
- Swerve, confectioners – 1/3 cup or to taste
- Water – 1 cup for the pot

Directions:

In a bowl, mix together the swerve, salt, almond butter, macadamia nuts, coconut oil, coconut butter, and chocolate. Mix well. Add 1 cup water to the Instant Pot and place in the trivet. Transfer the batter to a greased dish and place the dish onto the trivet. Cover the bowl with foil. Close the lid and press Manual. Cook on High for 20 minutes. Do a natural release. Open and remove the dish. Cool in the refrigerator until set. Break into pieces and serve.

Ice Cream Bites
Cook time: 5 minutes| Serves: 7| Per serving: Calories 170; Carbs 5.7g; Fat 16g; Protein 2.1g

Ingredients:

- Sugar-free chocolate chips – 6 tbsps.
- Full-fat cream cheese – 4 ounces, softened
- Full-fat coconut milk – ½ cup
- Heavy whipping cream – 1 cup
- Swerve, confectioners – ½ cup
- Vanilla extract – ½ tsp.

Directions:

Add 1 cup of water into the Instant Pot and insert the trivet. In a bowl, combine vanilla, swerve, whipping cream, coconut milk, cream cheese, and chocolate chips. Mix well and drop onto greased egg bites molds. Place molds on top of the trivet and cover loosely with foil. Close the lid and press Manual. Cook 5 minutes on High. Do a natural pressure release. Remove the molds and freeze for at least 1 hour. Serve.

Cupcakes

Cook time: 30 minutes| Serves: 7| Per serving: Calories 219; Carbs 2.8g; Fat 22.3g; Protein 3.3g

Ingredients:

- Almond flour – 2 cups
- Butter – 2 tbsps. softened
- Eggs – 2
- Unsweetened almond milk – ½ cup
- Swerve – ½ cup
- Nutmeg – ½ tsp. ground
- Baking powder – ½ tsp.

Frosting

- Full-fat cream cheese – 4 ounces, softened
- Butter – 4 tbsps. softened
- Heavy whipping cream – 2 cups
- Vanilla extract – 1 tsp.
- Swerve, confectioners – ½ cup
- Sugar-free chocolate chips – 6 tbsps.

Directions:

Add 1 cup water into the Instant Pot and place in the trivet. In a bowl, combine swerve, baking powder, nutmeg, almond milk, eggs, butter, and flour. Mix thoroughly. Transfer to a greased muffin mold. Place the molds onto the trivet and cover with foil. Close the lid and press Manual. Cook on manual for 30 minutes. Meanwhile, in a bowl, combine the frosting mixture and blend with a hand mixer until light and fluffy. Place the frosting in the refrigerator. Do a natural release when cooked. Open and cool. Top with frosting and serve.

Mini Chocolate Cakes

Cook time: 20 minutes| Serves: 4| Per serving: Calories 158; Carbs 9 g; Fat 11.5g; Protein 5.1g

Ingredients:

- Almond flour – 1 cup
- Egg- 1
- Sugar-free chocolate chips – ½ cup
- Baking soda – ¼ tsp.
- Unsweetened cocoa powder – ¼ cup
- Water – 1 cup

Directions:

Add 1-cup water into the Instant Pot and add in the trivet. In a bowl, add cocoa powder, baking soda, chocolate chips, almond flour, and egg. Mix with a hand mixer. Add the batter into 4 greased ramekins. Cover with foil and place on top of the trivet. Close the lid and press Manual. Cook for 20 minutes on High. Do a quick release and remove the ramekins. Serve.

Chocolate Chip Cheesecake
Cook time: 25 minutes| Serves: 6 | Per serving: Calories 339; Carbs 9g; Fat 31.2g; Protein 8.4g

Ingredients:

- Full-fat cream cheese – 16 ounces, softened
- Swerve, confectioners – ½ cup
- Eggs – 2
- Vanilla extract – 4 tsps.
- Sugar-free chocolate chips – 5 tbsps.
- Water – 2 cups

Directions:

Combine vanilla, eggs, swerve, and cream cheese in a bowl and mix well. Pour mixture into a greased pan and cover with foil. Add 2 cups of water into the Instant Pot and place in the trivet. Cover and press Manual. Cook for 25 minutes on High. Do a natural release, remove and cool. Then refrigerate to chill. Bring out the cheesecake and remove the foil. Sprinkle evenly with chocolate chips and serve.

Classic Brownies
Cook time: 40 minutes| Serves: 5 | Per serving: Calories 162; Carbs 8.9g; Fat 14.3g; Protein 5g

Ingredients:

- Sugar-free chocolate chips – 8 tbsps.
- Unsweetened cocoa powder – 3 tbsps.
- Butter – 2 tbsps. softened
- Chopped walnuts – ½ cup
- Egg – 1
- Swerve – ½ cup
- Almond flour – 1 cup
- Salt – ½ tsp.
- Vanilla extract – ½ tsp.

Directions:

Pour 1 cup water into the Instant Pot and place in the trivet. In a bowl, combine vanilla extract, salt, almond flour, swerve, egg, walnuts, butter, cocoa powder, and chocolate chips. Blend with a hand mixer and transfer the mixture into a greased dish. Place the dish onto the trivet and cover with foil. Close the lid and press Manual. Cook 40 minutes on High. Do a natural release and open. Remove, cool, slice and serve.

Chocolate Almond Squares
Cook time: 40 minutes |Serves: 8| Per serving: Calories 213; Carbs 8 g; Fat 18.1g; Protein 6g

Ingredients:

- Almond flour – 1 cup
- Sugar-free chocolate chips – 6 tbsps.
- Unsweetened cocoa powder – ¼ cup
- Coconut oil – 2 tbsps.
- Eggs – 2
- Cacao nibs – 2 tbsps. raw
- Chopped almonds – 1 cup
- Swerve – ½ cup, confectioners
- Full-fat coconut milk – ¼ cup
- Vanilla extract – ½ tsp.
- Salt – ½ tsp.
- Water – 1 cup for the pot

Directions:

In a bowl, mix together vanilla, salt, coconut milk, swerve, almonds, cacao nibs, eggs, coconut oil, cocoa powder, and chocolate chips. Combine well. Add 1-cup water into the Instant Pot and place the trivet. Transfer the chocolate mixture into a bowl and place on the trivet. Cover with a foil and close the lid. Press Manual and cook 40 minutes on High. Do a natural release. Open the pot and remove the dish. Refrigerate for 20 minutes. Cut into 8 squares and serve.

Easy Pecan Cookie Bars
Cook time: 40 minutes |Serves: 6| Per serving: Calories 147; Carbs 1.6g; Fat 15.6g; Protein 1.4g

Ingredients:

- Almond flour – 1 cup
- Butter – 2 tbsps. softened
- Swerve – ½ cup
- Chopped pecans – ½ cup
- Vanilla extract – ½ tsp.
- Cinnamon – ½ tsp. ground
- Nutmeg – ½ tsp. ground
- Baking soda – ¼ tsp.
- Water - 1 cup for the pot

Directions:

Mix butter and flour in a bowl. Add baking soda, nutmeg, cinnamon, vanilla, pecans, and swerve. Mix to make a dough. Add 1-cup water into the Instant Pot and place the trivet. Place the dough into a greased dish and place the dish on the trivet. Cover with the foil and close the lid. Press Manual and cook 40 minutes on High. Do a natural release. Open and cool. Cut into bars and serve.

Matcha Cheesecake

Cook time: 40 minutes| Serves: 8| Per serving: Calories 325; Carbs 4.6g; Fat 31.2g; Protein 8.6g

Ingredients:

- Full-fat cream cheese – 16 ounces, softened
- Almond flour – 3 tbsps.
- Heavy cream – 3 tbsps.
- Eggs – 2
- Matcha powder – 1 tbsp.
- Vanilla extract – ½ tsp.
- Swerve – 2/3 cup
- Sour cream – ½ cup, room temperature
- Sugar-free chocolate chips – ½ cup
- Water – 2 cups for the pot

Directions:

In a bowl, combine the vanilla, matcha powder, eggs, heavy cream, flour, and cream cheese. Mix well. Place the mixture in a springform pan and cover with foil. Add 2 cups water to the Instant Pot and add in trivet. Place the cake pan on top. Cover with the lid and press Manual. Cook 40 minutes on High. Do natural release. Remove and cool for 30 minutes. Refrigerate for 45 minutes. Remove foil. In a bowl, mix sour cream and swerve. Cover the cake with the mixture, and sprinkle with chocolate chips. Slice and serve.

Coconut Cookie Bites

Cook time: 20 minutes| Serves: 6| Per serving: Calories 129; Carbs 3.1g; Fat 11.9g; Protein 3.5g

Ingredients:

- Butter – 2 tbsps. softened
- Eggs – 2
- Almond flour – 1 cup
- Unsweetened coconut flakes – ¾ cup
- Swerve, - ½ cup
- Almond butter – ½ cup, smooth
- Baking powder – ½ tsp.
- Vanilla extract – ½ tsp.
- Salt – ½ tsp.
- Water – 1 cup for the pot

Directions:

In a bowl, mix together salt, vanilla, baking powder, almond butter, swerve, coconut, almond flour, eggs, and butter. Mix well. Add 1 cup water into the Instant Pot and place in the trivet. Transfer the mixture into a greased egg bites pan. Place the dish onto the trivet and cover with foil. Work in batches if necessary. Close the lid and press Manual. Cook for 20 minutes on High. Do a natural release. Open and remove, serve.

Lemon Squares
Cook time: 40 minutes| Serves: 6| Per serving: Calories 166; Carbs 2.8g; Fat 14.8g; Protein 6.2g

Ingredients:

- Eggs – 3
- Butter – 2 tbsps. Softened
- Full-fat coconut milk – ½ cup
- Baking powder - ½ tsp.
- Vanilla extract – ½ tsp.
- Swerve – ½ cup
- Lemon juice – ¼ cup
- Almond flour – 1 cup
- Water – 1 cup for the pot

Directions:

In a bowl, mix flour, lemon juice, swerve, vanilla, baking powder, coconut milk, butter, and eggs. Mix well. Add 1 cup water into the Instant Pot and place in the trivet. Transfer the mixture into a greased dish. Cover the dish with foil and place on top of the trivet. Cover the lid and cook for 40 minutes on High. Do a natural pressure release. Open the pot, remove and cool. Cut into squares and serve.

Pound Cake
Cook time: 40 minutes| Serves: 8| Per serving: Calories 213; Carbs 2.1g; Fat 20.2g; Protein 6.5g

Ingredients:

- Eggs – 3
- Almond flour – 1 cup
- Swerve – 2/3 cups
- Heavy cream – ¼ cup
- Full-fat cream cheese – 4 ounces, softened
- Butter – 2 tbsps. softened
- Baking powder – ½ tsp.
- Vanilla extract – ½ tsp.
- Salt – ½ tsp.
- Water – 1 cup for the pot

Directions:

In a bowl, whisk together the heavy cream, swerve, flour, and eggs. Stir in salt, vanilla, baking powder, butter, and cream cheese. Mix well. Add 1 cup water into the Instant Pot and place in the trivet. Transfer the mixture into a greased dish and cover with a foil. Place the bowl on top of the trivet. Close the lid and press Manual. Cook for 40 minutes on High. Do a natural release. Open and remove. Remove the foil. Cook in the oven at 350F for 2 to 5 minutes to brown the top. Cool, slice and serve.

Blueberry Cupcakes

Cook time: 25 minutes| Serves: 6| Per serving: Calories 223; Carbs 3.8g; Fat 20.4g; Protein 5.9g

Ingredients:

- Almond flour – 2 cups
- Baking powder – 2/3 tsps.
- Baking soda – ¼ tsp.
- Xanthan gum – ½ tsp.
- Swerve – 1 cup
- Eggs – 3
- Almond milk – 1 cup, unsweetened
- Blueberries – ¼ cup
- Butter – 1 tbsp. softened
- Coconut oil – 1 tbsp.
- Lemon zest – 1 tbsp. freshly grated
- Vanilla extract – 1 tsp.
- Water – 1 cup for the pot

Directions:

Combine all the dry ingredients into a large bowl. Mix thoroughly and gradually add milk. Beat and add eggs, one at a time. Add coconut oil, butter, lemon zest and vanilla extract. Mix well. Fold in blueberries and transfer to a 12-cup silicone cupcake pan. Add 1-cup water in the Instant Pot. Set the trivet in the pot and place the silicone pan on top. Cover loosely with aluminum foil and seal the lid. Press Manual and set the timer for 25 minutes. When done, do a quick pressure release and open the lid. Remove the muffin pan from the Instant Pot, and cool completely. Serve.

Chocolate Brownies

Cook time: 20 minutes |Serves: 8 | Per serving: Calories 180; Carbs 2.4g; Fat 17.5g; Protein 4.8g

Ingredients:

- Cocoa powder – ½ cup, unsweetened
- Unsweetened dark chocolate chunks – ¼ cup
- Cream cheese – 1 cup
- Large eggs – 2
- Coconut oil – 3 tbsps.
- Salt – ½ tsp.
- Swerve – ¾ cup

- Water – 1 cup for the pot

Directions:

In a bowl, combine the coconut oil, eggs, and cream cheese. Beat thoroughly until smooth. Add dark chocolate chunks, swerve, salt and cocoa powder. Beat until mixed thoroughly. Grease a cake pan with some oil and line with parchment paper. Dust the paper with some cocoa powder and pour in the butter. Flatten the surface and loosely cover with aluminum foil. Add 1 cup of water in the Instant Pot. Set the steam rack at the bottom of the steel insert and place the cake pan on top. Seal the lid and press Manual. Cook for 20 minutes. When done, release the pressure naturally. Open the lid and remove the pan. Cool and serve.

Peach Pie
Cook time: 25 minutes| Serves: 6 | Per serving: Calories 221; Carbs 4.4 g; Fat 19.4g; Protein 6.6g

Ingredients:

- Almond flour – 2 cups
- Medium peach – 1, sliced
- Raspberries – ¼ cup
- Eggs – 4
- Butter – 6 tbsps.
- Baking powder – 2 tsps.
- Salt – ½ tsp.
- Swerve – ¼ tsp.
- Vanilla extract – ¼ tsp.
- Lemon zest – 2 tsps.
- Water – 1 cup for the pot

Directions:

Brush cake pan with oil and line with parchment paper. Set aside. Whisk together the eggs and swerve in a bowl. Set aside. Combine all the remaining dry ingredients in another bowl and mix well. Slowly pour in the egg mixture, mixing constantly. Then add the remaining ingredients. Transfer to a mixing bowl and beat for 2 minutes on medium speed. Pour the mixture into the prepared cake pan and shake a few times to flatten the surface. Wrap with some aluminum foil. Add 1-cup water in the Instant Pot. Set the trivet at the bottom and place the wrapped pan on top. Cover and cook for 20 minutes on High. Do a quick release when done. Open the lid and remove from pan. Cool and serve.

Almond Butter Cookies
Cook time: 25 minutes| Serves: 15| Per serving: Calories 154; Carbs 1.5g; Fat 15.3g; Protein 2.9g

Ingredients:

- Almond flour – 1 ½ cup
- Coconut flour – ½ cup

- Eggs – 3
- Coconut oil – ¾ cup, melted
- Almond butter – 3 tbsp.
- Cocoa powder – ¼ cup, unsweetened
- Swerve – ½ cup
- Salt – ½ tsp.
- Water – 1 cup for the pot

Directions:

Add 1-cup water in the Instant Pot and place in the trivet. Line a round baking pan with parchment paper and set aside. In a bowl, add coconut flour, almond flour, swerve, cocoa butter, salt, and mix. Add almond butter, coconut oil, and eggs. Beat on high speed until fully mixed. Scoop out 15 cookies and place them in the prepared baking pan. Place the pan in the pot and cover with aluminum foil. Seal and cook for 25 minutes. When done, release the pressure naturally. Open the lid and remove the pan. Cool and serve.

Mini Brownie Cakes
Cook time: 15 minutes| Serves: 4| Per serving: Calories 404; Carbs 4.8g; Fat 39.1g; Protein 9.7g

Ingredients:

- Almond flour – 1 cup
- Cocoa powder – ½ cup, unsweetened
- Swerve – ¼ cup
- Eggs – 4
- Unsweetened dark chocolate – ¼ cup, cut into chunks
- Rum extract – 1 tsp.
- Coconut oil – ½ cup
- Water – 1 cup for the pot

Directions:

Add 1-cup water and a trivet into the Instant Pot. In a bowl, combine coconut oil, rum extract, dark chocolate chunks, swerve, and eggs. Mix until light and creamy. Sift almond flour and cocoa powder over the egg mixture and mix again. Divide the mixture between 4 ramekins and tightly wrap with aluminum foil. Place each ramekin on the trivet, seal and cook for 15 minutes. Open the lid and remove the ramekins. Cool and serve.

Eggnog
Cook time: 10 minutes| Serves: 4| Per serving: Calories 437; Carbs 5.3 g; Fat 41.7g; Protein 9.5g

Ingredients:

- Unsweetened almond milk – 3 cups
- Egg yolks – 10

- Swerve – 1 cup
- Whipped cream – 3 cups
- Vanilla extract – 1 tsp.
- Rum extract – 2 tsps.
- Ground cinnamon – ½ tsp.

Directions:

Press Sauté and add the almond milk, cinnamon and vanilla extract. Stir well and cook for 5 to 6 minutes. Meanwhile, place egg yolks in a deep bowl. Add one cup of swerve and stir well. Pour the mixture into the Instant Pot and mix well. Continue to cook for 2 minutes more. Stir in the rum extract and whipped cream. Gently simmer for 2 to 3 minutes and press Cancel. Transfer the eggnog to serving glasses and chill. Refrigerate for 1 hour before serving.

Chocolate Chip Cookies
Cook time: 15 minutes |Serves: 10 | Per serving: Calories 133; Carbs 3.2g; Fat 11.2g; Protein 4.2g

Ingredients:

- Almond flour – ½ cup
- Flax meal – ¼ cup
- Coconut flour – ¼ cup
- Almond butter – ½ cup
- Coconut oil – ¼ cup
- Salt – ¼ tsp.
- Swerve – ¼ cup
- Large eggs – 3
- Vanilla extract – 1 tsp.
- Dark chocolate chips – ¼ cup, unsweetened
- Water – 1 cup

Directions:

Combine the flax meal, almond flour, coconut flour, salt and swerve in a large bowl. Place in a food processor along with eggs, coconut oil, almond butter and vanilla extract. Process until it has a sandy texture. Transfer the mixture to a lightly floured work surface and fold in chocolate chips. Knead and shape into 10 balls. Press each ball to make a cookie. Line a baking pan with parchment paper and place on the cookies. Add 1-cup water in the Instant Pot. Set the trivet inside and place the pan on top. Seal and cook 15 minutes. When done, release pressure naturally and open the lid. Remove the cookies from the pot, cool and serve.

Cherry Pudding
Cook time: 6 minutes| Serves: 5| Per serving: Calories 153; Carbs 2g; Fat 14.2g; Protein 4.5g

Ingredients:

- Whipped cream – ¾ cup
- Almond milk – ¾ cup, unsweetened
- Egg whites – 4
- Powdered stevia – 3 tsps.
- Cherry extract – 1 tsp. sugar-free
- Xanthan gum – ¼ tsp.
- Water – 2 cups for the pot

Directions:

In a bowl, combine egg whites, almond milk, and heavy cream. Beat thoroughly on high for 3 minutes. Pour the mixture into 5 ramekins. Add 2 cups of water into the Instant Pot. Position a trivet at the bottom and place the ramekins on top. Lock and cook 3 minutes on High. When done, press Cancel and release the pressure naturally. Open the pot and cool. Refrigerate for 1 hour before serving.

Carrot Cake
Cook time: 40 minutes| Serves: 8| Per serving: Calories 126; Carbs 2.7g; Fat 10.1g; Protein 5.5g

Ingredients:

- Almond flour – 2 cups
- Almonds – ¼ cup, chopped
- Carrot – 1 small, shredded
- Large eggs – 4
- Heavy cream – ½ cup
- Baking powder – 1 tsp.
- Stevia powder – 1 tbsp.
- Apple pie seasoning – 1 tsp.
- Water – 2 cups for the pot

Directions:

Combine all ingredients in a large bowl. Mix well and set aside. Pour the mixture into a springform pan and cover with aluminum foil. Add 2 cups of water in the Instant Pot and position a trivet. Place the springform pan on top and lock the lid. Cook for 40 minutes on High. Press Cancel and turn off the pot. Release pressure naturally. Cool and serve.

Chocolate Bundt Cake
Cook time: 20 minutes| Serves: 10| Per serving: Calories 137; Carbs 1.9g; Fat 12.9g; Protein 4.6g

Ingredients:

- Almond flour – 1 cup
- Cocoa powder – ½ cup, unsweetened
- Walnuts – 3 tbsps.

- Large eggs – 4
- Coconut oil – 4 tbsps. melted
- Heavy cream – ½ cup
- Baking powder – 1 tsp.
- Powdered stevia – 1 tsp.
- Water – 2 cups for the pot

Directions:

Combine all dry ingredients in a bowl. Mix well and then add coconut oil, eggs, and heavy cream. Beat until well combined. Grease a bundt pan with cooking spray. Pour in the batter and set aside. Add 2 cups of water in the Instant Pot. Position a trivet and place in the bundt pan on top. Lock and cook 20 minutes on High. When done, press Cancel and release pressure naturally. Open the pot and remove. Cool, slice and serve.

Mug Cake
Cook time: 10 minutes| Serves: 3 | Per serving: Calories 151; Carbs 4.4g; Fat 10.2g; Protein 8.7g

Ingredients:

- Almond flour – 1 cup
- Fresh raspberries – ½ cup
- Dark chocolate chips – 1 tbsp. unsweetened
- Large eggs – 3
- Swerve – 1 tbsp.
- Vanilla extract – ¼ tsp.
- Salt – ¼ tsp.
- Water – 2 cups for the pot

Directions:

Mix all the ingredients in a bowl. Grease 3 mason jars with cooking spray and evenly divide the mixture between them. Add 2 cups of water in the Instant Pot. Place a trivet in the pot and place the jars on top. Cover each jar with aluminum foil and lock the lid. Cook for 10 minutes on High. When done, press Cancel and do a quick release. Remove the jars from the pot. Cool and serve.

Strawberry Cake
Cook time: 20 minutes |Serves: 6 | Per serving: Calories 195; Carbs 4.2g; Fat 16.4g; Protein 5.7g

Ingredients:

- Almond flour – 2 cups
- Coconut flour – 1 cup
- Unsweetened cocoa powder – ¼ cup
- Baking soda – 1 tsp.
- Baking powder – ½ tsp.

- Salt – ½ tsp.
- Unsweetened almond milk – 1 cup
- Eggs – 3
- Egg whites – 2
- Whipped cream – 3 cups, sugar-free
- Stevia extract – 1 tsp.
- Strawberry extract – 2 tsps.
- Water – 1 cup

Directions:

Line springform pan with parchment paper and set aside. Combine the coconut flour, almond flour, cocoa powder, baking soda, baking powder, and salt in a mixing bowl. Mix well and gradually add milk. With a hand mixer, beat on high speed. One at a time, add the eggs and beat constantly. Finally, add the egg whites and mix well. Transfer the batter to the prepared springform pan and flatten the surface with a spatula. Cover loosely with some aluminum foil. Add 1-cup water in the Instant Pot. Place the trivet in the pot and gently place the springform on top. Cover and press Manual. Cook 20 minutes. Open and carefully remove the pan. Place on a wire rack and cool. Meanwhile, place stevia, whipped cream, and strawberry extract in a bowl. Beat with a hand mixer to combine well. Pour the mixture over the chilled crust and refrigerate for 1 hour before use.

Almond Bars
Cook time: 15 minutes| Serves: 6| Per serving: Calories 253; Carbs 1.5g; Fat 25.7g; Protein 4.6g

Ingredients:

- Almond flour – 1 ¼ cup
- Coconut flour – ¼ cup
- Coconut oil – ½ cup
- Almond butter – 2 tbsps.
- Salt – ¼ tsp.
- Swerve – 3 tbsps.
- Vanilla extract – 1 tsp.
- Eggs – 2
- Water – 1 cup

Directions:

Place the trivet in the IP and add 1-cup water. Combine the ingredients in a food processor and process until a sandy texture. Line a baking pan with some parchment paper and add the dough. Press well with the palm of your hands and gently place in your Instant Pot. Cover with some parchment paper and seal the lid. Cook for 15 minutes on High. Release pressure naturally and open the lid. Carefully remove and chill. Slice into 6 bars and refrigerate for 1 hour before serving.

Creamy Raspberry Cake
Cook time: 10 minutes| Serves: 8| Per serving: Calories 222; Carbs 5.3g; Fat 18.3g; Protein 3.9g

Ingredients:

- Coconut flour – ½ cup
- Heavy cream – ¼ cup
- Fresh raspberries – ½ cup
- Egg yolks – 5
- Butter - ¼ cup
- Powdered stevia – 3 tsps.
- Baking powder – 1 tsp.
- Vanilla extract – 1 tsp. sugar-free
- Coconut oil – ¼ cup
- Water – 2 cups for the pot

Directions:

Except for raspberries, combine all dry ingredients in a bowl and mix well. Add all wet ingredients and beat unit fully combined. Line springform pan with some parchment paper and pour in the batter. Spread the raspberries on top by tucking them into the batter. Pour in 2 cups of water in the IP. Position a trivet in the pot and place the pan on top. Secure the lid cook 10 minutes on High. When done, press Cancel and do a quick release. Open the pot and let it chill before serving.

Bread Pudding
Cook time: 20 minutes| Serves: 4 | Per serving: Calories 300; Carbs 46g; Fat 7g; Protein 11g

Ingredients:

- Egg yolks – 4
- Brioche – 3 cups, cubed
- Half and half – 2 cups
- Vanilla extract – ½ tsp.
- Sugar – 1 cup
- Olive oil – 2 tbsps.
- Cranberries – 1 cup
- Warm water – 2 cups
- Raisins – ½ cup
- Zest of 1 lime

Directions:

Grease a baking dish with oil and set aside. In a bowl, mix egg yolks with half and half, cubed brioche, vanilla extract, sugar, cranberries, raisins, and lime zest and mix well. Pour the mixture into the greased dish and cover with aluminum foil. Set aside for 10 minutes. Add the warm water to the Instant Pot. Place the steamer basket in the Instant Pot and add the baking dish on top.

Cover the pot and cook on High for 20 minutes. Do a natural release and open. Cool, slice, and serve.

Ruby Pears
Cook time: 10 minutes| Serves: 4| Per serving: Calories 145; Carbs 12g; Fat 5.6g; Protein 12g

Ingredients:

- Pears – 4
- Juice and zest of 1 lemon
- Grape juice – 26 ounces
- Currant jelly – 11 ounces
- Garlic – 4 cloves, peeled
- Vanilla bean – ½
- Peppercorns – 4
- Rosemary sprigs – 2

Directions:

Pour the jelly and grape juice into the Instant Pot and mix with lemon zest and lemon juice. Dip each pear in this mix. Wrap them in aluminum foil and arrange them in the steamer basket of the Instant Pot. Add the garlic cloves, peppercorns, rosemary, and vanilla bean to the juice mixture. Place the steamer basket in the Instant Pot and cover the pot. Cook on High for 10 minutes. Take the pears out, unwrap them, and arrange them on plates. Serve cold with cooking juice poured on top.

Pumpkin Rice Pudding
Cook time: 25 minutes| Serves: 6| Per serving: Calories 100; Carbs 21g; Fat 1g; Protein 4.1g

Ingredients:

- Brown rice – 1 cup
- Boiling water – ½ cup
- Cashew milk – 3 cups
- Dates – ½ cup, chopped
- Salt to taste
- Cinnamon – 1 stick
- Pumpkin puree – 1 cup
- Maple syrup – ½ cup
- Pumpkin spice mix – 1 tsp.
- Vanilla extract – 1 tsp.

Directions:

Put the rice into a bowl, add boiling water to cover and set aside for 10 minutes. Then drain. Put the milk into the Instant Pot; add rice, cinnamon stick, dates, and salt. Stir and cover. Cook on

Rice for 20 minutes. Do a natural release and open. Add maple syrup, pie spice, and puree. Stir. Cover and cook on High for 5 minutes. Discard the cinnamon stick add the vanilla. Mix and transfer the pudding to bowls. Cool and serve.

Lemon Marmalade
Cook time: 16 minutes| Serves: 8| Per serving: Calories 458; Carbs 124g; Fat 1g; Protein 1.3g

Ingredients:

- Lemons – 2 pounds, washed, peeled, sliced and cut into quarters
- Sugar – 2 pounds
- Water – 2 cups

Directions:

Put the lemon pieces into the Instant Pot. Add water, cover, and cook on High for 10 minutes. Do a natural release and open. Add the sugar and mix. Cook and stir for 6 minutes on Sauté. Serve.

Ricotta Cake
Cook time: 20 minutes| Serves: 6| Per serving: Calories 211; Carbs 21g; Fat 8.6g; Protein 12g

Ingredients:

- Ricotta – 1 pound
- Dates – 6 ounces, soaked 15 minutes, then drained
- Honey – 2 ounces
- Eggs – 4
- Sugar – 2 ounces
- Vanilla extract to taste
- Water – 17 ounces
- Orange juice and zest from ½ orange

Directions:

Whisk the ricotta in a bowl until softens. In another bowl, whisk the eggs. Combine the two mixtures and mix well. Add the vanilla, honey, dates, orange zest, and juice to the ricotta mixture and mix. Pour the batter into a dish and cover with aluminum foil. Place the dish in the steamer basket of the Instant Pot and place the steamer basket in the Instant Pot. Add water to the pot. Cover the pot and cook on High for 20 minutes. Do a natural release and open. Cool, slice, and serve.

Berry Jam
Cook time: 20 minutes| Serves: 12| Per serving: Calories 331; Carbs 85g; Fat 0g; Protein 0g

Ingredients:

- Cranberries – 1 pound
- Strawberries – 1 pound

- Blueberries – ½ pound
- Blackcurrant – ¼ pound
- Sugar – 2 pounds
- Zest from 1 lemon
- Salt to taste
- Water – 2 tbsps.

Directions:

In the Instant Pot, mix all the berries, blackcurrants, lemon zest, and sugar. Stir and set aside for 1 hour. Add salt and water. Mix well. Press Sauté and bring the mixture to a boil. Then cover and cook 10 minutes on High. Do a natural release and open. Bring to a boil again and simmer for 4 minutes. Serve.

Raspberry Curd
Cook time: 4 minutes| Serves: 4 | Per serving: Calories 110; Carbs 16g; Fat 4g; Protein 1g

Ingredients:

- Sugar – 1 cup
- Raspberries – 12 ounces
- Egg yolks - 2
- Lemon juice – 2 tbsps.
- Olive oil – 2 tbsps.

Directions:

Put the raspberries into the Instant Pot. Add the sugar and lemon juice. Stir and cover. Cook on High for 2 minutes. Do a natural release and open. Strain the raspberries and discard the seeds. Mix the egg yolks with raspberries in a bowl and stir well. Return this to the Instant Pot. Cook on Sauté for 2 minutes. Add the oil and stir. Serve cold.

Pear Jam
Cook time: 4 minutes| Serves: 12| Per serving: Calories 90; Carbs 20g; Fat 0g; Protein 0g

Ingredients:

- Pears – 8, cored and cut into quarters
- Apples – 2, peeled, cored and cut into quarters
- Apple juice – ¼ cup
- Cinnamon – 1 tsp. ground

Directions:

In the Instant Pot, mix the pears with apples, cinnamon, and apple juice and stir. Cover the pot and cook on High for 4 minutes. Do a natural release and open. Blend with a hand mixer, cool, and serve.

Berry Compote

Cook time: 5 minutes | Serves: 8| Per serving: Calories 260; Carbs 23g; Fat 13g; Protein 3g

Ingredients:

- Blueberries – 1 cup
- Strawberries – 2 cups, sliced
- Lemon juice – 2 tbsps.
- Sugar – ¾ cup
- Cornstarch - 1 tbsp.
- Water – 1 tbsp.

Directions:

In the Instant Pot, mix the blueberries with lemon juice and sugar. Stir, and cover. Cook on High for 3 minutes. Do a natural release and open. In a bowl, mix the cornstarch with water, stir well, and add to the Instant Pot. Stir to mix. Press Sauté and cook for 2 minutes. Cool and serve.

Carrot Cake II

Cook time: 32 minutes| Serves: 6| Per serving: Calories 140; Carbs 23.4g; Fat 3.5g; Protein 4.3g

Ingredients:

- Flour – 5 ounces
- Salt to taste
- Baking powder – ¾ tsp.
- Baking soda – ½ tsp.
- Ground cinnamon – ½ tsp.
- Nutmeg – ¼ tsp.
- Allspice – ½ tsp.
- Egg – 1
- Yogurt – 3 tbsps.
- Sugar – ½ cup
- Pineapple juice – ¼ cup
- Olive oil – 4 tbsps.
- Carrots – 1/3 cup, peeled and grated
- Pecans – 1/3 cup, toasted and chopped
- Coconut flakes – 1/3 cup
- Cooking spray
- Water – 2 cups

Directions:

In a bowl, mix the flour with baking soda, baking powder, salt, allspice, cinnamon, and nutmeg and mix. In another bowl, mix the egg with yogurt, sugar, pineapple juice, oil, carrots, pecans, and coconut flakes and mix thoroughly. Combine the two mixtures and stir well. Pour this into a springform cake tin greased with cooking spray. Add water to the Instant Pot, then place a steamer basket. Place the springform tin on top of the steamer basket and cover the Instant Pot. Cook on High for 32 minutes. Do a natural release and open. Cool, slice, and serve.

Cranberry Cake
Cook time: 30 minutes| Serves: 6| Per serving: Calories 258; Carbs 48.8g; Fat 5.2g; Protein 4.4g

Ingredients:

- Wheat flour – 8 oz.
- Ground cinnamon – ¼ tsp.
- Ground cardamom - ½ tsp.
- Baking powder - ½ tsp.
- Coconut milk - ½ cup
- Brown sugar – ½ cup
- Cranberries – 4 oz. chopped
- Cooking spray
- Water – 1 cup, for cooking

Directions:

In a bowl, mix wheat flour, cinnamon, cardamom, baking powder, coconut milk, and sugar. Add chopped cranberries and mix well. Spray a bundt pan with cooking spray and transfer the mixed dough. Flatten the dough gently and cover the pan with parchment or foil. Secure the edges. Pour water in the Instant Pot. Insert the bundt pan and close the lid. Cook on High for 30 minutes. Then do a natural release. Cool and serve.

Raisin Pudding
Cook time: 20 minutes| Serves: 4| Per serving: Calories 404; Carbs 89.8 g; Fat 1g; Protein 3.6g

Ingredients:

- Raisins – 3 cups
- Rum – ½ cup
- Sugar – 1 tbsp.
- Cocoa powder – 1 tbsp.

Directions:

Cover everything in the Instant Pot and cover with the lid. Cook on Low for 20 minutes. Do a natural release. Serve.

Conclusion

The Instant Pot can assist you in adding variety and ease to your meal preparation. You can eat healthily and enjoy juicy meals that are perfectly cooked in a short time. As you have noticed, this book is suitable for both beginner and experienced cooks and has a wide variety of recipes for any taste. This Instant Pot cookbook is a must-have for every family. Recipes are created in a clear and understandable manner, and ingredients are easy to find. With this Instant Pot cookbook, you will cook much better, tastier, and faster meals for yourself and your family.